Foreword

Despite enormous economic progress – especially from 1965 to 1985 – millions, a vast majority of whom live in rural areas, continue to suffer acute and chronic deprivation in developing countries. This pervasive deprivation and misery calls for quick and effective remedial action.

Recent studies suggest that the failure to ameliorate deprivation is not so much because of government inaction or indifference towards the poor. Rather, the failure stems in many cases from inappropriate anti-poverty measures, a limited understanding of their direct and indirect effects, intertemporal equity-efficiency trade-offs and weak administrative structures. In particular, interventionist states' attempts to supplant operational market mechanisms have proved futile. The present FAO report, prepared by Prof. Gaiha, advocates a judicious combination of the market mechanism and state action, with a key role assigned to coalitions of the rural poor both as pressure groups and collaborators in poverty alleviation.

Significant contributions have been made in recent years, with a focus on measuring poverty, targeting anti-poverty interventions accompanied by imperfect information, and collective action. Much of this literature is highly specialized and narrow in its policy orientation. One merit of Prof. Gaiha's study is that it provides a coherent and meticulous synthesis of these contributions and draws out their policy implications.

While recognizing the importance of the rate and pattern of growth – especially agricultural growth – the present study argues that a major dent in rural poverty can be made through well-coordinated, direct anti-poverty interventions. Careful attention is paid to the nature of these interventions, the complementarities among them and their timing, financing and political feasibility.

Appropriate budgetary allocations for alleviating poverty make a difference but poverty alleviation requires more than this. Recognizing that fiscal stringency imposes hard choices, the present study argues that, given the budgetary outlays involved, it is vital that the poor benefit from them. In this context, contrary to some assertions in the recent literature, coalitions of the rural poor have a potentially signficant role.

The battle against poverty will be a long and hard one. An important first step is to devise a sound strategy. Through a careful and scholarly analysis of a wide range of issues and policy choices central to poverty alleviation, this report goes a long way towards identifying critical elements of such a strategy.

T. Kelly White
Director
Policy Analysis Division

Design of poverty alleviation strategy in rural areas

FAO
ECONOMIC
AND SOCIAL
DEVELOPMENT
PAPER

115

by
R. Gaiha
Faculty of Management Studies
University of Delhi

Food
and
Agriculture
Organization
of
the
United
Nations

Rome, 1993

M-60
ISBN 92-5-103283-1

Contents

Acknowledgements

This study was sponsored by the Policy Studies Group of FAO's Policy Analysis Division. It has benefited from the comments of Amartya Sen, Jere Behrman, Jean Drèze, Michael Lipton, David Newbery, Christopher Bliss, Harold Alderman, Nicholas Stern and Nikos Alexandratos, as well as from the generosity of Martin Ravallion, Anil Deolalikar and Timothy Besley who promptly supplied their unpublished manuscripts. Special thanks are due to Apostolos Condos for his interest, support and constructive suggestions at all stages of the study. However, the author alone is responsible for the views expressed herein.

Chapter 1
Introduction

PROBLEM

Despite enormous economic progress – especially from 1965 to 1985 – millions continue to suffer severe and chronic deprivation in developing countries. If account is taken of the numbers experiencing sharp, downward fluctuations in living standards as a result of exogenous shocks such as failure of the monsoon and associated abrupt price changes of food staples, the extent and severity of deprivation are staggering.[1] This pervasive deprivation and misery – largely in rural areas – calls for quick and effective remedial action.

As two recent studies (World Bank, 1990; FAO, 1991a) emphasize, the failure to reduce deprivation is not so much because of government inaction or indifference towards the poor and vulnerable. Rather, the failure stems in many cases from inappropriate anti-poverty measures, a limited understanding of their direct and indirect effects, intertemporal equity- efficiency trade-offs, and weak administrative structures. In particular, scepticism of the market mechanism in efficiently allocating resources and in generating incomes for the poorest paved the way for a highly interventionist role for the state, especially during the 1960s. In recent years, however, sufficient empirical evidence has accumulated to question, if not reject, this paradigm of an interventionist state. Just as markets do not always work, government policies also fail sometimes. Indeed, it is arguable that, in specific cases – the provision of credit in rural areas, for instance – both markets and

---

[1] According to FAO (1991a), the total number of rural poor increased from 783 million to 808 million between 1980 and 1987. A large majority of them lived in Asia. The intensity of poverty remained acute in some developing countries (for which estimates are available).

governments fail for the same reasons. Some recent theoretical and applied work (Drèze and Sen, 1989; Hoff and Stiglitz, 1990) has brought into sharp relief the futility of governments trying to supplant the market mechanism. What is in fact advocated is a judicious combination of the two, with a key role assigned to local communities both as pressure groups and collaborators in poverty alleviation (Drèze and Sen, 1989).

SCOPE

The aim of the present report is to review direct anti-poverty interventions (e.g. land reforms, rural public works, rural credit programmes), identify the sources of their failures and suggest reforms. The emphasis is more on the insights that emerge from such a reappraisal and not so much on empirical validation of largely theoretical propositions. Some of these insights are of course illustrated by empirical evidence.

The contribution of this report lies in its critical evaluation of a large body of recent, predominantly technical literature on imperfect information and related incentive issues, its largely intuitive but perceptive studies of the varied roles of local communities both as pressure groups and collaborators, and its mixture of technical and intuitive investigations of the political dimensions of anti-poverty interventions. The emphasis throughout is on the policy guidelines suggested by these studies.

The analysis reflects the belief that isolated, piecemeal interventions are not likely to make a dent in rural poverty. Instead, a whole package of simultaneous and well-coordinated interventions in land, labour and credit markets is necessary. This is because, in a given macroeconomic environment, poverty usually stems from a complex interaction of factors such as limited endowments (e.g. lack of access to land), skills, access to credit, and vulnerability to shocks affecting the production system (e.g. drought). Given this characterization of rural poverty, it follows that an isolated intervention is not likely to be effective – and may well be counterproductive when transactions in different rural markets are interlinked. As some sections of the poor – the aged, infirm and those in resource-poor areas – are not likely to benefit even from a successful implementation of such a strategy, a system of well-targeted transfers and safety nets is also required.

Above all, the political feasibility of anti-poverty interventions ought not to be overlooked. The trade-offs between political feasibility and the accuracy of targeting may, for example, leave no choice but to allow some "leakage" of benefits to those who are are not poor.

Some omissions may also be noted. One is the neglect of international aspects of poverty alleviation. This may seem surprising in the context of the debt crisis and the widespread concern for minimizing the hardships suffered by the poor as a result of structural adjustment programmes. Cut-backs and reallocations of public expenditure, and the downscaling of price and quantity controls – in both domestic and external sectors – may potentially influence the extent and severity of poverty in the short term. The actual effect would, however, depend largely on domestic policies and, in particular, on the effectiveness of direct anti-poverty interventions. So, while international aspects matter (their importance obviously varies from one country to another), domestic policies would undoubtedly be crucial. Another defect is that poverty alleviation and sustainable development linkages are not addressed. Although the literature has grown rapidly in recent years, the formulations continue to be tentative and have a weak empirical base.[2] As a result, the inferences are mostly conjectural and few definitive generalizations can thus be made. Given this state of knowledge, it was decided not to address these linkages.

SCHEME

Chapter 2 deals with conceptual and measurement problems in poverty analysis; more specifically, welfarist and non-welfarist perspectives on living standards, poverty threshold, equivalence scale, intrahousehold disparities and dominance conditions. In view of the understatement of poverty when intrahousehold disparities are ignored, some recent formulations and their policy implications are reviewed. Chapter 3 examines the relationship between economic growth and rural poverty. It is argued and demonstrated that feasible growth by itself is not likely to make a dent in poverty, as

---

[2] See, for example, FAO (1991a).

there is a hard core of poverty which persists even when incomes rise in general. As a prelude to the overview of direct anti-poverty interventions and their underlying rationale in Chapter 4, some proximate determinants of poverty are identified and their relative importance assessed in Chapter 3. The overview in Chapter 4 discusses the rationale and forms of anti-poverty interventions as well as their timing, financing and other related policy concerns.

Chapter 5 reviews the rationale of land reforms (i.e. land redistribution, tenancy reforms and land titling), assesses their performance and argues against certain anomalies. Whether or not the market mechanism could be combined with minimal intervention by the state is examined critically. Access to land or security of tenancy by itself is not likely to enhance the income prospects of poor cultivators unless access to credit is also ensured. Credit thus also has a key role in poverty alleviation. In Chapter 6, in the light of a monopolistically competitive characterisation of rural credit markets, reasons for the failure of subsidized credit programmes are analysed and a more appropriate role for government intervention, designed to overcome informational deficiencies and reduce transaction costs, is spelled out. In many developing countries, agricultural labourers are highly poverty prone, partly because of market imperfections and partly on account of limited employment opportunities in agricultural slack periods. In this context, rural public works (RPW) have a major role in poverty alleviation. A merit of RPW is their self-targeting nature. Based on a comprehensive framework, an assessment of RPW is carried out and followed in Chapter 7 by suggestions for enhancing their cost-effectiveness.

Chapter 8 critically evaluates the role of food subsidies as a form of safety net while Chapter 9 focuses on the role of human capital in poverty alleviation. Although human capital takes time to build and its benefits accrue over a period of time, it is nonetheless a major component of poverty alleviation strategies. The role of human capital is reviewed in the light of recent empirical evidence, and an approach combining the market mechanism with public action is elaborated with a view to ensuring the efficient allocation and effective targeting of public expenditure. Chapter 10 focuses on the political feasibility of a wide range of anti-poverty interventions, taking into account the formation of coalitions as well as their effectiveness. Chapter 11 draws together the main conclusions from a broad policy perspective, supplemented by observations on data requirements for monitoring changes in rural poverty.

Chapter 2
Conceptual and measurement issues in poverty analysis

An attempt is made here to review *i)* approaches to measurement of well-being; *ii)* the relationship between poverty and inequality; *iii)* poverty indices; *iv)* alternative approaches to specification of a poverty threshold; *v)* intrahousehold disparity and poverty; and *vi)* dominance conditions for assessing changes in poverty over time.

Poverty exists when one or more persons fail to attain a level of well-being (usually material) that is deemed to constitute a reasonable minimum by the standards of that society (Ravallion, 1992). For policy purposes, it is not enough to know that poverty exists. It is also necessary to know how much poverty exists.

This raises the following questions:
- How do we assess individual well-being or welfare?
- At what level of measured well-being do we say that a person is not poor?
- How do we aggregate individual indicators of well-being into a measure of poverty?

The first two questions relate to the identification problem (i.e. which individuals are poor and how poor are they?) while the third is referred to as the aggregation problem (i.e. how much poverty is there?). Much of the recent theoretical literature is concerned largely with the aggregation problem (notably, Sen, 1976; Foster, Greer and Thorbecke, 1984). However, there are also a number of difficult issues relating to the identification problem as discussed below.

ABSOLUTE AND RELATIVE POVERTY
Approaches to the measurement of well-being

Following Sen (1979), a distinction is drawn between welfarist and non-welfarist approaches to the measurement of well-being. While the former is based solely on individual utility levels, as assessed by the individuals themselves, the latter may pay little attention to utility considerations. Consider, for example, the importance attached to nutritional attainments in poverty alleviation programmes. While every individual values food consumption, it is doubtful whether individuals are good judges of the importance of nutrition to well-being. A non-welfarist poverty comparison may thus consider the poor to be better off even if the poor do not agree.

Welfarism involves two contentious issues. One relates to interpersonal utility comparisons. Another has to do with whether individuals know what is best for them. In certain situations personal judgements of well-being may be considered suspect, either because of a lack of information or because of the incapacity for rational choice even with perfect information (Akerlof, 1984). Even when aware of alternative employment opportunities, a bonded labourer in the Indian state of Bihar, for example, may be disinclined to consider seriously the option of breaking out of the feudal bondage. On the other hand, non-welfarist value judgements tend to dominate policy discussions on poverty. For example "workfare", i.e. the poor have to work to gain benefits, enjoys wide support among policy-makers as a non-welfarist consideration in poverty alleviation. If utility considerations are of greater importance, however, a cash transfer would be better. The emphasis on non-welfarist considerations should not be taken to imply that utility considerations are unimportant. In designing nutrition interventions, for example, taste considerations ought not to be overlooked.

The concept "standard of living" can be either welfarist or non-welfarist.[1] The welfarist approach typically emphasizes aggregate expenditure on all goods and services consumed (including consumption from one's own

---

[1] Note that the terms "standard of living" and "well-being" are used interchangeably.

production), valued at appropriate prices. By contrast, a common non-welfarist approach emphasizes specific commodity forms of deprivation, such as inadequate food consumption or, even more narrowly, inadequate nutrition.

A variation is to consider opportunity for consumption, rather than actual consumption. (From a non-welfarist perspective, the focus will be on whether a nutritionally adequate diet is affordable.) However, such a variation requires data on wealth, which are rare and unreliable. When savings are positive, income may be an appropriate measure of opportunity for consumption (Ravallion, 1992).

Sen (1987) advocates a broadening of the focus in assessing living standards. He rejects the welfarist approach with its emphasis on utility as being inadequate and potentially misleading when used as a basis for assessing living standards. Consider, for example, the interpretation of utility as desire fulfilment.[2] It is then arguable that the fulfilment of a person's desire may or may not be indicative of a high level of well-being or living standards. As Sen emphasizes, utility is essentially a psychic response that is conditioned by, among other things, present circumstances. As he elaborates: "The battered slave, the broken unemployed, the hopeless destitute, the tamed housewife, may have the courage to desire little, but the fulfilment of those disciplined desires is not a sign of great success and cannot be treated in the same way as the fulfilment of the confident and demanding desires of the better placed" (Sen, 1987, p. 11). He is equally critical of the emphasis on opulence or commodity possession in both narrowly formulated welfarist and non-welfarist approaches, as this is potentially misleading. Recognizing that opulence and the standard of living are closely linked, he points out that the two are not synonymous. An example clarifies the distinction: consider two persons, A and B. Both are quite poor but B is poorer. A has a higher income and, in particular, succeeds in buying more

---

[2] Utility could be interpreted as pleasure, happiness, desire fulfilment or simply as the reflection of choice. Sen expresses serious reservations about each of these interpretations. For further details, see Sen (1987) and the related comment by Muellbauer (1987).

food and consuming more of it. However, A also has a higher metabolic rate and a parasitic disease so, despite his higher food consumption, he is in fact more undernourished and debilitated than B. A may be richer or more opulent, but it cannot really be said that he has the higher standard of living of the two, since he is quite clearly more undernourished and more debilitated (Sen, 1987).

Instead, Sen (1987) argues persuasively, the focus must shift to the kind of life people can and choose to live. A distinction is then drawn between "functionings" and "capabilities". A functioning is an achievement, whereas a capability is the ability to achieve. Functionings are, in a sense, more directly related to living conditions, since they are different aspects of living conditions. Capabilities, in contrast, are notions of freedom in the positive sense: what real opportunities a person has regarding the life he or she may lead.[3]

Given the close connection between functionings and actual living, it is tempting to concentrate on functionings rather than capabilities when evaluating the living standard. This could be limiting in some ways. Capabilities also matter, since living standards are not quite independent of the perspective of freedom. To borrow an example from Sen (1987), suppose a person is able to choose various lifestyles – A, B, C and D – and decides to choose A. Consider that the other lifestyles – B, C and D – are unavailable, but that he or she can still choose A. It might be said that the standard of living is unchanged, since A is what this person would have chosen anyway. It is nevertheless legitimate to argue that there is some loss in this person's living standard as a consequence of the reduction of freedom.

Is this approach different from the basic needs approach? Sen (1987) clarifies the differences: first, the basic needs are typically formulated in terms of commodity possession (rather than functioning achievements); and second, it is not clear why the fulfilment of basic needs is important. Pigou (1952), for example, argued in favour of an approach similar to that of basic

---

[3] Note that the extent of freedom must not be judged by the number of alternatives only but also by the goodness of the alternatives (Sen, 1987).

needs but founded on utilitarian principles. In case the concern is with the kind of lives people do or can lead, the basic needs would have to be specified more selectively in line with functionings and capabilities – nourishment and shelter, for example, then have an instrumental value for the capability of living a long and healthy life.

The implementation of this approach is, however, problematic. Apart from the selection of basic capabilities, a rather difficult problem is the aggregation of different functionings and capabilities into an overall index. If, for example, there is an improvement in one indicator (e.g. nourishment) and a deterioration in another (e.g. shelter), it is difficult to judge whether there has been an overall improvement in living standards. Recognizing this difficulty, Sen (1987) points out that, for a wide range of weights, it may be possible to establish a partial ordering which could yield unequivocal judgements of whether there has been an overall improvement. But, even when such a partial ordering is highly sensitive to the range of weights, changes in individual functionings and capabilities (e.g. stemming from an improvement in nourishment and a deterioration in shelter) are of sufficient interest in themselves from a policy perspective. Undoubtedly, this is an intuitively appealing and promising approach but it requires further elaboration and refinement (as well as much more detailed data sets than those available now) for its empirical implementation.[4]

Subject to the limitations noted above, a somewhat narrow version of the non-welfarist approach limited to nutritional adequacy has been widely used in poverty analysis (although important theoretical contributions have been made using the welfarist approach). Hence, much of the discussion in this report inevitably also has a non-welfarist flavour.

Absolute poverty

Much of the literature in developing countries is concerned with absolute poverty. An absolute poverty threshold is determined using the living

---

[4] In this context, the Drèze and Sen (1989) study is an important contribution.

standard indicator and is fixed over the entire domain of the poverty comparison.[5] Thus, an absolute poverty comparison will deem two persons at the same real consumption income level to both be either "poor" or "not poor", irrespective of the time or place being considered, or with or without a particular policy change, within the relevant domain (Ravallion, 1992).

Domain. That the poverty threshold is specific to a domain requires further comment. In the context of a global comparison of poverty (e.g. World Bank, 1990), for example, there is a strong case for using the same poverty threshold for all countries. Depending on how the threshold is fixed, it may be high for some poor countries and low for other less poor countries. But the domain of that particular poverty comparison goes well beyond the borders of one country. If, however, a temporal poverty comparison is carried out for a country, the appropriateness of the threshold to that country cannot be overlooked. The choice of an absolute poverty threshold is thus conditional upon the domain.

Nutritional considerations. A common approach in defining an absolute poverty threshold is to estimate the cost of a bundle of goods deemed to ensure that basic consumption needs are met in the specific domain of poverty comparison.[6] The difficulty is in what constitutes basic needs. For developing countries, an important component is the food expenditure necessary to attain a recommended food energy intake. This is then augmented by a modest allowance for non-food goods.

The choice of food energy requirement remains contentious as it can vary across individuals and over time for a given individual. An assumption must be made about activity levels which determine energy requirements beyond

---

[5] This exposition is largely from a non-welfarist perspective and is based mainly on Ravallion (1992).

[6] The basic needs approach to defining poverty thresholds goes back to the study by Rowntree (1901) on poverty in York in the United Kingdom at the turn of the twentieth century.

those needed to maintain the human body's metabolic rate at rest.[7] Activity levels are, however, endogenous socio-economic variables rather than exogenous physiological ones. Another problem is that the minimum cost of recommended calories may be considerably less than the expenditure level at which a low-income person typically attains that calorie level. Obtaining adequate nutrition is not the sole motive for human behaviour, even for most of the poor, nor is it the sole motive in food consumption.[8]

Other considerations. Sometimes an allowance is made for non-food consumption. A common procedure is, first, to fix a food energy intake cut-off point in calories and then to determine the consumption expenditure or income level at which a person typically attains that food energy intake. This can be estimated from a regression of calorie intake against consumption expenditure or income.[9] This method makes an allowance for non-food consumption, when the total consumption expenditure at which a person typically attains the caloric requirement is located. It also has the merit of yielding a poverty threshold that is consistent with local tastes

---

[7] Among the sceptics, Srinivasan (1986) argues forcefully that a biological basis for defining a fixed energy requirement for humans does not exist. There is now increasing support for the view that the energy balance (i.e. intake minus expenditure) of a healthy individual maintaining body weight and performing the same activity is a stationary, stochastic process with a zero mean. In other words, the energy balance on successive days is not independent but correlated. Specifically, there is a physiological regulatory mechanism which controls appetite and energy expenditure so that variations in intakes within certain homeostatic limits are absorbed without leading to under- or overnutrition. This in turn means that energy requirement is not a fixed number.

[8] A recent econometric analysis (Behrman and Deolalikar, 1987), based on a rural southern Indian sample, for example, confirms that higher income does not result in substantial improvements in nutrient intake. Food expenditures increase substantially – more or less proportionally to income – but the marginal increments in food expenditure are not devoted primarily to obtaining more nutrients. With more education about the relation between nutrients and other food characteristics, or with the development of other food varieties in which the nutritional benefits are more highly associated with the food attributes that consumers value highly at the margin, stronger associations between nutrient intakes and increases in income could perhaps be developed.

[9] See, for example, Greer and Thorbecke (1986).

as well as prices. However, it is still debatable whether non-food "requirements" can be specified in a precise way.

Equivalence scale. The poverty threshold is usually specified on a per caput income or consumption expenditure basis. Since households of a given size may vary in composition (i.e. age and gender), a refinement of this method is to construct an adult male equivalence scale as a basis for the normalization of household income/consumption. The presumption is that children and adult females have lower needs than adult males.

The equivalence scale is constructed from household surveys. The focus is on how aggregate consumption during a period varies with household size and composition. Specifically, a demand model is constructed in which the share of food expenditure of each household is regressed on the log of total consumption expenditure per person, and the number of household members classified by age and gender. Assuming that food share is a welfare indicator, a reference welfare level and, hence, food share are fixed. Using the regression results, a calculation is made of the difference in total consumption per caput needed to compensate a household for its compositional difference relative to that of the reference household. The equivalence scale is then constructed from these differences.[10]

This procedure is, however, problematic. One difficulty is that the welfare interpretation of observed consumption behaviour is rendered difficult by the possibility that multiple (indeed, infinitely many) utility functions will generate the same behaviour. Relevant parameters of well-being will not then be identifiable from that behaviour (Ravallion, 1992).

The welfare interpretation of equivalence scales constructed from consumption behaviour also depends on how consumption allocations are made within the household. As elaborated later, the interpretation of the empirical evidence would vary depending on whether household decision-making is embedded in a Beckerian common preference formulation or a bargaining formulation. If the latter is the more plausible formulation, the intrahouse-

---

[10] For more details, see Deaton and Muellbauer (1980) and Muellbauer (1987).

TABLE 1
Consumption within two hypothetical households

Household	Individual consumption				Household consumption	
	Male adult	Female adult	First child	Second child	Per person	Per equivalent male adult
A	40	20	10	10	20	40
B	30	–	–	–	30	30

Source: Ravallion (1992).

hold allocation will be influenced by outside options. The equivalence scale derived from consumption behaviour can then be taken to embody two distinct sets of considerations: real difference in needs between certain age and gender groups; and inequalities in outside options or bargaining power. A failure to separate these considerations may result in inappropriate policy interventions.

An example from Ravallion (1992) illustrates this potential policy problem. Suppose there are two households, A and B. Household A has one adult male, one adult female and two children, while B comprises a single adult male. Individual consumptions are given in Table 1.

Suppose the government wants to make a transfer to the poorer household but cannot observe the distribution within a household; all the government knows is the aggregate consumption and household composition. Assuming that the criterion for transfer is per caput consumption, household A will be chosen.

As an alternative, consider a scale which assigns weights proportionally to actual consumption levels. The equivalence scale would then be 0.5 for an adult female and 0.25 for each child. There are thus two equivalent adult males in household A, which then has a consumption per equivalent adult male which is more than that of household B. Hence B will receive help first. If much of the inequality within a household is due to the weak bargaining power of certain members (i.e. women and children), the use of an adult equivalence scale for targeting transfers, constructed from observed consumption patterns, may aggravate intrahousehold disparities.

TABLE 2

Incidence of rural poverty in India using different price deflators

NSS[1] rounds	Survey period	Percentage	CPIMR	Percentage	CPIAL
			(million persons)		*(million persons)*
25	July 1970 - June 1971	53.4	231	55.4	239
27	Oct. 1972 - Sept. 1973	57.4	258	56.5	254
28	Oct. 1973 - June 1974	56.4	258	56.4	258
32	July 1977 - June 1978	51.5	253	50.1	246
38	Jan. 1983 - Dec. 1983	45.3	248	42.9	235

[1] National sample survey.
Source: Minhas *et al.* (1987).

Price adjustment. The income/consumption poverty cut-off point is specific to a set of prices for a particular year. For poverty comparisons over time, it is therefore necessary to convert the cut-off point to current prices for different years. If the prices for low-income households do not diverge from those facing others, the price conversion would be a more or less straightforward exercise. This is, however, not generally true. In fact, according to carefully collected data on fractile group-specific price indices for the whole of rural India, it seems that the price rise for low-income households was larger than for rich households. Prices for the bottom 5 percent of the rural population, for example, went up from 100 in 1960-61 to 191.13 in 1967-68; for the top 5 per cent of the rural population the corresponding rise was from 100 to 172.98.[11] This divergence may be due to two related reasons. One is that the poor typically buy small quantities. The daily wage of casual agricultural labourers, for example, constrains their ability to buy food grains and other necessities. The other is the timing of purchasing. At the time of harvest, prices tend to drop. However, low-income households are unable to take advantage of these prices because they lack resources to buy food grains in bulk and to store them for later use.

As the price adjustment has been a controversial issue in Indian literature

---

[11] For further details, see Bardhan (1974a).

and policy discussions, some illustrations may be helpful. In Table 2, the incidence of poverty in rural India (i.e. the proportion of poor in the rural population) is computed by using two alternative price deflators, viz. the Consumer Price Index for the Middle Rural Population (CPIMR), i.e. from the 31st to the 60th percentile of the rural population, and the Consumer Price Index for Agricultural Labourers (CPIAL).

In a recent study a strong case was made in favour of the CPIMR in rural poverty analysis on the grounds that there "is a broad band in the middle constituting about 30 percent of the rural population (approximately from the 30th percentile to the 60th percentile of the distribution), large chunks of which either come into poverty or get excluded from poverty, depending on the price, production and employment conditions in a particular year (Minhas *et al.*, 1987, p. 16). This implies that the bottom 30 percent of the rural population remains perpetually poor. Such a claim can only be sub-stantiated with a panel survey. Unfortunately, no supporting evidence was cited. Indeed, a detailed analysis presented elsewhere casts doubts on this claim, as its results do not support the contention that the poorest 30 percent of the rural population are necessarily chronically poor. A substantial num-ber, in fact, are not. Nor is the obverse – that is, the chronically poor are necessarily the poorest – corroborated (Gaiha, 1989a). It is arguable that the CPIAL is the more appropriate deflator on the grounds that agricultural labour households are the largest occupational group among the rural poor. Not only are the bulk of them poor, but they also account for a large share of the rural poor.[12] More important, since agricultural labour households are net buyers of food, the CPIAL can be expected to provide a close approximation to the prices confronting net buyers of food among the rural poor (which, incidentally, would be much larger than the share of agricul-tural labour households among the rural poor).

As is evident from Table 2, the choice of a price deflator makes a

---

[12] In an analysis based on a pan-Indian panel survey of rural households, it was found that from 67 percent to 78 percent of casual agricultural labour households were poor and that these accounted for 42 to 44 percent of the rural poor in 1968, depending on the specification of the poverty cut-off point (Gaiha and Kazmi, 1981).

difference. With the CPIMR, there is a moderate reduction in the incidence of poverty while there is a substantial increase in the absolute number of the poor during the period 1970 to 1983. There is a more rapid reduction in the incidence of poverty when the CPIAL is used and, more strikingly, even the absolute number of the rural poor registers a reduction.

At a general level, two observations follow from this illustration. One is that the estimates of rural poverty are sensitive to the choice of price deflator. The other is that, in the absence of fractile group-specific price indices, a price index for the single largest occupational group among the rural poor would be appropriate.

Income versus consumption poverty thresholds. There is often a preference for a specification of the poverty cut-off point based on consumption expenditure (as opposed to an income-based specification). Consumption expenditure – as a living standard indicator – has the merit of being less variable than income. To the extent that consumption smoothing takes place by drawing on past savings and/or community support, income variation is not necessarily reflected in consumption variation. However, the constraints for consumption smoothing may vary across different groups. The landless poor, for example, are more constrained in their borrowing options than small landholders. While consumption smoothing and risk-sharing arrangements do exist in certain communities, they tend to break down when there is an all-round reduction in production and/or income. Another issue is the reliability of a consumption expenditure estimate relative to income estimates. While both consumption and income estimates are to some extent distorted by ad hoc procedures for imputing value to goods produced for self-consumption, income estimates tend to be further distorted by underreporting (especially among, but not necessarily limited to, the more affluent sections of the population).

Admittedly, consumption expenditure has some advantages over income in assessing living standards but it would be naïve to assume that the former is usually much more reliable. If the divergence in poverty estimates is not negligible, it is imperative from a policy perspective to investigate the reasons.

An illustration based on a pan-Indian survey may be helpful. Deciles of households ranked by per caput consumption expenditure in 1968 were cross-classified by per caput income in 1968. The diagonal elements (among the poor deciles) were low, implying that there was considerable mismatching among the rankings of households on these two criteria. For the third consumption expenditure decile, for example, the diagonal element was barely 16 percent. The intersections of the poor were also low, about 63 percent and 45 percent of the poor on the consumption expenditure criteria were also poor on the income criteria (note that the lower figure corresponds to the lower poverty cut-off point). If, at lower income levels, a higher consumption expenditure is maintained through sale of assets and/or borrowing for a certain period, the welfare implications may well be serious.[13] Thus, consumption expenditure by itself may be a limited and somewhat misleading living standard indicator.

Sensitivity analysis. Given a cumulative income/consumption expenditure distribution and a poverty threshold, the percentage of poor in a population may be determined. This is the so-called identification exercise to which a reference was made earlier in this chapter. Once the number of poor households and their share in the total population are determined, a profile of the poor can be constructed, focusing on household, demographic and employment characteristics. Such a profile serves as a starting point for an investigation of the underlying causal factors and for identifying broad areas of policy intervention. This is attempted in Chapter 5, Policy interventions.

One difficulty must, however, be noted. Given the nature of the calculations and the poor quality of data, a great deal of confidence cannot be placed in the estimates of rural poverty. Usually, therefore, two alternative poverty thresholds are specified and, thus, two point estimates of rural poverty are obtained. Following the terminology in a recent study (World Bank, 1990), those below the lower poverty threshold are sometimes designated as

---

[13] For more details, see Gaiha and Kazmi (1981).

"extremely" or "ultra poor". For each point estimate, a confidence interval may also be worked out. For a given point estimate, if the confidence interval (at the 95 percent level, for instance) is narrow, it implies that there is a high probability of actual poverty lying in that interval.

Relative poverty

The role of contemporary living standards in the measurement of poverty has long been recognized. Adam Smith (1776), for example, observed in a widely quoted passage:

"By necessaries, I understand not only the commodities which are indispensably necessary for the support of life but whatever the custom of the country renders it indecent for creditable people, even of the lowest order, to be without. A linen shirt, for example, is strictly speaking not a necessity of life. The Greeks and Romans lived, I suppose, very comfortably though they had no linen. But in the present time ... a creditable day-labourer would be ashamed to appear in public without a linen shirt, the want of which would be supposed to denote that disgraceful state of poverty" (p. 691).

In the same way, Marx referred to the fact that for the worker, "the number and extent of his so-called necessary wants ... are themselves the product of historical development and depend, therefore, to a great extent on the degree of civilization of a country" (cit. Atkinson, 1975, p. 227).

These considerations underlie an explicitly relative standard of poverty. As pointed out by Townsend (1973), "individuals and families are in poverty whose resources, over time, fall seriously short of the resources commanded by the average individual or family, in the community in which they live" (p. 48).

The relative approach has been widely used in developed countries in recent years, notably in the United Kingdom and the United States. The use of a relative poverty standard, however, does not imply that the poor are necessarily always with us. If, for example, the poverty threshold is taken to be half the average income, rising with the general standard of living, the income distribution may be such that no one has an income below this threshold. Nor does the fact that the poverty threshold may rise with the general level of income mean that it is a matter of "keeping up with the Jones's". Rather, it is a reflection of the interdependence of living standards (Atkinson, 1975).

Translation of the relative poverty concept into a concrete measure is far from straightforward. One approach has been to take the standard set by the government either explicitly, as in the United States, or implicitly, as in the United Kingdom in the form of social security benefits. Both approaches have their limitations. These measures rely on money income and ignore other aspects of deprivation. No account is taken of poor-quality housing, schools or health care, which may or may not be associated with low incomes. Moreover, poverty may represent only one aspect of a more general powerlessness, an inability to influence one's environment (Atkinson, 1975).

An alternative approach relies on a "participation" standard for poverty, taking account "of the many roles people play as citizens, workers, parents, householders, neighbours and members of the local community" (Cripps *et al.*, 1981, p. 184). Such a participation criterion was first used in Townsend's 1968-69 survey of poverty in the United Kingdom (Townsend, 1979). His aim was to investigate whether, below a certain income level, a significant number of families reduce their participation in the community's style of living. As he recognizes, there is no unitary and clear-cut national "style of living", but he suggests that there are types of consumption and custom that may be indicative; for example, owning a refrigerator, having had a holiday away from home in the past year and having sole use of an indoor toilet. How far a definite cut-off point emerges is of course a matter of debate.

What about its relevance for developing countries? Although both absolute and relative deprivation figure in common perceptions of poverty, it may be noted that it is the former that tends to dominate. Poverty tends to take particularly nasty, brutish and depressing forms (e.g. the use of violence to secure access to food, the consumption of debilitating and often poisonous berries found in local forests, the sale of children) in large parts of the developing world, and these manifestations are better captured as absolute deprivation. Yet another issue is whether relative poverty is distinguishable from inequality. Consider, for example, a poverty measure that is a function of a poverty threshold as a fixed proportion of the average income and a set of parameters specifying the Lorenz curve of the income or consumption distribution. The question is whether or not a ranking of the distributions in terms of this measure will preserve their ranking in terms of an appropriate measure of inequality. Any measure of inequality must have the property that, whenever income is transferred from a rich to a poor person, inequality should decrease and vice versa. Examples can be constructed to demonstrate that distribution A Lorenz dominates B – so that A has lower inequality than B for any well-behaved measure of inequality – and yet the poverty index in question is higher for the A distribution (Ravallion, 1992). Similar examples can be constructed when there are transfers among the poor.[14] Hence, the concepts of relative poverty and inequality are distinct.

POVERTY INDICES

Having identified the poor for a given poverty threshold in income/consumption expenditure, the next task is to take into account the distributional aspects. The headcount measure of poverty, for example, simply calculates the number of people whose income/consumption expenditure falls short of the poverty threshold, irrespective of how far short each happens to be. This requires the aggregation of different indicators (e.g. the number of poor and their income shortfalls) into an overall index.

There is now a large literature on poverty measures.[15] A short review of the well-known measures is given below and is followed by an observation on their policy implications.

A widely used measure is the headcount ratio, i.e. the proportion of units (individuals/households) in the population that are classified as poor in relation to a norm or a poverty threshold. Let y_i denote per caput income of the ith unit and let z denote the poverty threshold. Suppose there are N units in the population, then $P = [i/y_i \leq z]$ constitutes the set of poor units.

Let the number of units in P be N_p, then the headcount ratio will be:

---

[14] For a formal exposition, see Ravallion (1992).
[15] See, for example, Sen (1979), Atkinson (1987) and Srinivasan (1990).

$$H = N_p / N \tag{1}$$

This is a measure of the incidence of poverty. A limitation of this measure is that it does not take into account the severity/intensity of poverty. Often, therefore, the headcount ratio is supplemented by another, the average income shortfall. The latter, denoted by G, is defined as follows:

$$G = \frac{1}{N_p} \sum_{i \in p} \left[\frac{z - y_i}{z} \right] \tag{2}$$

But this index does not register an increase if there is a transfer from an acutely poor unit to a moderately poor unit (since the aggregate income shortfall is unaffected). In order to overcome this difficulty, *distributionally sensitive measures of poverty* have been formulated. Notable among these are the Sen index and the Foster-Greer-Thorbecke index. The Sen index takes the form,

$$S = H \left[G + (1 - G) \, g \right] \tag{3}$$

where g denotes the Gini coefficient of income distribution among the poor. While this index takes note of changes in the severity of poverty – specifically, it registers an increase if there is a transfer from an acutely poor unit to a moderately poor unit (or if there is an increase in g without a change in G) – it is not decomposable.

The Foster-Greer-Thorbecke index, specified below, has a number of attractive features:

$$F_{(\alpha)} = \frac{1}{N} \sum_{i \in p} \left[\frac{z - y_i}{z} \right]^{\alpha}, \quad \alpha \geq 0 \tag{4}$$

It is easily seen that $F_{(o)} = H$ and $F_{(1)} = HG$. In the event of a transfer from an acutely poor unit to a moderately poor unit, $F_{(\alpha)}$ will register an increase for $\alpha > 1$.[16] This index is also decomposable in the sense that, if a population of N units is divided into M subgroups with the number of units in the jth subgroup being N_j, the aggregate index $F_{(\alpha)}$ for the entire population is a weighted average of the aggregate indices of the subgroups, the weights being their population shares; that is

$$F_{(\alpha)} = \sum_{J=1}^{N} \left(\frac{N_j}{N} \right) F_{j(\alpha)} \tag{5}$$

This feature ensures that, if poverty increases (decreases) within a subgroup, *ceteris paribus,* aggregate poverty will also increase (decrease).

Given the large number of poverty indices to choose from, it is of interest to ask: Does it really matter in poverty comparisons which of these measures is used? The answer depends on whether income/expenditure inequality has changed. In case there is distributionally neutral growth or contraction, all of these poverty measures will yield the same ranking, and the ranking in terms of absolute poverty will be determined solely by the direction of change in the income/consumption expenditure distribution.

However, the differences between these measures can be quite pronounced in other situations. Consider, for example, two policies: Policy A entails a small redistribution from people around the mode of the distribution, where (by assumption) the poverty cut-off point is also located, to the poorest households. Policy B entails the opposite change – the poorest lose while those at the mode gain. The headcount index, H, will prefer policy B, since $H_A > H_B$. However, a measure such as $F_{(2)}$ will indicate the opposite ranking, $F_{(2)A} < F_{(2)B}$, since it will respond relatively more to the gains among the poorest than among those who are less poor (Ravallion, 1992). A more structured exposition of some of these issues, together with some empirical applications, is discussed later in this report.

---

[16] The higher the value of α, the more sensitive is the measure to the well-being of the poorest person.

POVERTY AND INEQUALITY

In the first section of this chapter, it was argued that poverty and inequality are related but distinct problems. This relation is pursued here from a welfarist perspective, in order to identify and elaborate some specific policy concerns.[17]

Alternative specifications

Following Atkinson (1987), at least four different specifications of the relation between poverty and inequality can be distinguished, as summarized below. I denotes the "cost" of inequality to be deducted from the mean income $\bar{y}$ while the equally distributed equivalent income[18] is $\bar{y} - I$. P similarly denotes the "cost" of poverty to be subtracted:

i) no specific weight to poverty: maximize $\bar{y} - I$;
ii) lexicographic approach: maximize $- P$, then $\bar{y} - I$, where ranking on P identical;
iii) concern only for poverty: maximize $\bar{y} - P$;
iv) trade-off between poverty and equality: maximize $\bar{y} - I - P$.

Rationale

In the first specification, the concern is limited to inequality. If poverty is taken into account, it is as a component of inequality. To illustrate, inequality is sometimes decomposed into that which is due to people having incomes below a poverty threshold and other components.[19] In case the measurement of inequality is based on the Rawlsian difference principle (Rawls, 1971), the focus is on the poor.

Although this principle is usually interpreted as maximizing the welfare of the least advantaged group without any reference to a poverty threshold, Atkinson (1987) points out that this could be misleading, since identification

---

[17] Some of the important contributions are Atkinson (1970, 1987). For an alternative non-welfarist view, see Sen (1973, 1992b).

[18] Or the level of income per head which, if equally distributed, would give the same level of social welfare as the present distribution.

[19] Such a decomposition into a poverty effect and an affluence effect is attempted in Watts (1968) and Pyatt (1984).

of such a group is likely to involve a poverty threshold (less than half of the median income).

More important, the difference principle is the second of Rawls' two principles, and a concern for poverty may enter through the first principle which gives priority to basic liberties. These liberties, which include participation in society, may depend on a minimum level of income. This motivates the second view, embodying a lexicographic approach that gives priority to poverty in ensuring "effective" liberty, followed by a concern for inequality.

As regards the remaining two specifications, an assessment of social welfare may be viewed as comprising two stages. The first stage consists of identification of an income level as being below the poverty threshold and evaluation of the costs associated with this deprivation. In the second stage, an aggregation across individuals is carried out to arrive at an overall social judgement. The first stage reflects a concern for poverty only, or the third view. Since the aggregation at the second stage involves social weights derived from a principle of justice, there is a trade-off between poverty and inequality, or the fourth view.

INTRAHOUSEHOLD INEQUALITY AND POVERTY

Some recent studies (e.g. Sen, 1988 and Chen, Huq and D'Souza, 1980) have drawn attention to sharp disparities in the allocation of household resources by gender – especially food and medical care. That these disparities are in part due to differences in gender-specific needs is generally not disputed. The dispute is usually about how many of these disparities are due to differences in needs and how to account for the remaining ones. This section comments on the latter, drawing on some recent contributions.[20] Implications of intrahousehold disparity in calorie intake for the assessment of poverty are also brought out.

---

[20] This section is based largely on Haddad and Kanbur (1989), Hoddinott (1992) and Sen (1983).

Common preference versus bargaining models

Of particular importance is Becker's (1981) common preference or altruistic model of household behaviour. It assumes a household utility function that reflects the preferences of all members. Maximizing this subject to the appropriate budget constraint yields demand functions for goods and leisure. In this model, all household resources (capital, labour and land) are pooled and all expenditures are made with pooled income.

As its point of departure, the alternative model assumes differences in preferences among household members, which are resolved by a bargaining process. The bargaining generates an agreed, self-enforcing utility function. Using cooperative Nash, non-cooperative Nash and other related solutions, bargaining models of household behaviour are formulated (e.g. Sen, 1983; Manser and Brown, 1980; McElroy and Horney, 1981; Lundberg and Pollak, 1991). A key concept is the threat point (or fall-back position) which determines an individual's bargaining power.

One major difficulty in choosing between the common preference and bargaining models is that they lead to similar predictions in many cases (Hoddinott, 1992). Suppose an exogenous change occurs that increases the return to women's labour outside the household. Both models predict that this may lead to changes in the allocation of women's time. In the common preference model, the household head or benefactor may decide to reorganize household production so as to increase women's labour market participation.

In a bargaining context, women may decide to renegotiate the conjugal contract on the basis of the enhanced earning opportunity. Further, increased women's labour force participation may alter the distribution of income within the household and this could affect the pattern of household expenditure. But again, this would be predicted by both the models. In the common preference model, the change in expenditure may reflect the reallocation of members' time. For example, households may purchase fuel rather than gather it.

Alternatively, the increase in women's earnings outside the household raises their bargaining power within it either because their threat point is higher or because their perceived contribution within the household is greater.[21] However, there are pieces of evidence that lend greater plausibility to the bargaining models. Monetary transfers in the common preference model, for example, would be negatively linked to the income or wealth of the recipient. The available evidence for Botswana (Lucas and Stark, 1985) and Kenya (Hoddinott, 1992) does not corroborate this. This could imply that donor-recipient relations are guided not so much by altruism as by self-interested exchange. Further, evidence available on the high incidence of physical violence within a family – a cross-cultural ethnographic study (Levinson, 1989) found that wife-beating occurred in 84 percent of the developing societies studied – is hardly reassuring from the point of view of altruistic household behaviour.

Understatement of poverty

Two types of evidence, one relating to disparities in intrahousehold allocation of food and health care, and another to the "outcomes" of such disparities, are frequently cited. Although such disparities are observed in different regions, in most cases (except in South Asia) the evidence continues to be patchy and anecdotal (Sen, 1988). Accordingly, the review here concentrates on the South Asian evidence.

Among the most careful and detailed quantitative studies are those based on the 1977-79 Food and Nutrition Study for Matlab Thana in Bangladesh, reported in Chen (1982). According to this study, from June to August 1978, male daily per caput calorie consumption was an average 16 percent higher among children under five years (for protein it was 14 percent higher). This significant female disadvantage in forms of food intake remains even after adjustments for gender-specific food requirements. This also shows up in the anthropometric assessment of nutritional status; by using the weight-for-age standard, a much larger percentage of female children was classified as severely or moderately malnourished compared with males.

As for medical care, Miller (1981) provides ethnographic evidence on the inferior kind and amount of medical care given to girls as compared with

---

[21] These illustrations are taken from Hoddinott (1992).

boys. Relative tardiness by parents in cases of girls' illness in approaching medical facilities even when they are accessible, premature stopping of medical treatment, more frequent recourse to faith healing and traditional medicine, for example, are quite common. Such discrimination is confirmed in Dandekar (1975) for rural Maharashtra, and Singh, Wyon and Gordon (1962) for Punjab (both Indian states). Chen (1982) reports from the Matlab study of Bangladesh that, in spite of offers of free transport and treatment for diarrhoeal diseases, and even though the disease incidence was roughly comparable between genders, male children were brought to the Matlab treatment facility by their guardians more frequently than female children.

Such intrahousehold disparities manifest themselves in lower survival chances for females in South Asia. The Indian evidence is illustrative: according to Sample Registration System data in 1976-78, the female death rate in rural India was 6 percent higher than the male death rate. But this average over age groups conceals the much larger differential in childhood and reproductive years: it is, for example, 17 percent higher in the age group up to four years, 31 percent higher in the five to nine age group, and 65 percent higher in the 20 to 24 age group. In the 15 to 34 age group, in general, maternity risk is of course mainly responsible for the differential. For children, however, other socio-economic and cultural factors matter. Even within the zero to four age group, the female disadvantage is much larger in the postneonatal (one to 11 months) and one to four age group than in the neonatal (less than one month) group. The female child is sturdier at birth (as in most countries) than the male but soon loses her relative advantage (in contrast to most countries). In 1977, of all deaths in rural India, for males, about 26 percent were in the age group of one month to four years while, for females, it was about 33 percent, underlining the quantitative importance of differential mortality in that age group (Bardhan, 1988).

The regional contrast in the differential chance of survival for the female child, as depicted in Table 3, is indeed striking. As it turns out, this contrast is closely linked to differential female employment prospects (Bardhan, 1988).

The death rate of rural female children (in the zero to four years age group) was as much as 47 percent higher than that of males in Punjab, 37 percent

TABLE 3

Death rate per thousand in zero to four years age group in different states of rural India, 1970

State	Males	Females	Ratio of females to males
Andhra Pradesh	50.8	43.6	0.86
Assam	43.4	43.0	0.99
Bihar	35.7	37.5	1.05
Gujarat	72.6	79.6	1.10
Haryana	25.5	34.6	1.36
Himachal Pradesh	52.9	46.0	0.87
Jammu/Kashmir	32.7	31.8	0.97
Karnataka	43.6	42.8	0.98
Kerala	22.0	22.1	1.00
Madhya Pradesh	64.8	60.2	0.93
Maharashtra	41.6	42.3	1.02
Orissa	64.0	55.3	0.86
Punjab	32.1	47.2	1.47
Rajasthan	64.2	78.9	1.23
Tamil Nadu	53.3	54.4	1.02
Uttar Pradesh	68.6	93.9	1.37
West Bengal	35.4	34.2	0.97

Source: Bardhan (1988).

higher in Uttar Pradesh, 36 percent higher in Haryana, 23 percent higher in Rajasthan and 10 percent higher in Gujarat. In contrast, most states in eastern and southern India had a female-to-male child death rate ratio that was below the average for rural India.

Bardhan (1974b) conjectures that the regional contrast is closely linked to, among other factors, ecological variations in crop production and associated female employment prospects. In all the states of eastern and southern India (except Karnataka), the predominant crop is paddy, which – unlike wheat and dry-region crops – tends to require relatively intensive female labour. Transplanting paddy is an exclusively female job in many paddy areas; besides, female labour plays a very important role in weeding, harvesting, threshing and various kinds of paddy processing. By contrast, in dry cultivation, and even in wheat cultivation under irrigation, the work involves more muscle power and less tedious, often back-breaking but delicate operations done by males.

This conjecture is supported by an econometric analysis, based on a sample of 1 334 rural households in India in 1971 (Rosenzweig and Schultz, 1982). In a two-stage regression analysis, the first stage confirms that there is a significant positive relationship between normal district-level rainfall and the probability of a woman being employed in rural India – thus supporting Bardhan's (1974b) conjecture about wet agriculture being relatively intensive in female labour. The second stage confirms that the differential survival chance of the female child improves with a higher female employment rate or with a lower male-female earning differential per day. "... [T]his means that expanding employment opportunities for women or lowering the male-female earning differential in rural India is not just another feminist cause: it may actually save the lives of many little girls in rural households" (Bardhan, 1988, p. 478).

That there is some correspondence between intrahousehold disparity and poverty is obvious. What is not so obvious is the precise relationship between them. A recent study (Haddad and Kanbur, 1989) throws valuable light on this relationship. In a formal exposition, the direction of the effect of intrahousehold inequality on the Foster-Greer-Thorbecke class of poverty indices is worked out and then illustrated with the Philippines' data. For a subset of the Foster-Greer-Thorbecke class of poverty indices ($\alpha \geq 1$), it turns out that neglect of intrahousehold inequality understates true poverty.

This is not a surprising conclusion. What is somewhat surprising is the extent of the difference between poverty measured with and without taking into account intrahousehold disparity. Restricting the analysis to food poverty (or calorie shortfall), it appears that the understatement in $P_{(1)}$ is over 18 percent and in $P_{(2)}$ 23 percent when intrahousehold inequality is ignored.[22] These discrepancies are by no means negligible.

---

[22] This analysis is based on a predominantly rural household survey in the southern Philippines in 1984-85, covering 448 households comprising 2 880 individuals. Calorie intake represented mothers' 24 hour recalls of food eaten by individual family members. Recommended daily allowance (RDA) calorie figures were disaggregated into 32 age, gender and pregnancy status categories. The limitations of RDA are well known. In particular, it does not take into account individual adaptation to food availability in the form of activity patterns, longitudinal growth retardation and, to a lesser extent, basal metabolic rate adjustment.

Shifts in threat points

To the extent that the bargaining model is a more plausible representation of household behaviour, there is a case for shifting threat points for women or, to use McElroy's (1990) terminology, influencing extrahousehold environmental parameters. In particular, assigning rights of property to women on par with men (e.g. land rights), the promotion of female literacy and employment could make a substantial difference to the amelioration of intrahousehold disparities and poverty. However, a caveat is necessary. Some Indian evidence suggests that human capital attributes, such as education, are not as important for women as they are for men in explaining differences in wages (Walker and Ryan, 1990). Less mobility among women workers, because of household obligations and social norms, may partly explain this. This suggests that higher female literacy may accomplish little unless impediments to female mobility are removed.

DOMINANCE CONDITIONS

As discussed earlier, various poverty measures have been proposed in recent years. Central to their measurement is the specification of a poverty threshold. Even if the poverty threshold is restricted to the cost of a nutritionally adequate diet, some rather difficult measurement problems arise.[23] It is, therefore, not surprising that often the poverty threshold is fixed in a somewhat arbitrary manner. In view of alternative specifications of the poverty threshold together with the wide range of poverty measures used in empirical work, assessments of whether poverty increased or decreased over a given period tend to vary. This is clearly unsatisfactory from a policy perspective. In order to overcome this difficulty, stochastic dominance conditions were proposed in a recent contribution by Atkinson (1987). These dominance conditions facilitate an unambiguous assessment of temporal changes in poverty even when both the poverty threshold and

---

[23] One difficulty, for example, stems from individual adaptation to shortfalls in nutrient intake. If individuals typically adapt within limits, it is doubtful whether a precise nutritional norm can be specified. See, for example, Srinivasan (1979).

the poverty index vary. An intuitive exposition of the dominance conditions is given below.[24]

First order dominance condition

Assuming a range of poverty thresholds, with the maximum defined as the highest permissible income level, and a class of poverty measures that satisfy mild conditions (viz. the measures are continuous, separable, symmetric and weakly monotonic), poverty has unambiguously declined between two dates (e.g. before and after the policy change) if the cumulative income distribution for the latter date is no higher than that for the former date over the entire interval up to the maximum poverty threshold.

This is the first order dominance condition. If the result is unambiguous, then poverty has declined irrespective of the poverty thresholds and the poverty measures used. However, if the cumulative distribution curves intersect within the range of permissible poverty thresholds, then the result is ambiguous – different poverty thresholds and measures will yield conflicting assessments.

Second order dominance condition

If the first order condition fails, the second order dominance condition may prove useful. The latter is, however, restricted to distributionally sensitive measures such as Foster-Greer-Thorbecke measures with $\alpha > 1$. The second order condition states that poverty has fallen if the area under the old cumulative distribution function is greater than that under the new distribution over the entire range of permissible poverty thresholds.[25] As is obvious, the second order condition requires more restrictions than the first order condition to achieve an unambiguous ranking (Fig. 1).

---

[24] For a more detailed exposition, see Ravallion (1992).

[25] When the second order dominance condition is inconclusive, a third order dominance condition could be used by further restricting the range of poverty measures. For details, see Atkinson (1987). *Note:* For an application of dominance conditions to Indonesian data, see Ravallion and Van de Walle (1991).

Conceptual and measurement issues in poverty analysis

FIGURE 1
Cumulative income distributions before and after policy change

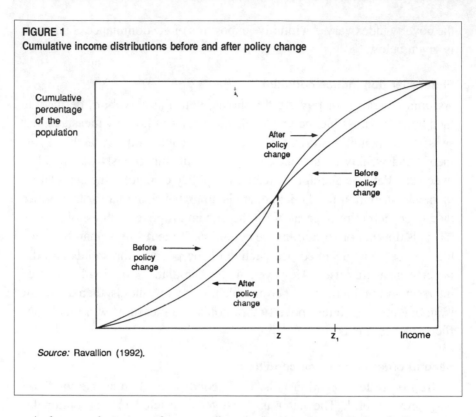

Source: Ravallion (1992).

As long as the range of poverty lines is restricted to z, the level of poverty is unambiguously higher before than after the policy change. This follows from the fact that, in accordance with the first order dominance condition, the cumulative income distribution curve before the policy change lies above the one for after the policy change over the range for poverty thresholds. However, if the range is extended up to z_1 then the first order dominance condition fails. The second order condition, for poverty to be higher before than after the change, is that the area under the cumulative distribution curve up to z_1 for before the change exceeds that for after.

Application

Since the dominance tests are relatively recent, there are few applications to actual data sets. Two interesting applications are based on Indonesian data for 1984 and 1987 (Ravallion, 1992). This was a period of external shocks and macroeconomic adjustment. A number of indicators of poverty, based on real consumption per person, real income per person and food energy intake per person were considered. For all indicators, the first order dominance held over the period in question: the 1984 distributions were entirely above those for 1987, suggesting that poverty fell. At the regional level the changes in a measure of undernutrition were, however, not so clear-cut. The first order dominance test indicated an unambiguous improvement for 29 of the 52 regions, while an unambiguous worsening was indicated for only three over the period 1984-1987. However, the first order test was ambiguous for 20 regions. For each of these, the 1987 (food energy intake) distribution crossed the 1984 distribution just once from below, i.e. there was an improvement in the lower segment of the distribution. The average crossover point was at about 1 950 calories per person per day. The second order test resolved this ambiguity for 12 regions, all but one of which showed an unambiguous improvement. Thus, there was unevenness across regions in reducing undernutrition, although first order or second order dominance tests indicated a reduction in undernutrition for about 80 percent of the regions. The extent of this improvement also varied considerably across regions.

Chapter 3
Does economic growth trickle down to the poor?

In this chapter, an attempt is made to examine the relationship between poverty and economic growth. Much of the recent literature – including the influential World Bank report on poverty (World Bank, 1990) – emphasizes an inverse relationship between poverty and economic growth. In the context of rural areas, the focus is on the poverty-alleviating role of agricultural growth. That agricultural growth reduces poverty is unexceptionable (Gaiha, 1989c).[1] This effect varies, however, depending on the nature of the agricultural growth process. If, for example, growth takes place in a setting of extreme inequality in endowments, its benefits are not likely to "trickle down" to large segments of the poor. In fact, some growth processes impoverish (Bardhan, 1985; Gaiha, 1987). Relevant evidence is therefore reviewed here to illustrate the conditions under which impoverishment occurs.

A related but distinct problem is the *persistence* of poverty in rural areas. To the extent that there is a large hard core of poverty (measured by the share of chronically poor in total poor), the overall reduction in rural poverty that is consequent on a significant improvement in agricultural performance may be small. Either large transfers or specific interventions, designed to help the chronically poor overcome their constraints or disabilities (e.g. negligible human capital), may therefore be necessary. Some illustrative evidence on the incidence of chronic poverty is summarized and its policy

---

[1] See, for example, the econometric evidence summarized in FAO (1991a). For further details, see FAO (1990b).

implications are noted. Finally, as a prelude to the overview of direct anti-poverty interventions in Chapter 4, a detailed analysis of causation of poverty is reviewed. Although the specific mechanisms resulting in poverty are not captured in this analysis, some (proximate) causal factors are identified and their relative importance assessed.

DECOMPOSITION OF CHANGE IN POVERTY

Some recent investigations (FAO, 1991; World Bank, 1990) confirm that growth reduces poverty. However, the strength of this relationship weakened during the 1980s, mainly because of larger fluctuations in income inequality (World Bank, 1990). In this context, the contrast between India and Brazil (mostly during the 1980s) is instructive. Some useful insights emerge from a decomposition of change in poverty into a *growth* component, a *distributional* component and the *residual*.[2] If poverty falls over time, part of the reduction may be due to a higher average income without any change in its distribution (i.e. the growth component), some reduction may be due to a change in the distribution itself without any change in the average income (i.e. the distributional component), while the remaining reduction may be due to the interdependence between growth and distributional change (i.e. the residual). The issue is whether the favourable effect of growth is neutralized or reinforced by income distributional changes. The results summarized below are striking.

Table 4 contains different measures of poverty for India and Brazil,[3] viz. the headcount ratio, H; the poverty gap index, HG; and the Foster-Greer-

---

[2] Expressing a poverty index as a function of the poverty threshold, the mean income and the Lorenz curve of income distribution, the growth component is measured as the difference in the poverty index (over a specified period) when only the mean changes, while the Lorenz curve (or the distribution of income) remains unchanged; the distributional component refers to the difference in the poverty index when the Lorenz curve changes but not the mean; and, finally, the residual exists whenever the marginal effects on the poverty measure of changes in the mean (Lorenz curve) depend on the Lorenz curve (mean). For a formal exposition, see Datt and Ravallion (1990).

[3] Note that the analysis reviewed here covers rural India and all of Brazil (in the absence of a rural/urban disaggregation of income distribution data in the latter).

TABLE 4
Poverty in India and Brazil since the late 1970s

Poverty measure/country	1977-78	1981	1983	1985	1986-87	1987	1988
Rural India							
Headcount index	52.68	–	45.13	–	36.84	–	38.66
Poverty gap index	16.03	–	12.74	–	9.44	–	9.40
Distributionally sensitive index	6.67	–	4.97	–	3.48	–	3.25
Brazil							
Headcount index	26.46	32.14	26.13	–	24.23	–	–
Poverty gap index	10.07	13.09	9.90	–	9.46	–	–
Distributionally sensitive index	4.96	6.81	4.82	–	4.79	–	–

Source: Datt and Ravallion (1990).

Thorbecke index, $F_{(2)}$; with $\alpha = 2$ referred to as the distributionally sensitive index.

All poverty measures for rural India fell during the period, although not all continuously, with an increase in the headcount index between 1986-87 and 1988. However, the increase was small.[4]

The decomposition is shown in Table 5. In most cases (1986-87 to 1988 being an exception) the growth component dominated. For example, the growth component accounted for a reduction of about 13 percentage points in a total reduction of over 14 percentage points in the headcount ratio during the period 1977-78. But the relative importance of the growth and distributional components varied greatly, depending on the measure of poverty used. This is most striking for the subperiod 1986-87 to 1988.

As regards the headcount index, both the growth and distribution components contributed to the increase in poverty. However, for the other two measures, changes in distribution mitigated the adverse effect of the decrease in the mean expenditure. In fact, those around the poverty threshold became worse off over this subperiod, while the poorest became better off. Finally, the residuals varied considerably in size. For example, for the

---

[4] Note that the samples for 1986-87 and 1988 are not comparable, since the latter covered only six months of that year.

Does economic growth trickle down to the poor?

TABLE 5

Decomposition of change in poverty in rural India

Period	Growth component	Distributional component	Residual	Total change in poverty
		(Percentage points)		
Headcount index				
1977-78 to 1983	– 6.45	– 1.18	0.09	– 7.54
1983 to 1986-87	– 7.33	– 0.72	– 0.24	– 8.29
1986-87 to 1988	1.04	1.44	– 0.66	1.82
1977-78 to 1988	– 12.74	– 0.46	– 0.82	– 14.02
Poverty gap index				
1977-78 to 1983	– 2.82	– 0.53	0.06	– 3.29
1983 to 1986-87	– 2.87	– 0.54	0.11	– 3.30
1986-87 to 1988	0.39	– 0.19	– 0.24	– 0.04
1977-78 to 1988	– 5.31	– 1.26	– 0.06	– 6.63
Distributionally sensitive index				
1977-78 to 1983	– 1.40	– 0.34	0.04	– 1.70
1983 to 1986-87	– 1.34	– 0.28	0.13	– 1.49
1986-87 to 1988	0.17	– 0.37	– 0.03	– 0.23
1977-78 to 1988	– 2.56	– 0.99	0.13	– 3.42

Source: Datt and Ravallion (1990).

headcount index over the entire period 1977-78 to 1988, the residual was larger in absolute value than the distributional component. However, in all other cases, the residual was small relative to both growth and distribution components.

The period 1981-1983 was one of recession and macroeconomic adjustment in Brazil, with the latter achieved through a combination of tight monetary policies, exchange rate policies and fiscal restraint. The latter half of the 1980s saw a return to the higher growth rates of the 1970s. Table 4 contains estimates of three indices of national poverty for Brazil during the period 1981 to 1987. These indices show a slight decrease in poverty in this period. However, there was considerable variation across subperiods, with a sharp increase from 1981 to 1983 by all measures, followed by a decline from 1983 to 1987. The results of the decomposition are given in Table 6.

During the period 1981 to 1987, the growth component was responsible for the reduction in poverty while the distributional component substantially weakened this effect. The relative strength of these two components varied depending on the poverty index used. In the case of the distributionally sensitive index, for example, the distributional component almost neu-

TABLE 6
Decomposition of change in poverty in Brazil

Period	Growth component	Distributional component	Residual	Total change in poverty
		(Percentage points)		
Headcount index				
1981-1983	3.96	1.65	0.07	5.68
1983-1985	− 5.84	0.02	− 0.10	− 5.91
1985-1987	− 2.61	0.46	0.15	− 2.00
1981-1987	− 4.48	2.13	0.12	− 2.23
Poverty gap index				
1981-1983	2.18	0.72	0.11	3.02
1983-1985	− 3.18	0.15	− 0.16	− 3.19
1985-1987	− 1.34	0.92	− 0.01	− 0.44
1981-1987	− 2.34	1.80	− 0.06	− 0.66
Distributionally sensitive index				
1981 to 1983	1.39	0.37	0.09	1.85
1983 to 1985	− 2.00	0.15	− 0.14	− 1.99
1985 to 1987	− 0.81	0.87	− 0.09	− 0.03
1981 to 1987	− 1.42	1.39	− 0.14	− 0.16

Source: Datt and Ravallion (1990).

tralized the growth component. During 1981-83, the poverty indices increased as a result of a reduction in mean income and adverse distributional changes, with the former exerting the larger effect. The recovery during 1983-85 was associated with a reduction in poverty indices, mainly because of the growth component. As regards the distributionally sensitive index, the growth component was more than neutralized by the distributional component. Nevertheless, there was a slight reduction in this index due to the stronger combined effect of the growth component and the residual.

The contrast between Brazil and India is striking. Both recorded reductions in poverty. In the former, the favourable effects of growth were partly offset by adverse distributional changes, implying that the poor did not participate in the growth. In India, while growth was the decisive factor in poverty alleviation, distributional changes further contributed to poverty alleviation.

AGRICULTURAL GROWTH AND IMPOVERISHMENT
Given that the decomposition is concerned with change in a poverty index over time, it is unable to capture the impoverishment of certain sections as a direct consequence of growth processes dominated by large landhold-

ers. If, for example, a subset of the moderately poor becomes poorer while many of the poorest gain during a period of growth, the poverty index (including the distributionally sensitive index) may register an improvement, with part of the improvement attributable to the rise in mean income. Another limitation of the decomposition is that it does not throw any light on the causal linkages.

It is important to know, for example, whether the reduction in poverty occurred as a consequence of higher farm productivity or higher wages or simply better rainfall. Ideally, in order to link income distributional changes to some of these factors, panel data (i.e. data collected from a given panel of households at different points of time) are required. Whether particular subsets of households (e.g. agricultural labourers, smallholders) earned higher or lower incomes over a period of time can then be related to changes in endowments, prices and cropping pattern and intensity. Even though the evidence reviewed below has been taken from Indian surveys, the findings are likely to be of wider interest.

Bardhan (1985) drew attention to agricultural growth aggravating rural poverty, through a logit analysis of poverty among cultivating and agricultural labour households, based on a sample of 550 villages in the Indian state of West Bengal in 1977-78. A distinguishing feature of this analysis is that both village- and household-specific characteristics are taken into account.

Among agricultural labour households, the village irrigation level was inversely related to the risk of poverty (derived from an *ex post* measure) while the distance from the nearest town was positively related. On the other hand, household characteristics – such as area cultivated and number of men with more than a primary education in the 15 to 60 age group – were negatively associated with the risk of poverty. These results are not surprising. What is surprising is the highly significant positive coefficient of the growth rate of agricultural production. With a few minor differences, similar results (including a highly significant positive coefficient of the growth rate of agricultural production) were obtained for cultivating households. Subject to some caveats, the overall conclusion is that, other things being equal, both agricultural labour and cultivating households faced a higher risk of poverty in districts where agricultural production grew at a faster rate. It is arguable that Bardhan's (1985) use of cross-sectional data to infer the effect of agricultural growth on poverty is subject to the usual problem of deriving time-series conclusions from a cross-section. It is possible, for example, that if the faster growing districts in West Bengal also happened to be the ones with above-average poverty in the initial year, and, if the growth rate was not sufficient to offset those initial conditions, one could arrive at Bardhan's conclusion (Srinivasan, 1985). The other difficulty is that the headcount measure used by Bardhan (1985) is insensitive to income distribution among the poor. Given that Bardhan based his analysis on a cross-section of headcount ratios, it would have been more interesting to examine whether other poverty measures bore a similar relationship to agricultural growth.

Gaiha (1987) builds on Bardhan's (1985) analysis, basing his study on a panel survey of rural households in India. It contains three cross-sections on a panel of 4 118 households, each of which was interviewed in 1968-69, 1969-70 and 1970-71. Even though the period of analysis was short, it nevertheless provided an appropriate setting for a study of impoverishment, as it was marked by a rapid spread of the new agricultural technology – consisting of biochemical innovations – and, consequently, a rapid growth of agricultural production.

During the period in question, the headcount ratio among the cultivating households fell sharply from about 48 percent to about 36 percent. The average income shortfall among the poor also fell sharply – from 0.4 to 0.27 percent – in the same period. On the basis of these poverty indices, an altogether favourable view of this period would be taken. The following observations, however, demonstrate that such a view is misleading.

Three points follow from the results in Table 7:
- the reduction in the headcount ratio was due to the fact that the poor who ceased to be poor (i.e. category 3) exceeded the non-poor who became poor (i.e. category 5);
- both among the poor and the non-poor, and especially among the latter, the share of the impoverished (i.e. poor who became poorer and non-poor who became poor) was far from negligible;

TABLE 7

Cultivating households by poverty status in rural India, 1968-70

Poverty status	Percentage of cultivating households
1. Poor who remained poor without becoming poorer	17.07
2. Poor who became poorer	6.00
3. Poor who became non-poor	24.57
4. Non-poor who remained non-poor	39.94
5. Non-poor who became poor	12.42

Source: Gaiha (1987).

- among the impoverished (i.e. categories 2 and 5), the non-poor who became poor were the larger subset.

In Table 8, categories 1 and 3 recorded very substantial income gains, with the latter gaining more than twice as much. This contrasts with the little more than marginal increase in the average income of category 4. Between the two impoverished categories, 2 and 5, the latter was subjected to more acute impoverishment, as the reduction in the average per caput income for this group was more than 2.5 times that of the former.

After it had been established that transitory variations resulting from random shocks (associated with weather or abrupt price movements, for instance) were negligible, it was demonstrated that the impoverishment was a direct consequence of the greater dominance of large landholders (i.e. those cultivating households with a gross cropped area ≥10 ha) in the growth process unleashed by the new agricultural technology. Following is a somewhat stylized description of how the dominance grew.

With the advent of the new technology, investment in agriculture became much more profitable. Since smallholders enjoyed restricted access to institutional credit and consequently modern agricultural inputs, the benefits of the new technology accrued mainly to large landholders. The latter expanded acreage through the resumption of land for personal cultivation (by evicting tenants) and/or through the leasing or outright purchase of land from small landowners. As a result, the distribution of gross cropped area

TABLE 8

Change in real income of cultivating households by poverty status in rural India, 1968-70

Poverty status	Average per caput income		Percentage change in average income[1]
	1968	1970	
1. Poor who remained poor without becoming poorer	88.16	146.15	65.78
2. Poor who became poorer	144.14	111.86	(–)22.40
3. Poor who became non-poor	126.29	310.01	145.47
4. Non-poor who remained non-poor	433.65	460.89	6.28
5. Non-poor who became poor	334.21	144.09	(–)56.91

[1] Percentage change in real income = $\dfrac{\text{Average per caput income in 1970} - \text{Average per caput income in 1968}}{\text{Average per caput income in 1968}} \times 100$

Source: Gaiha (1987).

became more unequal (the Gini coefficient increased from .602 to .698 in the period 1968-70) and there was a much higher incidence of landlessness (the share of landless households rose from 25 percent to 35 percent over the same period). The loss of income from cultivation among erstwhile tenants and small landowners could only be partly compensated by higher wage incomes. A rather striking piece of evidence is that the share of poor small cultivators (i.e. households with a gross cropped area ≤ 2.5 ha) who supplemented their primary source of income through wages more than doubled – from over 24 percent in 1968 to over 62 percent in 1970. If this is any indication of the pressure on rural labour markets, it would tend to depress the daily wage rate. Furthermore, a strengthening of oligopsonistic tendencies in rural labour markets further restricted the rise in wages. As a result, among the impoverished, additional wage income could only compensate for a small fraction of the loss of income from cultivation. The more acute impoverishment of the cultivating non-poor (i.e. the non-poor who became poor) resulted from more substantial losses of income from cultivation and a more acute failure in compensating for these losses through higher wage earnings.[5] If this analysis has any general validity, it suggests that the benefits of growth processes dominated by large landholders do not necessarily trickle down to all poor and other low-income segments, many of them in fact lose.

CHRONIC POVERTY

For some sections of the rural population, poverty is not a transitory phenomenon; it is more or less a permanent condition. Typically, these sections comprise: people living in remote, resource-poor regions, without any infrastructure, barely managing to survive; backward sections of society (euphemistically referred to as scheduled castes and tribes in India), debarred from owning assets, denied access to education and condemned to menial occupations; and the disabled and aged, incapable of augmenting their incomes above a bare subsistence level. Even when agricultural growth takes place, their plight seldom improves.

Despite a growing concern for the chronically poor, there are few empirical analyses. The major difficulty is the relatively small number of panel surveys. In the absence of a panel survey, an estimate of chronic poverty cannot be worked out. India is one of the few developing countries with two panel surveys, one for all of rural India (to which a reference was made earlier) and another for the semi-arid tract in south India. As few studies of chronic poverty based on these surveys are available (Gaiha, 1989b and 1992; and Gaiha and Deolalikar, 1992), their findings are reviewed below.

Using an income cut-off point, the incidence of chronic poverty (i.e. the share of chronically poor in the sample households) was calculated to be 27 percent in the pan-Indian sample for the period 1968-70. Alternatively, with an expenditure specification of the poverty cut-off point, a higher estimate was obtained (about 33 percent). The overlap between the chronically poor identified using income and expenditure criteria was large. About 23 percent of the sample households (or about 83 percent of the chronically poor using the income criterion) turned out to be chronically poor, using either the

---

[5] For further details, see Gaiha (1987).

TABLE 9

Chronically poor by per caput income decile in rural India, 1968

Income decile	Percentage of chronically poor within each decile	Percentage of total chronically poor
I	56.7	21.0
II	54.2	20.1
III	53.3	19.5
IV	44.2	16.5
V	43.6	16.0
VI	18.5	6.9

Note: Figures in the third column total 100.
Source: Gaiha (1989b).

income or expenditure criterion. The chronically poor accounted for 47 percent of the total poor in 1968 (using the income criterion).

The average income shortfall of the chronically poor in 1968 was 41 percent. A key question is whether the chronically poor were also the poorest.[6]

It follows from Table 9 that the incidence of chronic poverty was high in each of the five bottom deciles (note that all households in the bottom six deciles were poor in 1968), with higher values in each of the bottom three deciles. In fact, the percentages of the chronically poor fell steadily with higher deciles, with a rather sharp drop in the sixth decile. Referring to the third column of Table 9, while over 60 percent of the chronically poor belonged to the bottom three deciles, the remainder – by no means a small share – belonged to the higher deciles.[7] Besides, within each of the bottom five deciles the chronically poor were not necessarily the poorest. This is illustrated by the fact that, in these deciles, the average per caput income of the chronically poor was either as much as, or slightly higher than, the decile average.

---

[6] In a few recent studies (Lipton, 1988; and Minhas *et al.*, 1987) the obverse has been asserted, i.e. the poorest tend to be chronically poor.
[7] For a further corroboration through a logit analysis, see Gaiha (1992).

TABLE 10
Chronically poor by primary occupation in rural India, 1968

Occupation	Percentage of chronically poor within each occupation	Percentage of total chronically poor
Cultivators	16.20	26.90
Casual agricultural labourers	46.98	56.27
Casual non-agricultural labourers	22.28	4.37
Permanent wage earners	10.00	2.28
Artisans	26.83	8.52
Dependent on transfer income	15.64	1.67

Note: Figures in the third column total 100.
Source: Gaiha (1989b).

TABLE 11
Chronically poor by gross cropped area in rural India, 1968

Gross cropped area class	Percentage of chronically poor within each class	Percentage of total chronically poor
(hectares)		
0– ≤ 1	33.79	71.47
1.1– ≤ 2.5	23.27	17.04
2.6– ≤ 5.5	16.53	8.82
≥ 5.6	8.4	2.67

Note: Figures in the third column total 100.
Source: Gaiha (1989b).

Table 10 shows that the highest incidence of chronic poverty was among casual agricultural labourers. Among artisans and casual non-agricultural labourers the incidence was high, while among cultivators it was moderate. The lowest incidence was among permanent wage earners. Referring to the third column of Table 10, while casual agricultural labourers were the largest group among the chronically poor, cultivators were the second largest. With the exception of artisans, all other groups accounted for relatively small shares of the chronically poor.

Table 11 classifies the chronically poor by size classes of gross cropped

TABLE 12
Chronically poor by education level in rural India, 1968

Education level[1]	Percentage of chronically poor in each educational category	Percentage of total chronically poor
Illiterate	32.2	56.2
Primary or below	29.1	22.8
Above primary but below matriculation	21.1	17.8
Matriculation	11.5	3.2
Graduate and above	1.4	_[2]

[1] Education level represents the highest level attained by any household member.
[2] Negligible.
Note: Figures in the third column total 100.
Source: Gaiha (1989b).

area in 1968. Based on the results in the second column, the incidence of chronic poverty fell as size classes of gross cropped area increased. The third column illustrates clearly that the bulk of the chronically poor were either landless or near landless. Specifically, the bottom two classes (i.e. ≤ 2.5 ha) accounted for about 89 percent of the chronically poor.

Table 12 shows the proportion of chronically poor according to education level. Among the illiterates and those with few years of schooling, slightly below one-third in each category were chronically poor. However, the bulk of the chronically poor (79 percent) belonged to these two education categories. About 56 percent of the chronically poor were illiterate.

A cross-classification of the chronically poor by range of dependency burden is given in Table 13. The second column shows that relatively high percentages of the households in the dependency burden ranges of 21 to ≤ 40 percent and 41 to ≤ 60 percent were chronically poor, while moderate shares of the households in the remaining two ranges, i.e. the lowest (0 to ≤ 20 percent) and the highest (>60 percent), turned out to be so. The pattern displayed in the third column is, however, different. The shares of the chronically poor rose with higher ranges of dependency burden, with the highest range (>60 percent) accounting for over 52 percent of the chronically poor. Another noteworthy feature (not shown here) is the positive

TABLE 13
Chronically poor by dependency burden in rural India, 1968

Dependency burden	Percentage of chronically poor within each interval	Percentage of total chronically poor
(Percentage)		
0 – ≤ 20	16.85	4.51
21 – ≤ 40	37.69	13.42
41 – ≤ 60	37.47	29.77
> 60	22.87	52.30

Note: Dependency burden $= \dfrac{\text{Household size} - \text{earners}}{\text{Household size}} \times 100$.

Source: Gaiha (1989b).

association between dependency burden and household size. In other words, the greater the dependency burden, the larger was the household size.

To summarize, the chronically poor were not necessarily the poorest; in fact, a substantial number were moderately poor. However, the bulk of them were either landless or near landless, with virtually no formal education. The majority of the chronically poor households were large, with a high dependency burden (or, equivalently, with a low participation rate).

Although this is a useful and plausible characterization, it is in a sense incomplete. The incompleteness regards chronic poverty as a characteristic of a household over a period of time. The characterization presented above refers to some initial features in a particular year. In order to supplement this characterization, account therefore has to be taken of variation in some key magnitudes over time. Another analysis based on this panel survey (Gaiha, 1992) addresses this issue. A major conclusion that emerges from this analysis is that the chronically poor were distinguishable from the "just poor" (i.e. poor in 1968 – chronically poor during 1968-70) in terms of low variation in both household income and per caput income over the survey period (1968-70). The contrast with the non-poor was even sharper. The observations made in the following section are confined to variation in per caput income.

First, a decomposition of variation in per caput income for each of the three groups, viz. chronically poor, just poor and non-poor, was carried out separately for 1968 and 1970. Second, given the variations in per caput income, a decomposition of variation in (incremental) per caput income over the period in question was obtained.[8] The results confirm that the lowest variation was associated with the chronically poor, the next larger with the just poor and the largest with the non-poor. More specifically, among the chronically poor, the sum of the variation in the measure of per caput incomes in 1968 and 1970 was smaller than that for the just poor, and the sum for the latter was considerably smaller than that for the non-poor. Besides, the absolute value of the covariation between the measures of per caput incomes in 1968 and 1970 was lowest among the chronically poor and highest among the non-poor.

Further investigations revealed that the low variation in per caput incomes among the chronically poor reflected low variation in participation rates (i.e. share of earners among household members) and in earnings per worker – especially the latter. Since differences in earnings per worker signify differences in endowments (e.g. arable land, quality of soil, etc.) and/or ability (e.g. skills) to augment earnings from them, another feature of the chronically poor is suggested, namely their endowments and/or the ability to augment earnings from them varied much less relative to the just poor and non-poor over the period in question.

A major limitation of the pan-Indian panel survey is that it covers a short period of three years and therefore doubts may arise about the validity of these findings over a longer period of time. Supplementary evidence is provided by another study (Gaiha and Deolalikar, 1992), based on a smaller sample of households in the semi-arid tract in southern India (170 households) but covering a longer period of nine years from 1976 to 1984. Four measures of poverty are computed, of which two are particularly relevant in the present context. One is a measure of persistent poverty, based on an income specification of the poverty cut-off point, taking into account the

---

[8] This decomposition comprises three components, viz. variance of (log of) per caput income in 1968, variance of (log of) per caput income in 1970 and twice the covariance of (log of) per caput incomes in 1968 and 1970. From the sum of the first two components, the third is subtracted to arrive at the variance in the incremental (log of) per caput income.

TABLE 14

Persistent poverty estimates for semi-arid rural southern India, 1975-76 to 1983-84

	Number of years spent in poverty					
0 *(Never)*	1 *(Some time in poverty)*	2	3	4	5 .... 9 *(Always poor)*	
Percentage of poor households 12.4	87.8	80.2	73.1	68.4	61.3	21.8

Source: Gaiha and Deolalikar (1992).

duration of poverty. Another is a measure of innate poverty, which allows for random variation in income. More important, it incorporates a further refinement (made possible by the availability of panel data) of control for unobserved household fixed effects (representing managerial ability, indus-triousness and other household endowments) in the estimation of the income equation.[9] The incidence of innate poverty is worked out on the assumption that time-varying characteristics are fixed at sample values (note that the use of mean values is only for illustrative purposes). This measure thus focuses on households that are poor because of deep-rooted characteristics that cannot be easily changed in the short or medium term, such as schooling of the household head (which is observed), and managerial ability and industriousness (which are unobserved). An implication is that innately poor households will remain in poverty even if their physical assets, for example, are raised to the sample mean levels through redistribution.

Table 14 shows the proportion of households whose incomes fell under the poverty cut-off point for a varying number of years between 1975-76 and 1983-84 (viz. the persistently poor). What is surprising – indeed startling – about these figures is the persistence of poverty.

A very large number – indeed, an overwhelming majority – of sample

---

[9] The income equation includes time-invariant household characteristics such as schooling of the household head, time-varying household characteristics such as assets, proportion of non-earners, and village characteristics such as mean monthly rainfall during a year. For further details, see Gaiha and Deolalikar (1992).

households (87.8 percent) were poor for some time (i.e. in at least one year) during the nine-year sample period. Slightly more than 60 percent of households were poor for about half of the time (i.e. during five of the nine sample years) and, finally, a little more than one-fifth of the households were poor during all nine years. Thus, the persistently poor were by no means a small subset. The magnitude of innate poverty averaged 48 percent during the sample period. It is surprisingly large, considering that it identifies those households that would remain poor in spite of short-term changes in their assets and other characteristics (e.g. family size).

Admittedly, this is a small sample and there are obvious difficulties in generalizing from it – especially because the semi-arid tract is a special case from an agroclimatic point of view. The high magnitude of persistent poverty may therefore be specific to this region. Nevertheless, combining the different pieces of empirical evidence presented here, it is legitimate to infer that the chronically poor are not a small subset of the rural population, and therefore call for special measures. What the above analysis suggests is that drastic measures, such as income transfers on a continuing basis or a heavy concentration of physical and human assets, may be necessary to compensate subsets of the persistently poor for their innate disadvantages.

DETERMINANTS OF RURAL POVERTY

Econometric models employed in estimating poverty in developing countries in recent studies (e.g. World Bank, 1990; FAO, 1991a) throw hardly any light on the underlying causal mechanisms. If, for example, an inverse relationship is observed between rural poverty and agricultural performance, it does not offer any clues as to why certain sections of the rural population benefit while others do not. This issue is best addressed in a specific context. Accordingly, two analyses, based on a pan-Indian panel survey are reviewed below (Gaiha, 1985; 1988).[10] An important feature of these analyses is that they take into account village-specific, technol-

---

[10] The analysis for 1968 is reported in Gaiha (1988), while a comparative analysis for 1968 and 1970 is reported in Gaiha (1985).

ogical and household-specific variables.[11] Since the survey period (1968-70) was marked by a rapid spread of the new agricultural technology and, consequently, an acceleration of agricultural growth, the analyses in question yield insights into why certain sections failed to benefit from it.

The relationship explored may, however, be more complex than posited in this study. Consider, for example, the relationship between poverty and household size. Other things being equal, the larger the household size, the lower the per caput income would be and, consequently, the greater the likelihood of this household's being poor. On the other hand, the jointness of a household may itself be a response to acute poverty of nuclear units. For this reason, the variables associated with poverty are appropriately viewed as proximate determinants of poverty. Whether most of these factors would show up as important in other contexts as well cannot be ascertained, except that there are pieces of evidence suggesting that they also matter elsewhere. Two sets of logit exercises were carried out for 1968 and 1970, focusing on the risk of poverty in the aggregate sample as well as among subsamples of major occupational groups. In each case, an *ex post* measure of the risk of poverty was specified as a function of village-specific, technological and household-specific variables. First, the results for 1968 are reviewed, followed by a comparison of the results for 1968 and 1970.

In the aggregate sample (for different specifications of the poverty cut-off point) for 1968, the village-specific variables, viz. the availability of a bus or railway service between the nearest market and the village, the availability of health and/or veterinary services in the village and the existence of a small-scale factory in or near the village, reduced the risk of poverty. Among the technological variables, three bore a negative relationship to the risk of poverty. They were: whether a household used electricity for farming; gross cropped area devoted to high-yielding varieties (HYVs) of seeds; and whether agricultural extension services were provided in the village.

---

[11] Note that some technological variables e.g. high-yielding varieties (HYVs) are household-specific while others (e.g. the use of a tractor) are village-specific. For further details, see Gaiha (1988).

Among the household-specific variables, both household size and the age of the household head exercised a positive but diminishing effect on the risk of poverty; the dependency burden, the participation rate (number of workers/number of household members) and the proportion of male wage earners among total workers bore a positive relationship to this risk; education, however, reduced the risk of poverty.

Some additional causal linkages were identified in the disaggregated occupation analyses. Among cultivating households, tractor usage lowered the risk of poverty; among casual labour households, the ratio of female workers to male workers was negatively associated with this risk; and, among artisan households, the availability of institutional credit reduced the risk of poverty.

As cultivating and casual labour households accounted for the bulk of the rural poor (about 85 percent in 1968), the contrast between them is of particular interest. Among the village-specific variables, the availability of medical services reduced the risk of poverty among casual labour households but not among cultivating households. This seems plausible since the loss of employment on account of sickness and a consequent termination of contract may entail a more substantial loss of income for casual labourers than for cultivating households. Another important difference regards agricultural extension, which benefited cultivating households but not casual labour households. Since extension was intended to help smallholders, it is not surprising that it did not have any effect on the risk of poverty among casual labour households. Finally, while among cultivating households, the age of the household head exercised a positive but diminishing effect on the risk of poverty; among casual labour households, on the other hand, this variable did not have any effect. It is possible that, among the latter group, the life cycle effect is weak (in other words, poverty is more or less a permanent condition).

Some key relationships observed for these two occupations changed significantly over the period 1968-70. Among the cultivating households, the availability of institutional credit was associated with a reduction in the risk of poverty in 1970 (but not in 1968). The share of agricultural advances in total institutional credit was higher in 1970 than in 1968. While the distribution of credit continued to be skewed in favour of large landowners, there was a marked increase in the amount of institutional credit (per hectare) among small and medium landowners over the period 1968-70. Given that there was a substantial increase in the adoption rate of the new technology among small and medium landowners, it is plausible that much of the reduction in the risk of poverty resulted from a higher adoption rate of this technology, made possible by the larger amounts of institutional credit secured by this group (Gaiha, 1985). Other significant changes relate to the two employment variables: the participation rate and the proportion of male wage earners among total workers. While the former was positively associated with the risk of poverty only in 1970, the latter was positively associated in both 1968 and 1970. Moreover, the association of the latter was stronger in 1970. These results are consistent with the impoverishment of certain sections reported earlier in this chapter. As a result of agriculture becoming more profitable with the introduction of the new technology, small landowners were unable to resist the pressure from richer landowners to part with portions of their land – through forced sales or leasing out – and tenants who were not evicted were required to pay higher rents or share costs (with a given rent). Given the meagre income which smaller gross cropped areas yielded on average, adult members of these households (as well as children, in some cases) were forced to supplement the farm income by working on other farms, usually on a casual wage basis. It is significant that the negative correlation between the earnings per worker and the overall participation rate (earners/household size) among the poor cultivating households changed substantially from $-.577$ to $-.796$ in the villages where the new technology was adopted during the period 1968-70.

Among casual labour households too, some of the observed relationships changed over the same period. While there was a weakening of the effect of tractor usage on the risk of poverty, the evidence was not quite conclusive. More significant changes relate to the effects of the two employment variables, i.e. the participation rate and the ratio of female workers to male workers. The participation rate was negatively associated with the risk of poverty in 1968 but the sign reversed in 1970. While the latter relationship was not significant statistically, the sign reversal is of some importance in itself. A clue is provided by the fact that, while the overall participation rate rose within this occupation, in general (and not just among the subset of the poor), the negative correlation between the overall participation rate and the earnings per worker changed drastically (from −.677 to −.755) among the poor casual labour households during 1968-70. What thus distinguished the poor from the non-poor within this occupation in 1970 was not so much a difference in participation but in earnings per worker, since participation was uniformly high among both the poor and the non-poor. While the ratio of female workers to male workers exercised a negative effect on the risk of poverty in 1968, it ceased to do so in 1970. There was a substantial increase in female participation among households in this group and, thus, the difference in the average female participation rate between the poor and the non-poor was considerably reduced. Mechanization had the effect of pushing female workers out of certain agricultural operations, which were increasingly taken over by permanent farm workers, and into those which were less remunerative. The reduction in demand in these operations was more than offset by the augmented demand in other operations as a result of a higher cropping intensity. The all-round increase in female participation and the stagnant or lower earnings per female worker among some sections explain why the role of female workers (relative to male workers) ceased to be effective in alleviating the risk of poverty in 1970.

In order to link this analysis to anti-poverty interventions, it is necessary to assess the relative importance of some of the proximate determinants of the risk of poverty. A case could then be made for fixing some broad priorities in rural poverty alleviation although, admittedly, any generalization outside a given context is likely to be risky. Clearly, the analysis reviewed here is not enough and much more work is necessary. Nevertheless, some useful pointers emerge.

In the aggregate sample for 1968, out of the village-specific variables, the availability of transport and medical facilities reduced the risk of poverty by well over 9 percent relative to the reference value; among households dependent on transfer income, the availability of medical services alone caused a reduction of nearly 17 percent in the risk of poverty; while the availability of institutional credit brought about a reduction of about 11 percent among artisan households. The technological variables – the availability of extension services, the use of tractors and electricity for farming – taken together accounted for a reduction of over 51 percent in the risk of poverty among cultivating households. The use of tractors alone brought about a reduction of over 13 percent in the risk of poverty among casual labour households. Among the household-specific variables, the contribution of education was substantial; in the aggregate sample, the reduction in the reference probability of being poor was as much as 20 percent and even higher among some occupational groups, e.g. among cultivating households over 22 percent and, among artisan households, about 27 percent. Another important variable was dependency burden which, if reduced to half the sample mean, resulted in a reduction in the risk of poverty ranging from more than 8 percent among casual labour households to about 17 percent among permanent wage labour households.

Regarding changes over time, among cultivating households the contribution of technological variables (the availability of extension, the use of tractors and electricity for farming) taken together was slightly smaller in 1970 relative to that in 1968 – the reduction in the risk of poverty being 45 percent in 1970 as against 51 percent in 1968. Institutional credit was, however, associated with a substantial reduction in the risk of poverty in 1970, i.e. about 16 percent (note that the effect of credit in 1968 was negligible). Among casual labour households, the reduction in the probability of being poor associated with the use of tractors fell from 13 percent to about 9 percent over the period 1968-70.

POLICY INTERVENTIONS

To sum up, even when agricultural growth reduces poverty, the "entitlements" of different sections may change quite drastically, with many gainers and some losers. Although the evidence presented here is limited to India and, for the most part, covers a short period, it suggests that the extent and severity of impoverishment may well not be negligible while some indices of poverty register substantial improvement. Besides, there is often a hard core of poverty which is largely unrelated to changes in agricultural performance. If the Indian evidence reviewed here is anything to go by, poverty tends to persist among large subsets of the poor over several years. What is more disturbing is the finding that many of them would continue to be poor, despite a substantial redistribution of physical assets, because of certain innate disadvantages (e.g. morbidity and lack of managerial ability). Thus, special policy interventions may be necessary, for example income transfers on a continuing basis or a heavy concentration of physical and human assets.

Some broad areas of policy intervention are suggested: the provision of transport services, electricity, education and health care facilities and credit; access to arable land, biochemical innovations and extension services; the creation of non-farm employment activities in rural areas in order to open new avenues of employment for rural labourers and to add to their bargaining power; and the provision of safety nets (e.g. food subsidies) for mitigating acute and chronic deprivation – especially for those unable to participate in the growth process. As regards the chronically poor, more attention needs to be paid to their disabilities – both physical and social such as caste barriers – in order to devise interventions for specific contexts. All that can be inferred from the evidence reviewed here is that short-term relief measures may not make a dent in chronic poverty and longer-term and more concentrated interventions may be required. Thus, the prospects of eliminating chronic poverty – even when appropriate policy interventions are chosen – may be quite limited in the short term.

Having delineated these areas of intervention, the nature and forms of intervention in different markets, complementaries between these interventions and their timing, financing and political feasibility are examined in Chapter 4 which sets the stage for a more detailed exploration of direct anti-poverty interventions in the subsequent chapters. Although growth matters, the evidence reviewed here suggests that direct anti-poverty interventions have a crucial role. The rest of this report therefore concentrates on the latter in designing an effective anti-poverty strategy for rural areas in developing countries. Since some key causal relationships are likely to change even in a short period, careful monitoring of poverty alleviation programmes is vital to their success. Observations on the data requirements of such an exercise will be made in Chapter 11.

Chapter 4

Issues in anti-poverty interventions – an overview

This chapter critically evaluates the role of government in poverty alleviation. First, the rationale and forms of government intervention are spelled out; second, complementarities and trade-offs between government and private (including community) support are examined; third, financial and administrative aspects of implementation – basically, the choice between targeting and universalism – are discussed; and, finally, the timing of interventions is considered.[1]

RATIONALE AND FORMS OF GOVERNMENT INTERVENTION

A basic issue is whether government intervention is necessary. Usually, government intervention is justified when *i)* there is a market failure, in the sense that a Pareto optimal outcome is not likely or ruled out; *ii)* the income distribution is unjust; and *iii)* some fundamental rights are violated. An attempt is made below to elaborate these arguments in the context of poverty alleviation in rural areas.

In the present context, the labour market, the capital market and the insurance markets are directly relevant. The land market is dealt with later in the context of redistribution of assets. Essentially, the problem is that markets are either incomplete or highly imperfect, with serious welfare consequences for large subsets of the rural population.

---

[1] Although, in parts, this chapter relies on Burgess and Stern (1989), it extends their focus by incorporating some more recent results.

Market imperfections

Consider the rural labour market first. It is well known that, since agricultural employment is seasonal and non-farm employment opportunities are generally limited, there are typically long spells of inactivity primarily for casual labour households in rural areas.[2] Low levels of earnings are thus compounded by high seasonal variation and the two together account for the high incidence of poverty among casual labour households.[3]

Labour market imperfections take different forms. There is, for example, some evidence of segmentation in rural labour markets, making it difficult for labourers from one village to work in another. Also, in some cases there is an interlinking of transactions in land, labour and credit markets.[4] The associated inefficiencies and transaction costs are detrimental to the interests of rural labour households (e.g. job search is costly). Since rural labour households are usually not well organized, some interventions may be necessary.

Legislation of minimum wages in rural areas is often counterproductive. When there is surplus labour, it is hard to enforce minimum wages. Weak enforcement machinery is a major obstacle.[5] However, even when there is effective enforcement – in exceptional cases – it is doubtful whether the enforcement of minimum wages is beneficial to rural labourers, since it induces employment rationing.

Another important intervention is rural public works. Used initially in emergency situations, such as droughts and famines, RPW are now being more widely used as a regular component of an anti-poverty strategy in

---

[2] Some evidence summarized in Lipton (1983) is illustrative. A sample survey of villages in West Bengal in 1972-73 revealed major seasonal variation in the very low daily male wages. Rates below Rs 2 prevailed for 7 percent of villages in the period July-September, but for 21 to 23 percent in the January-June period. Moreover, employment and wage rates tended to fall in the slack season. Many of these households were forced to rely on loans to restrict the variation in consumption expenditure.

[3] See, for example, Gaiha (1988).

[4] For a review of the evidence, see FAO (1990b).

[5] A review of recent evidence suggests that even government agencies frequently violate minimum wage legislation (FAO, 1991b).

developing countries. An important reason for their popularity is their self-targeting nature. Given that the poor's opportunity cost of time is relatively low, the work-requirement condition acts as an effective screening mechanism. But there may be incentive effects as well. Dependence on RPW may act as a disincentive for seeking more rewarding employment. The effectiveness of RPW in poverty alleviation, however, varies depending on how they are designed. For example, for a fixed long-term budget, a low wage rate implies a wide coverage of RPW while a high wage rate implies low coverage. These and other related choices in designing RPW are addressed elsewhere in this report.

If capital markets function efficiently in rural areas, borrowing against future income could smooth consumption when income fluctuates. Capital markets are, however, far from perfect. The fundamental reasons are the high risk of default and weak enforcement mechanisms. An individual cannot expect to borrow as much as he or she desires at the prevailing interest rate, since lenders regard a higher indebtedness of a particular borrower as a sign that repayment will be more uncertain and they may therefore wish to alter the terms of the loan in case there is any willingness to lend further sums. Besides, higher interest rates attract less dependable borrowers. As a result, some degree of credit rationing may occur (Hoff and Stiglitz, 1990). Government intervention in the form of a credit programme is justified on the grounds of better information, risk pooling and powers of enforcement. However, the very high default rates reported for government credit programmes and the substantially better recovery rates for local moneylenders are not consistent with this justification. The insights emerging from the imperfect information paradigm (taking note of information asymmetry and enforcement problems) suggest an altogether different role for governments in rural credit markets. Rather than act as a provider of subsidized credit, a more appropriate role for the government would be to reduce information and enforcement costs. Rural credit markets, together with the role of the government, are discussed in Chapter 6.

While capital markets may allow an individual to borrow in difficult circumstances, insurance markets can protect him or her against certain outcomes (e.g. crop losses, disease, disability). Problems similar to those that constrain the satisfactory functioning of capital markets arise in insurance markets. Specifically, the information and enforcement problems are equally severe. It may be difficult for an insurance company to ascertain, for example, whether the loss of a crop is due to an accident or negligence on the part of the insured. Given the magnitude of these difficulties, it is not surprising that there is little insurance against crop loss, unemployment, disease, disability or widowhood in rural areas. Government insurance schemes are not widespread in developing countries either and, where they do exist, the poor are usually not covered. Given the importance of the events insurance schemes are designed to protect against, this is an area where properly designed government intervention may carry substantial benefits (Ahmad, 1989).

Externalities

So far, market failure has been attributable to market imperfections and incomplete markets. Market failure is also linked to externalities, however. The action of a group of individuals may, for example, impose a cost on others, i.e. a negative externality. Environmental degradation is a case in point. For example, it is argued that deforestation and consequent soil erosion in Nepal contribute significantly to the silting of rivers and thus the size and probability of floods in Bangladesh (Burgess and Stern, 1989). Markets cannot cope with an externality on this scale.[6] Even at the local level, exploitation of a resource (e.g. excessive grazing) by one group can threaten the livelihood of another. However, at the local level, cooperation may be more feasible and it may therefore be more effective for governments to support local initiatives and institutions (Wade, 1987). Voluntary collective action, together with the nature of government support to strengthen it, are discussed in Chapter 10.

---

[6] Not even the most fervent devotees of the "Coase Theorem" would suggest that the current (and future) peasants and landless labourers of Bangladesh, recognizing the potential for a Pareto improvement, would seek out their counterparts in Nepal and negotiate to reduce the amount of silt flowing down the rivers (Burgess and Stern, 1989).

Income inequality

Another set of considerations favouring government intervention is independent of market failure. One of these considerations is whether the prevailing distribution of income is fair. Even though views differ on what a fair distribution is, there may be a broad agreement on a wide range of observed distributions as being unfair. Theoretically, of course, this could be remedied by lump sum taxes and transfers. In fact, however, lump sum taxes (which do not have any effects on individual incentives to work and save) are not easy to devise. Taxation of income/wealth, therefore, involves a trade-off between efficiency and equity.

Given the incentive and administrative problems, a highly uneven distribution of assets (e.g. land), together with deprivation associated with a lack of assets (e.g. landlessness), may lead a government to consider straightforward redistribution as an alternative. Specifically, the redistribution of land in rural areas has largely been a failure. A systematic exposition of the failure of land redistribution in the new political economy framework is given later. Support for certain coalitions – e.g. the rural landless and urban middle class, the latter being concerned mainly with social stability (Hayami, 1991) – may in this framework shift the political equilibrium in such a way that a higher level of redistribution becomes feasible.

Rights

Yet another justification for government intervention reflects the concern for the fulfilment of certain basic rights, e.g. the protection of law, basic education, health and housing (Burgess and Stern, 1989). This concern stems from some notions of liberty and equality (as, for example, in Rawls, 1971). The liberty to pursue one's own life and income opportunities may conflict with ideas of equality of outcomes. It could, however, be argued that equality refers to the right to a basic position from which to pursue the opportunities provided by these liberties while being accorded equal protection against deprivation and adversity. This right is fundamental in the sense that it would be wrong for the government to deny it even if it were in the general interest to do so. Consider, for example, utilitarian arguments based on the Bergson-Samuelson social welfare function. If, in the interest of maximization of social welfare, distinctions are made between individuals on the grounds of personal preference and interpersonal judgement (as embodied in the Bergson-Samuelson approach), these distinctions would violate the conception of equality emphasized here. It is the latter, i.e. the basic right of everyone to be treated with equal concern and respect, that takes priority over maximization of social welfare (Burgess and Stern, 1989).

COMPLEMENTARIES AND TRADE-OFFS BETWEEN GOVERNMENT AND PRIVATE SUPPORT

In the previous section, the rationale and forms of government intervention in alleviating deprivation were spelled out. It is argued below that government intervention is only one component of public action. Other components comprise family and community support. Following the exposition in Burgess and Stern (1989), this raises at least three sets of issues. The first relates to the extent of family and community support and the underlying motivation. If, for example, it is motivated by altruism, it is likely to be withdrawn when government support is provided. The second set of issues relates to whether specific forms of support are provided most efficiently by the family, community or government. Information considerations in alleviating certain forms of distress may, for instance, favour family support while covariant risks in a community may favour an outside agency. A third set concerns communities as pressure groups and collaborators in poverty alleviation programmes or, following Drèze and Sen (1989), a distinction may be drawn between the adversarial and collaborative roles of a community.

Intrahousehold and interhousehold transfers are far from negligible in developing countries[7]. To a large extent, the family or community performs

---

[7] Ninety-three percent of a rural southern Indian sample received transfers from other households. In Malaysia, private transfers accounted for almost half the income of the poorest fifth of households. Nearly three-quarters of rural households in Java, Indonesia, gave private transfers to other households. About half a sample of households in the Philippines received private cash transfers (Cox and Jimenez, 1990).

the role of formal institutions in developed countries. Information problems and resource constraints make it difficult to set up formal institutions or operate them effectively (Rosenzweig, 1988). Transfers between related or proximate individuals serve the purposes of risk mitigation, insurance against income shortfalls, help during illness and educational loans, both in rural and urban households (Cox and Jimenez, 1990; Ravallion and Dearden, 1988; and Rosenzweig, 1988). The underlying motivation, however, has elements of both altruism and self-interested exchange in a risky environment.[8] It is therefore not surprising that public transfers do not result in the complete withdrawal of private transfers.

The immediate family and community have some advantages in overcoming moral hazard and adverse selection problems. Both are well placed to judge, for example, whether an individual has fallen on hard times and whether this is the result of his own carelessness or factors beyond his or her control. Besides, the sanction of social opprobrium which may arise from fraud or neglect can be very strong within the family or community. On the other hand, insurance and risk-spreading considerations tend not to favour local entities. Since members of a family or community are likely to be affected in the same way by, for instance, adverse weather conditions, or be subject to covariant risks, this form of insurance has an obvious limitation. The diversification of rural activity (e.g. through rural industry) and rural-urban migration may help to some extent to mitigate income shortfall risk and facilitate consumption smoothing in such an environment.[9] However, in an extreme situation (e.g. drought) government support (e.g. by releasing foodgrains on the market) may be vital to avert mass suffering.

---

[8] Empirical evidence suggests that patterns of private transfers are generated either by altruism or by self-interested exchange or by a combination of both. Private transfers tend to even out income inequality. In particular, they tend to raise the incomes of the poorest households. There is strong evidence that higher-income households give more transfers, whereas lower-income households are more likely to receive transfers (Cox and Jimenez, 1990).

[9] Alderman and Paxson (1992) point out that covariant income risk may limit the usefulness of credit markets as a tool for consumption smoothing if credit markets are regionally segmented.

Finally, communities can play an effective role in social provisioning both as pressure groups and collaborators. Given the powerlessness of the poor and limited awareness of their needs, grassroots organizations often serve as a vital link between government agencies and the poor. Rural health and literacy programmes in the Indian state of Kerala, for example, owe much to the work of social activists. Not only are the basic needs of the poor and vulnerable given due importance in various government programmes, but their targeting improves significantly.[10] Cost-effectiveness is thus likely to be greater.[11]

FINANCIAL, ADMINISTRATIVE AND OTHER ASPECTS OF IMPLEMENTATION

Limited success in poverty alleviation is often attributed to resource constraints. Few tax instruments and low levels of income yield low revenues. There are usually many other claims – including defence – on these limited resources and they therefore have to be rationed. On the other hand, given the widespread deprivation in rural areas, the cost of poverty alleviation is likely to be enormous. A case is then made for the self-financing of anti-poverty interventions. There is some merit in these arguments. It is, however, arguable that, even within these constraints, a reallocation of the budget and better targeting of anti-poverty interventions could yield better results.

Allocation of anti-poverty budget

There are two aspects to the allocation of anti-poverty resources: one is the allocation of the outlay among different poverty alleviation programmes (e.g. among RPW and food subsidies); the other is the pattern of allocation within a specific programme (e.g. whether RPW should concentrate on the poorest or on the moderately poor or on a combination of both).

---

[10] For other illustrations of the collaborative and adversarial roles, see Drèze and Sen (1989) and Gaiha (1990b).
[11] For a more detailed exposition, see Gaiha and Spinedi (1992).

As regards the first aspect, a measure of cost-effectiveness for each poverty alleviation programme is necessary. By their very nature, such calculations tend to be conditional on a number of (usually simplifying) assumptions; efficiency in targeting and implementation, for instance.[12] Another major difficulty is that some of these programmes cater to different sections of the rural poor. For example, while RPW would benefit those willing to engage in physically demanding tasks, food subsidies may cater to the old, infirm and disabled. The point is that the allocation of the anti-poverty outlay among different programmes on cost-effectiveness considerations may imply unacceptably high trade-offs in the well-being of different groups in poverty.

The second aspect, i.e. the allocation of an outlay within a poverty alleviation programme, has received considerable attention in some recent studies (e.g. Bourguignon and Fields, 1990). The policy significance of whether to spend the given outlay on the poorest, the moderately poor or a combination of both is obvious – especially in view of stringent budgetary constraints. A review of some recent theoretical results is given here while applications are considered later.

Assuming that the targeting of benefits is administratively feasible and that no serious incentive problems arise, e.g. the beneficiaries do not withdraw from productive employment when the state provides supplementary income, some recent studies (notably Bourguignon and Fields, 1990) have shown that whether a particular anti-poverty allocation is optimal depends on the poverty index.[13] This implies that policy-makers must first decide what particular poverty measure they are seeking to minimize. Then and only then will they be in a position to evaluate the effects that alternative allocations of their budget have on property.[14]

---

[12] See, for example, the simulations reported in Narayana, Parikh and Srinivasan (1988); and Parikh and Srinivasan (1989).

[13] The complications arising from imperfect targeting and incentive issues are dealt with in the section Targeting, p. 71.

[14] It makes sense to think of the budget constraint as a long-term constraint, as there may be sharp fluctuations in the short term.

Allocations. The issue is how to allocate an anti-poverty budget so that a measure of poverty – H or HG or S or $F_{(\alpha)}$ – is minimized over a fixed period of time.[15] Any allocation involves a reduction in the number of poor and/or an increase in the incomes of those who remain poor. All transfers are positive. The budget is financed either by foreign aid or taxation. Three possible allocations of the anti-poverty budget are distinguished:

- Type-r: allocate the entire sum to the least poor;
- Type-p: allocate the entire sum to the poorest;
- Mixed allocation: allocate a (strictly positive) fraction of the amount to the least poor and another (strictly positive) fraction to the poorest.

Results. The important results, together with the underlying intuition, are summarized here.[16] For the headcount ratio H, and the Foster-Greer-Thorbecke class of measures, $F_{(\alpha)}$ with $\alpha < 1$, the optimal allocation consists of transferring the given amount to the least poor so as to have as few people as possible remaining in poverty (i.e. Type-r allocation). By contrast, for the F class of measures, with $\alpha > 1$, the optimal allocation is a Type-p allocation such that only the poorest receive a transfer.[17] For the index HG, the optimal allocation is, however, indeterminate since HG is reduced by the same amount under each allocation.

Specifically, as long as no poor person receives a transfer that would put him or her above the poverty threshold (i.e. $t_i = z - y_i$), any allocation of the budget – whether Type-r, Type-p, or mixed – will lead to exactly the same amount of reduction in poverty. With the Sen index, it turns out that a Type-r allocation is optimal in some circumstances, a Type-p allocation in others

---

[15] HG denotes the fraction of the poverty threshold, z, that would have to be spent per head of the whole population to eliminate poverty.

[16] For a more formal exposition, refer to Bourguignon and Fields (1990).

[17] Note that $F_{(\alpha)}$, with $\alpha < 1$, is a concave decreasing function of individual incomes such that total poverty is more sensitive to a dollar given to the least poor than to somebody lower on the poverty scale. On the other hand, $F_{(\alpha)}$ with $\alpha > 1$, is a decreasing convex function of individual incomes more sensitive to transfers at the bottom than at the top of the distribution.

and a mixed allocation in yet another set of circumstances.[18] Consider, for example, the case when the distribution of income on the interval (o,z) is uniform with density $1/z$. The optimal allocation is Type-r if the amount of the transfer is small. Lifting those people close to the poverty threshold out of poverty costs little and is best to be done when the total budget is limited. For larger budgets, however, it becomes increasingly costly to lift more people out of poverty, and this allocation is less advantageous than raising the incomes of the remaining poor.

An observation on the contrast between $F_{(\alpha)}$, with $\alpha > 1$, and the Sen index may be helpful from a policy perspective. The Sen index gives a higher weight to a reduction in the headcount ratio than does the $F_{(\alpha)}$ class. The latter is, however, limited to the poor segment of a given population. Accordingly, no particular weight is assigned to a transfer which permits somebody to be lifted out of poverty.[19]

An important application, based on Bangladesh data, was carried out by Ravallion (1989). For a given outlay, he investigated the effects of low wages and a wide coverage, as against high wages and a low coverage, of RPW on alternative poverty indices. As elaborated later in this report, besides the poverty index, the size of the outlay also makes a difference.

Targeting

Should poverty alleviation programmes be targeted or universalistic? The answer is not as obvious as is usually supposed. In other words, when the costs and benefits of strict targeting are taken into account, the case for strict targeting is not quite as persuasive (Sen, 1992a).

---

[18] Note that the presence of g (i.e. the Gini coefficient of income distribution among the poor) makes it difficult to determine analytically how poverty varies with the allocation of the anti-poverty budget.

[19] When a person $\in$ below the poverty threshold ceases to be poor, the Sen index values that reduction as the average income shortfall adjusted for the extent of inequality among the poor. The $F_{(\alpha)}$ class, with $\alpha > 1$, gives that same change a much smaller weight: the $F_{(\alpha)}$ changes by $\in^{\alpha}$, which is necessarily smaller than the average income shortfall. In the limit, as $\in \to 0$, the change in $F_{(\alpha)}$ goes to zero, whereas the change in the Sen index remains finite (Bourguignon and Fields, 1990).

The basic argument in favour of strict targeting is that it saves resources. Efficient selection of beneficiaries reduces the cost of the support programmes. The transfer of income, subsidized food, the free availability of health services and education and other such programmes all cost resources. The cost of such programmes may be reduced if the beneficiaries can be selected according to a strict criterion of needs and the non-poor are excluded from receiving the benefits of such programmes.

However, targeting also involves losses and costs.[20] Sen (1992a) provides a useful classification.

First, there are the administrative costs of selecting beneficiaries. Second, it is hard to maintain the quality of a service that is reserved for the poor, as they often lack the power or influence to monitor the quality of the services offered – particularly in rural areas. Third, other costs arise from information and incentive distortions. Any system of targeting the needy tends to produce attempts by some to distort the relevant information to qualify for the support. In order to exclude such cases, elaborate procedures are usually devised. Yet such procedures can and do result in the denial of support to the needy as well (the food ration system in India, for example, excludes migrant workers in urban areas), since some of the relevant information about needs is hard to obtain and verify. Targeting may also result in incentive distortions. Potential beneficiaries may adjust their work and other activities to qualify for the support and this could result in a substantial loss of output and activity. Fourth, from a political economy perspective, the support for strictly targeted interventions may be quite limited, as they tend to isolate the poor. On the other hand, schemes whose benefits accrue to the non-poor as well (as in the case of food subsidies for all urban residents) tend to enjoy wide support.

Finally, an economy based on targeting can be a very "invasive" one, involving constant policing and probing investigation into the lives of the poor to make sure that they are genuinely in need of support. No matter how

---

[20] For a formal exposition of these and other related issues, see Besley and Kanbur (1991) and Kanbur (1987).

specific the criterion is, any need-based selection tends to give the government officials a good deal of power over the lives of the potential recipients. As Sen (1992a) stresses, these social costs may be no less important than the financial expenses of running a targeted programme.

The case for strict targeting is thus not so transparent.[21] On the other hand, the principle of universalism is appealing in certain areas. Whether from the perspective of rights or from the economic perspective of merit goods, there is a strong case for universal coverage of elementary education and primary health care programmes. Yet, even in these areas, effectiveness of the public policy may warrant some sort of selection. If the aim is, for example, to vaccinate children or to increase female literacy, it is necessary to ensure that the respective policies concentrate on the unvaccinated children and illiterate women. But the mere fact of selection does not imply that these are targeted interventions, except perhaps in a trivial sense. As Sen (1992) emphasizes, the key issue in targeting is not whether some kind of selection is involved – most policies do involve selection – but how far to push the selection process.

There are other areas, however, where the choice of appropriate policies depends on balancing the advantages of selection against the various costs and losses identified earlier. For example, in evaluating programmes of nutrition support (such as midday meals for schoolchildren), note must be taken of the cost of covering all the children of a particular age group. Yet at the same time, the costs of selection according to a criterion of needs must be given due importance. The choice of where to draw the line would then depend on an appropriately broad view of the social and economic effects of alternative policies (Sen, 1992a).

---

[21] In this context, the simulations in Besley (1990) are of considerable interest. Assuming first that means testing is accurate and that the poor incur a cost to be means tested, it is demonstrated that, for a given budget, means testing is generally superior to universal coverage. This is not surprising. What is surprising is that, when imperfect information and incentive effects are taken into account, the superiority of means testing is not overturned. This, of course, does not take into account the psychic costs of means testing emphasized by Sen (1992a).

There is also the possibility of making use of self-selection in some cases. One example is work requirement as a screening mechanism (to which a reference was made earlier). Another is the quality of a service. Consider, for example, health care and educational facilities which are typically available at different quality levels. If the government can identify the quality level at which the demand for the publicly provided service comes from the poor only, the quality choice provides a self-acting test on the basis of which the poor can be targeted. If such a quality level cannot be found, cash transfers of the same value would be better (Besley and Kanbur, 1991).

Timing of interventions

An important issue in designing anti-poverty interventions is their timing. Two alternative paradigms have been suggested:[22] one is *growth-mediated security* and the other is *support-led security.* Governments may either wait for the level of income to rise before embarking on a poverty alleviation strategy (i.e. growth-mediated security) or try and protect the poor even at low levels of income (i.e. support-led security).[23] Growth-mediated security could be justified on the grounds that, without resources for poverty alleviation, adequate protection of the poor cannot be ensured. There is some merit in this argument. On the other hand, given the pervasiveness and severity of deprivation in many developing countries, the immediacy of relief may well be a decisive consideration – in some cases more so in the context of structural adjustment. That effective relief is feasible even at low levels of income is already well documented.[24] Some detailed illustrations are given in Chapter 9, Markets, prices and public action.

---

[22] The exposition is based on Drèze and Sen (1990).
[23] Note that support-led security does not imply neglect of long-term growth considerations.
[24] See, for example, Drèze and Sen (1989) and FAO (1990b).

Chapter 5
Land reforms

The relationship between rural poverty and access to land is complex. Many factors are involved, including differences in land quality, the availability of complementary inputs, access to credit and markets and opportunities for off-farm employment. When the land quality is poor and access to inputs and markets is limited, access to land – even large quantities – may not significantly reduce the risk of poverty.[1] Nevertheless, to the extent that land is a major source of income in rural areas and its distribution has important linkages with the non-farm sector, land reforms are crucial to poverty alleviation.

It is sometimes surmised that population pressure will render land reforms more important from the point of view of poverty alleviation. One possibility is that land distribution becomes more concentrated with a higher incidence of landlessness. Given the laws of inheritance, rapid subdivision of smallholdings and the failure of these smaller plots to yield a subsistence income may, for example, force their owners to sell the plots to large landowners and, consequently, the distribution of land may become more concentrated. In such a situation, land reforms may acquire greater urgency. Bell (1990a) is sceptical for two reasons, however: *i)* he points out that there is no conclusive evidence that population growth concentrates the ownership of land in fewer hands even as the size of holding contracts; and *ii)* population growth may be fully offset by technical progress, as has happened in many countries. Indeed, if technical progress in agriculture has

---

[1] In Bangladesh, while the proportion of landless and marginal farmers among the poor was as high as 93 percent in 1978-79, more than one-fifth of all households with more than 25 acres of land were also among the poor (Ravallion, 1989).

the effect of augmenting land availability and urbanization proceeds fairly rapidly, the effective supply of land may increase more rapidly than the rural population. Even if Bell's scepticism is justified, it does not follow that land reforms will lose much of their importance. Indeed, if the bulk of the rural population continues to depend on agriculture and distribution inequalities persist, land reforms will have a major role in poverty alleviation.

The first section of this chapter sketches the major components of land reform, viz. land redistribution, regulation of tenancy and land titling. The following three sections seek to assess (largely qualitatively) their impact on the poor. The next section focuses on the political constraints to land reforms while the final section draws together the policy guidelines.

FORMS

Land reform comprises a wide range of measures, including land redistribution, regulation of tenancy contracts and land titling, with varying degrees of targeting on the poorer population segments (the landless, smallholders, etc.). While some aspects of land reform have received attention in the recent literature (e.g. World Bank, 1990), there has been a waning of interest in the redistribution of land as a key component of reform. This is in a large measure attributable to the dismal record of land redistribution in many developing countries. In the few countries that undertook land redistribution, it met with strong resistance and the pace consequently slowed down. Moreover, the benefits to the poorest groups were quite limited.[2] Nevertheless, it is argued below that land redistribution plays a major role in poverty alleviation (Lipton, 1974; 1991).

LAND REDISTRIBUTION
Rationale

The equity case for land redistribution from large to landless and/or small

---

[2] Lipton and Van der Gaag (1991) point out that most major land reforms were the direct result of social revolution or war and, even then, not all achieved the stated goal of reducing poverty (for example, in Mexico and Bolivia).

landowners rests on two facts: *i)* landless/small landowners are usually poorer than large landowners; and *ii)* total employment per hectare, especially of the poorest (comprising mainly casual unskilled workers), increases as farm size decreases. The efficiency case requires that land redistribution increases, or at least does not reduce, farm output. An inverse relationship between farm size and land output per hectare is invoked to support the efficiency of land redistribution.[3] Most of the observed instances of the inverse relationship rest mainly on higher cropping intensity, a more labour-intensive and valuable crop mix and on smaller farms.[4]

If the inverse relationship is strong, this reinforces the equity case for land redistribution. However, many question whether a redistribution from large to small farmers will in fact raise farm output. If, for example, the observed differences are in part due to land quality differences between small and large farmers, the expected increase in farm output may not occur.[5] But this objection is specious if land quality is endogenous. As Lipton (1991) elaborates, land quality on small farms is raised in part by the actions of the family, e.g. bunding, levelling and irrigation construction or maintenance – especially in slack periods – for the familiar reasons of lower transaction costs and fewer information deficiencies in using labour. Another objection has to do with marketed surplus. It is sometimes asserted that the efficiency case for land redistribution is weakened by the likelihood of a reduction in marketed surplus as smallholders may retain a larger share for self-consumption. This is, however, not corroborated by empirical evidence.[6] Fi-

---

[3] The inverse relationship refers to land productivity as opposed to total productivity and is, in fact, generally associated with a higher level of inputs per hectare on small farms, particularly labour per hectare. However, in countries where labour is abundant, capital use low and land the scarce input, the efficiency of land use is of primary concern.

[4] See, for example, Berry and Cline (1979), Cornia (1985) and Thiesenhusen and Melmed-Sanjak (1990).

[5] Bhalla and Roy (1988) show with Indian data that controlling land quality substantially weakened or removed the inverse relationship. In a similar analysis for northeast Brazil, Kutcher and Scandizzo (1981) note that productivity differences between large and small farms decline but do not disappear.

[6] In Kenya, for example, smallholders' higher land productivity outweighs their greater propensity to retain food crops for self-consumption. In any case, it is only for food staples

nally, farm/non-farm linkages may further support land redistribution. Some South Asian evidence, for example, suggests that places with relatively equal land and farm income distributions have a higher share of non-farm consumption that is produced locally and presumably labour-intensively (Islam, 1986). Thus, depending on the strength of these linkages, the multiplier effect on the incomes of the poor (comprising smallholders and unskilled labourers) would be greater, the more equal the land distribution.[7]

Experience

It is well documented that most attempts to redistribute land without a restructuring of power relations has had, at best, limited success (FAO, 1991a). For example, between the 1950s and the mid-1980s, only about 1.2 percent of cultivated land in India was redistributed. A significant proportion of the recipients of the redistributed land belonged to the scheduled castes and tribes (often the poorest), and their economic security was no doubt enhanced by the transfer. However, the total number affected represented only a tiny proportion of the land-poor households in India (Osmani, 1988). Success is more likely to be achieved when distributing state-owned land, where resistance is less than it is when trying to redistribute away from large landholders. In the Philippines between 1987 and 1990, while two-thirds of total land distribution targets were fulfilled, only 2 percent of the targets for private land redistribution were achieved. This was because of conflicts with owners over appropriate compensation (Government of the Philippines, 1990).

The modernization of agriculture does not necessarily facilitate land redistribution. Subsidies on inputs, tax breaks and the threat of expropriation in Latin American countries were successful in modernizing larger farms and hence in increasing agricultural output. One outcome of this modernization, however, was to render expropriation with compensation very

---

that smallholders are likely to show high retention ratios. For other crops (tea, vegetables) the ratio of marketed surplus to output is normally very high in all size groups (Lipton, 1991).
[7] For a more detailed exposition, see Lipton (1991).

costly. Further, as recently found in Colombia, larger farmers often success-fully used their influence to extract promises from the government that their land would not be expropriated if they modernized. As a consequence, the redistribution of land to the poor was negligible. Interestingly, the modern-ization of agriculture had the opposite effect on land redistribution in the Philippines. There, since compensation had been fixed at pre-Green Revo-lution land values, the economic gains associated with modern seed and fertilizer rice technology allowed the beneficiaries to compensate the ex-propriated landlords at pre-Green Revolution land values while capturing significant economic surpluses.

One reason why land redistribution was not accompanied by large produc-tivity gains was the failure to understand why wealthier farmers adopted new technologies first. India, Kenya and Mexico, for example, demonstrate that, while large farmers adopted modern seed varieties first, small farmers frequently succeeded in catching up. In most cases where catching up occurred, an important role was played by specific policies encouraging small farmers' adoption of these varieties. Such policies typically included credit provision, irrigation and extension services.[8]

The experiments with producer cooperatives produced disappointing re-sults – particularly in some Latin American countries.[9] Earlier reforms in Peru had led to some two-thirds of agricultural land being controlled by producer cooperatives in 1979. However, since these cooperatives suffered serious diseconomies of scale and work incentive problems, many were broken up in the early 1980s and the land distributed as individual holdings. In Nicaragua, producer cooperatives were initially thought to be better suited for the large-scale production of export products such as coffee, cotton and beef. Subsequently, the emphasis on land redistribution moved

---

[8] For a comprehensive review of the evidence, see Lipton and Longhurst (1989).

[9] In some respects, producer cooperatives in general operated like large private farms. In Peru, for example, the costs of labour supervision led cooperatives to choose lower levels of labour per hectare than small private farms. Also, cooperatives tended to choose a higher ratio of hired labour to family labour than did family farms. Costs of shirking were reduced by preferring family members for permanent tasks and by keeping other employees casual and in fear (Lipton, 1991).

away from the establishment of producer cooperatives towards direct distribution to individuals. This followed the realization that dividing large farming units into smaller holdings would not necessarily cause a reduction in output, provided that adequate credit and infrastructural support were provided (FAO, 1991a).

TENANCY REFORMS
Rationale

Tenancy reforms comprise legislation to regulate property rights and land sales and rentals in an effort to help alleviate poverty and improve equity. In addition, these reforms also seek to improve productivity, enhance investment opportunities and encourage better husbandry through the provision of greater security. But, as elaborated in the next section, the results have been mixed. This is partly because the functions performed by different forms of tenancy contract have not been understood. Some recent work, for example, has drawn attention to the efficiency and equity aspects of sharecropping contracts. In the absence of insurance markets, sharecropping is an important vehicle for risk-sharing.[10] Evidence shows that there is a higher implicit rent on sharecropped rented land (which may reflect

---

[10] This is an important point. A landowner has the option of either cultivating the land himself with the help of hired workers or leasing it out to a tenant for a fixed rent or for a fixed share of the output. Suppose, first, that the only kind of risk is in production. Output depends, not only on the inputs, but on the weather. In the owner-operated system, the entire risk is borne by the landowner because the labourers earn a fixed wage and the owner earns the residual. In a fixed-rent system, the tenant bears the entire risk. Thus, given risk aversion, share tenancy may be optimal, since it allows for risk-sharing. Newbery (1977), however, proved that, if a landlord was free to partition his land between fixed-rent and owner-operated tenancy, he could always earn as much as he would by giving the entire land to a share tenant. This could weaken the case for share tenancy. There are, however, two further arguments that support share tenancy. First, Newbery established his result under the assumption of constant returns to scale. So, if there are increasing returns to scale, a partitioning of land may turn out to be sufficiently inefficient to make it unattractive. Production risk coupled with increasing returns, may thus be a possible explanation of share tenancy (Basu, 1984). Second, Newbery also demonstrated that if, along with production risk, labour markets are risky, even with constant returns, fixed-rent tenancy and risky wage contracts would not achieve production efficiency, while share tenancy would.

a risk premium) and a higher frequency of share tenancy in areas with variable weather. Moreover, sharecropping may be important as a form of credit where other sources of credit are rationed or expensive. Cost-sharing arrangements in share contracts allow tenants to obtain easier access to capital inputs (Sharma and Drèze, 1990). Likewise, because rents on leased lands must generally be paid in advance, poor farmers without access to credit may be prevented from leasing-in land. This constraint is overcome under share tenancy as payments are made only at harvest. Hence share tenancy enables poorer sections to obtain land for cultivation.

In general, studies of farming practices in Asian countries have found no significant differences in yields per hectare between sharecropped and rented or owner-farmed land for the same crop. However, Shaban (1987), using Indian data on individual farmers – each cultivating under more than one form of tenure to control for farmer characteristics (since pure tenants and pure owners may be special cases) – found lower inputs and outputs per hectare for the same crop on sharecropped as opposed to rented or owned land. The observed inefficiency, however, may be due to short-term share tenancy. Contract choice and the relative efficiency of share tenancy, as pointed out by Bell (1990a), depend to a large extent on the ability of landlords to monitor work effort. Thus, the case against share tenancy in terms of efficiency and equity does not appear tenable.

Experience

Tenancy reforms in some cases produced unintended negative effects. In the Philippines, land reform legislation of the early 1970s applied only to tenanted areas, with a ceiling of 7 ha. Not only did this induce landowners to register excess holdings in the names of relatives, but tenants were also evicted. Similar effects of tenancy reform occurred in India and Sri Lanka in South Asia, and in numerous Latin American countries (FAO, 1991a). Even without eviction, the regulation of tenancy contracts could result in a contraction of the supply of land for tenancy and may thus contribute to the increasing number of landless in rural areas.

The change from the production team system to the household responsibility system (HRS), initiated in China in 1979, together with a set of market-oriented reforms introduced subsequently, was associated with a dramatic growth in agriculture during the period 1979-1984. These reforms were particularly impressive in that efficiency improved together with a sharp reduction in rural poverty. Households were initially allocated land tenancy rights on an equal per caput basis, taking into account different qualities of land. They were permitted to make their own cropping choices, adopt new technologies and sell on the market any surpluses above the amount they were contracted to sell to the state. Special encouragement was given to those households judged to have special farming abilities. Although income distribution widened following the reforms, this was not so much a result of the impoverishment of some households as of the rapid enrichment of others. However, as a way to reduce the state's burden and to increase the role of markets, the mandatory quotas were abolished (for cotton in 1984 and for grain in 1985) and replaced by procurement contracts negotiated between the government and the farmers. This change resulted in a reduction in the price margin paid to farmers (about 9 percent). The area devoted to cash crops expanded while grain area declined. (A separate estimate for cotton area is not available.) As a result of these adjustments, agriculture still grew at a respectable rate of 4.1 percent per annum during the period 1984-1987 (as against 7.7 percent during the period 1978-1984), although the grain and cotton production declined (especially the latter). Since the one-time discrete effect of the HRS reform had ended in 1984, as nearly all production teams had adopted HRS, the sharp drop in the state procurement prices relative to input prices and the consequent deceleration of agricultural growth were directly responsible for the exodus of labour from rural areas (Lin, 1992). The Chinese experience confirms that, with remunerative prices, decollectivization gives substantial efficiency and equity gains.

Following the reforms initiated in China in 1979, Laos and Viet Nam implemented far-reaching land tenancy reforms in 1988, making the farm household the basic production unit and issuing families inheritable, long-term property rights (up to 50 years in Viet Nam).[11] In Viet Nam, the current

---

[11] However, whether the lease will be renewed continues to be a source of uncertainty.

role of the state farms is to open up new lands and introduce new crops. After the new land is cleared, the state farms lease parcels to farmers, negotiating prices for land, seedlings and other inputs (FAO, 1991a). A recent assessment suggests that price policy reforms alone will not bring about sustained growth in agricultural output. These reforms have to be accompanied by investments in irrigation, water control, transport and soil conservation (Pingali and Vo Tong Xuan, 1992). The severe foreign exchange crisis in recent years has prevented the government from maintaining, let alone increasing, investments in irrigation. As a consequence, irrigation and water control infrastructure is in severe disrepair. The same is true of road infrastructure – especially in the northern and central parts of the country. Excessive transport costs prevent the movement of rice from the traditionally surplus southern provinces to the traditionally deficit northern provinces. Rapid population growth and the lack of security of land tenure have restricted farm-level investment in sustaining the productivity of the soil. The problem is most acute in central and northern Viet Nam. Without adequate erosion control and fertility management investments, these soils face declining productivity. Erosion control efforts, in addition to requiring high levels of investment, will also need collective action by the farmers affected.

Recent evidence on Africa suggests that most indigenous land tenure systems are adapting efficiently to changes in resource availability. As a policy option, it may therefore be better to concentrate on providing an appropriate legal and institutional environment for more efficient transactions than to restrict land sales and rental markets with tenancy legislation (Migot-Adholla *et al.*, 1990).

LAND TITLING
Rationale
It is sometimes claimed that land titling increases tenure security which in turn may promote investment in long-term improvements to the land and in capital inputs, and may induce appropriate crop choices. Furthermore, it may help in obtaining credit if titled land is used as collateral. Specifically, in the context of the food crisis in sub-Saharan Africa, tradi-

tional land tenure systems are often regarded as a major impediment to the growth of agricultural output and productivity. There is believed to be a mismatch between existing land arrangements, characterized by extensive farming practices, and the intensification of agriculture to accelerate growth. Basically, communal control over access to land and the absence of active rural land markets are supposed to discourage investment in land improvement and the use of appropriate soil husbandry practices. As Platteau (1990) points out in an illuminating essay, there are two separate theses in this connection, which are often not clearly distinguished.

The first thesis focuses on diffused decision-making among many persons (a management problem), high risk of labour shirking and supervision problems (a transaction cost problem) and sharing of the produce in accordance with social norms (an incentive problem). This thesis is distinguishable from that which emphasizes insecurity of tenure. As a result of this insecurity, it is argued, farmers are reluctant to invest in physical capital and other innovations because they fear that the benefits may not accrue to their progeny. Moreover, under communal tenure, land cannot be used as collateral, thus limiting the tenant's ability to invest. Sometimes it is further asserted that communal tenure limits the flexibility in land use that is vital for agricultural growth. Essentially, the belief is that land cannot be used efficiently unless it is transformed through individual titles into a fully marketable asset.

Platteau (1990) argues that these objections are somewhat exaggerated. First, security of tenure under communal systems is often greater than the critics seem to believe. Although the possession of land under communal tenure is neither exclusive nor definite, usually the allottee's right of access is protected as long as he keeps cultivating the land. Moreover, the heirs normally have access to the lands that were cultivated at the time of the death of the allottee. Finally, land can be exchanged, loaned or gifted (or even pledged) among members of the same landholding group, but transfers of land outside the group are restricted. Thus the allottee's right is more than a usufructurory one.

As regards communal tenure being a barrier to agricultural growth, Platteau (1990) points out that there is a clear underestimation of the flexibility and adaptation capacity of traditional communal systems. As a matter of fact, under the impact of population pressure and growing commercialization of agriculture, the pace of the individualization of tenure and land transactions has accelerated. Besides, inefficient collective management of productive resources may reflect not only maladjustments to changing environmental conditions (declining land/population ratios) but also the dissolution of solidarity structure or the erosion of authority patterns in traditional landholding groups. Thus, the management of watering points, for instance, has never been as efficient than when these points were the property and responsibility of well-defined social groups. It may therefore be wiser to revive or support such groups than to interfere with their normal functioning by superimposing new structures on them (Putterman, 1985). In any case, the granting of individual titles to land should not be taken to imply unregulated land transactions. Indeed, land transactions need to be regulated since free market transactions can easily lead to land concentration and a higher incidence of landlessness. The important point is, however, that the same undesirable effects may result from the free operation of customary systems of land tenure (Platteau, 1990). Therefore, in a context of increasing land scarcity, it is essential for the state to take on the task of regulating access to land and guaranteeing land titles with a view to avoiding all the efficiency and equity costs of non-intervention.

Against this background, following is a selective review of evidence on the effects of land titling.

Evidence

Recent evidence from Africa suggests that the link between tenure security and long-term investment is weak. In Kenya, Ghana and Rwanda, a positive relationship between the extent of land rights, particularly inheritance, and land improvements held in some areas but not in others (Migot-Adholla *et al.*, 1990). Further, formal ownership titles are not necessary for tenure security, since long-term leases may fulfil the same function. In addition, as pointed out above, under most communal tenure systems, a farmer has usage and other rights to an individual plot as long as it is under cultivation. These rights are often hereditary and may be maintained through generations. Thus, the absence of title does not necessarily imply tenure insecurity. On the other hand, security concerns may lead to inefficient cropping choices on untitled land. In Côte d'Ivoire, for example, cocoa farmers refused to intensify production because widely spaced trees allowed them to retain more land (Bruce, 1988). In other situations, a lack of title biased decisions in favour of short-cycle crops. For instance, squatters on government land in Jamaica devoted half the proportion of area to permanent and semi-permanent crops than did titled farmers. One-third of recipients under a government titling programme moved away from short-cycle crops after the change in their status (Feder and Noronha, 1987).

The granting of land titles in order to create collateral and improve access to credit may be desirable regardless of the effect of titling on investment incentives. Land titles, by lowering the default risk to the lender, may lower the cost of credit. If, however, farmers are unwilling to use their land as collateral, titling may not have a significant effect on credit access.

Evidence from Africa shows that titling did not have a significant effect on credit access. Within Kenya, for example, only half the formal sector loans were backed by land collateral and they were not significantly different in size or maturity from those not secured by land (Migot-Adholla *et al.*, 1990). Evidence outside Africa is rather more favourable. Feder *et al.*, (1986) report that Thai farmers frequently use their titled land as loan collateral. In the authors' sample, drawn from four provinces, titled farmers received 90 percent of institutional long- and medium-term loans while representing just 50 percent of the population. Similarly, an impact study of a land titling programme in Costa Rica found that, while 18 percent of respondents had received bank credit before titling, the proportion increased to 32 percent after they were granted titles. But this occurred during a period which saw a fall in total bank credit to small farmers. It is thus plausible that titling farmers merely redistributed a falling supply of credit among themselves without any positive impact on the welfare of small farmers as a group (Seligson, 1982). Land titling often aggravates inequality both because of the success of wealthier individuals in obtaining greater rights during implementation than they had under former tenure rules and because of the increased risk of landlessness after implementation.

Jodha (1986), in a study of common property resources in 21 districts of India, found that 84 to 100 percent of poor families dependend on common property for food, fuel and fodder as against 10 to 28 percent of wealthier families, and that activities on common property were the largest source of employment for the poor. Between the early 1950s and the early 1980s, there were declines in common property of 32 to 63 percent as a result of privatization under various welfare schemes. While they were meant to benefit the poor, in all districts the parcels received by poor households were smaller and the total area less than that which moved under the exclusive control of wealthier individuals. Because fuel and fodder gathering are primarily female tasks, it is plausible that the distributional changes had an unfavourable effect on poor rural women, one likely consequence being an increase in time allocated to these tasks. This study also shows that 63 to 91 percent of the land distributed to the poor was sold because of a lack of complementary inputs and because of pressing cash needs.

It is of course debatable whether the communal system would have worked as equitably as it did under the growing population pressure. If Platteau (1990) is right, there would have been some increase in inequality in access to these resources.

NEW POLITICAL ECONOMY FRAMEWORK

An attempt is made here to explore the reasons for the failure of land reforms – specifically land redistribution – in a new political economy framework. The key issue is whether this framework offers any additional insights that could then be used for designing land redistribution in order to make it politically feasible. The framework reviewed below is drawn from Hayami (1991). While it has the merit of focusing on the conflicting interests of different coalitions (in a democratic setting) as a factor impeding land redistribution, it is argued here that, in some respects, it is a limited framework.

Consider a market for land reform measures, as shown in Figure 2. The horizontal axis represents levels of land redistribution (= income transfers) while the vertical axis measures the marginal gain or loss of land redistribution to politicians or policy-makers. The gain may be measured by the

FIGURE 2
Determination of equilibrium in the market for land distribution policies

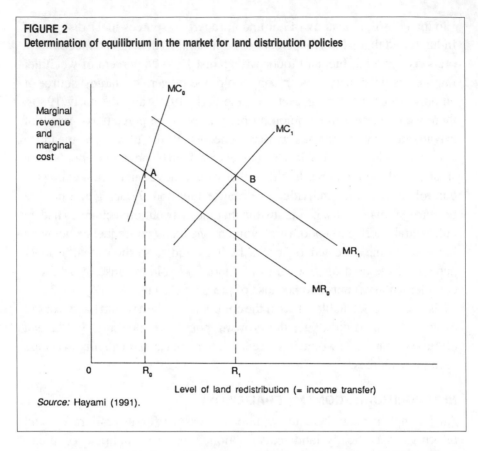

Source: Hayami (1991).

expected increase in the number of votes in support of the politicians from those in favour of land redistribution, while the loss may be measured by the expected decrease in votes from those opposed to the redistribution. More generally, the marginal revenue (MR) and the marginal cost (MC) curves in Figure 2 may be seen as the schedules of marginal increases and decreases of the probability of staying in office expected by the politicians, based on expected gains and losses in political support from various interest groups.

The MR curve is downward sloping as the intensity of support is likely to diminish at a high level of redistribution while the resistance is likely to multiply, thereby resulting in the upward sloping MC curve. The intersection of the MR and MC curves determines the equilibrium. In the present context, the key issue is the location of these two curves.

Essentially, the location of these two curves depends on the power and efforts of the groups supporting and opposing the reform in question. The group demanding reform consists of not only the rural landless, but also urban business and middle-class people seeking social stability and expansion of rural markets for urban goods and services. Landed interests constitute a strong opposition group. In addition, bureaucrats and local politicians tend to join the opposition in protests and sabotage if the government tries to increase the transfer to the landless by reducing bureaucrats' opportunities for rent-seeking through strengthened supervision and penalties.

The groups supporting land redistribution tend to be large but scattered and not well organized, while those opposed to it are usually better organized. Under these conditions, the marginal revenue is likely to be low, as represented by MR_0 in Figure 2, and the marginal cost is likely to be high, as represented by MC_0, with an equilibrium at A corresponding to a very low level of land redistribution or income transfer to the landless, as represented by OR_0.

During a crisis, however, a new equilibrium may emerge. If the expected gain from supporting land redistribution rises – the landless might threaten to revolt – the marginal revenue curve shifts up, as represented by MR_1. Guided by their instincts for survival, the landed interests might also weaken their resistance to this reform. In that case, the appropriate marginal cost curve would be MC_1. The MR_1 and MC_1 curves intersect at B, resulting in a higher level of land redistribution, as denoted by OR_1.

The upshot of this analysis is that conditions must be created so that the equilibrium shifts to a position such as B. In other words, widening of the support for land reforms must be combined with a lowering of the marginal cost of carrying out these reforms within the existing political market.

While this framework is useful in focusing on the conflicting interests of different coalitions in determining the politically feasible scale of redistribution of land, it is in some respects a limited one. Given the salient features, it can only indicate that a stronger coalition favouring land redistribution will shift the equilibrium to the right of the existing one. Since the demand

and supply curves are not parametrized through an empirical analysis, nothing more than a directional shift in the equilibrium can be surmised. Furthermore, whether this directional shift will be slow or quick cannot be inferred. The predictive power of this framework is thus limited.

Another issue is the stability of the equilibrium. Even if the equilibrium shifts to the right, it does not necessarily follow that the poor will be better off, except perhaps for a short spell. If, for example, the coalitions change as a result of a shock, the land redistribution may be reversed with serious hardships to the beneficiaries of the first round of redistribution. A striking illustration is provided by the Chilean experience.

According to Jarvis (1989), here the land reform process had three distinct phases. The reform began with the Eduardo Frei administration from 1964 to 1970 and was extended and amplified by the Salvador Allende administration from 1970 through September 1973. It was then curtailed by the military government after 1973, although its effects are still evolving.

After the coup in late 1973, the military government stopped expropriation and began returning land that was still in government hands to the private sector. The production cooperatives were dismantled, some land was returned to previous owners, other properties were parcelled out to land reform beneficiaries while additional land was auctioned off and some land was transferred to government agencies for development purposes. More than half the land expropriated was ultimately given to beneficiaries. This process was nearly complete by 1976 (Jarvis, 1989).

The effects of the land reform did not end with the distribution of expropriated land, however; sales of parcels thus created began almost simultaneously with their distribution and increased once such sales had become legal. Other farms were also bought and sold as a result of the relaxation of restrictions on land transactions. Thus, land reform had both a direct and indirect impact on the distribution of landholdings; the latter is still unfolding.

Although there is some evidence of the inequality in the size and distribution of landholdings lessening over the period 1965-1979, it cannot be accepted at face value because of the manipulation of land records and transactions by large landowners. The income distributional changes were, however, not likely to be favourable because the military government denied assistance of any kind (e.g. credit, marketing, procurement of inputs) to the new beneficiaries. Perhaps the most striking change was the disenfranchisement of the poor during the counter-reform through the suppression of agricultural labour unions and smallholders' organizations.

The land reform law was passed by a coalition of urban voters, with grudging support from many progressive farmers who felt the change was inevitable. As the reform progressed and became more extreme in the early 1970s, opposition from large landowners intensified. They were able to secure the support of small landowners fearing the same treatment, while those who failed to benefit – especially casual agricultural labourers – clamoured for more reforms. A sharp decline in output associated with widespread social and political conflict resulted in a conservative backlash, paving the way for a military government, supported and guided by large landowners. While land reforms may still have some progressive impact, in the long term, the changes since 1973 have largely reversed what the reformers had intended (Jarvis, 1989).

This illustration draws attention to a basic inadequacy of the Hayami (1991) framework in distinguishing an unstable equilibrium from a stable one. If the coalitions are as fragile as in Chile, Hayami's comparative static analysis is of limited value unless combined with an analysis of the formation and breakdown of coalitions.

DESIGN

As stated earlier, reform of the structure of landowning is only a part – albeit an important part – of a strategy to provide smallholders with the incentives, skills and infrastructure to increase their productivity. Among the major components of this strategy are improved infrastructure, price policies and marketing structures, and agricultural research and extension services designed to enhance both overall economic performance and the living conditions of the poor. Although contextual considerations are important, some guidelines can be provided for designing land reforms that ensure the efficient and equitable use of land in addition to the smooth redistribution of landownership titles. Of particular importance are mechanisms that would penalize landlords who hold land for the sake of hoarding and speculation to the extent that they impede efficient land use.[12]

- A prerequisite to designing land reforms is the compilation and regular updating of land records. Where such records exist, they are usually incomplete and outdated and are seldom reliable. This is a major constraint in both designing and monitoring the implementation of land reforms. To the extent feasible, attempts should be made to involve representatives of the local community – especially the poor – in the verification and updating of such records. Compilation of comprehensive land records is sometimes rejected for being prohibitively expensive. This, however, overlooks the advances in computerized storage and retrieval of information. An expert committee appointed recently by the Government of India, for example, estimated that the total cost of computerizing land records for 450 districts (including aerial photography units) would be Rs 150 crores over a five-year period. A time-bound programme for the compilation of land records may thus be financially feasible even in a country of India's large size.

- The ceiling on landholding must be imposed on the amount of land owned, regardless of crops and tenure status.[13] The smaller the land ceiling, the greater the improvement in income distribution and, probably, the gain in efficiency. Moreover, following Hayami (1991), a much greater constituency can be mobilized in favour of redistributions that benefit most of the rural poor as against a redistribution designed to benefit only smallholders. Frequent revisions in land ceilings create uncertainty and disincentives for investment. Once a ceiling is fixed, more attention could be given to eliminating loopholes, such as higher ceiling limits for larger families, separate provisions for adult sons,

---

[12] For a more detailed discussion, see Hayami (1991) and Otsuka (1990).

[13] Land reform in the Philippines, for example, was limited to rice and corn lands where tenancy arrangements predominated. This limitation induced landlords to divert their land to other crops, often at the expense of both efficiency and equity. Several potentially productive rice lands, with higher income-earning and labour absorptive capacities were converted into farms planting labour-saving crops such as coconuts.

etc. Landholders could be encouraged to sell the excess land directly to smallholders within a stipulated period. Provision of long-term credit would make it easier for the poor to acquire land.

- A progressive land tax according to the size of holding may facilitate land transfers to the poor (Hayami, 1991).[14] It may induce the intensive use of land and discourage the holding of land for speculative purposes. As a result, the supply of land may increase and the price of land will decrease. Many large landholders may also find it advantageous to subdivide their land into small parcels and rent them to tenants. In addition, the dismantling of input subsidies may further reduce the attractiveness of land to the rich.

- Scrapping all regulations concerning land tenure contracts, including tenancy reforms and land rent, is necessary (Hayami, 1991). In particular, restrictions on share tenancy in the absence of insurance markets may not help the poor. If the ownership of land is not highly concentrated, the tenancy market may function efficiently. However, in case there is extreme inequality, a large-scale intervention in the rural labour market (along the lines of the Employment Guarantee Scheme in the Indian state of Maharashtra) may well be more effective than tenancy regulation. At the same time, the rights of leaseholders already established must be preserved and made transferable.

- A progressive land tax on plantations and agribusiness firms operating plantations on leased public land may promote contract farming with small growers. Similarly, extensive cattle ranches on underused public land may turn into productive, family-sized agroforestry farms, resulting in greater employment and income in marginal upland areas (Hayami, 1991). The revenue collected could be used for strengthening infrastructural support and for providing extension and credit.

- Women require a special focus. Land titling programmes, for example,

---

[14] Bell (1990a), however, remains sceptical. He maintains it is not obvious that "the trick ... of distributing the burden in a manner acceptable to contending parties" (p. 157) is so much easier to perform for radical tax reform than for overt land redistribution.

tend to concentrate on households as the relevant target unit, while paying little attention to the distribution of land rights within them. As a result, the relative position of women sometimes worsens with the implementation of land titling schemes. Land titling, for example, may cause the loss of secondary land rights which are or particular import-ance to women, such as the right to gather fuelwood. Also, the common practice of granting land titles to male heads of household may diminish women's control over land usage and transfers. There is thus a strong case for designing land legislation and reforms to target women as direct beneficiaries. It is also imperative that complementary policies for the provision of credit, agricultural inputs and extension services be designed appropriately for women (FAO, 1991a).

Two caveats are in order:

i) Admittedly, under the suggested scheme, much of the land owned by large landowners will be purchased by the rural middle class rather than by the landless. The landless, however, will have the opportunity to climb the "agricultural ladder" from landless workers to tenants, to leaseholders and, finally, to owner-cultivators. The likelihood of climbing the ladder will be greater in cases where government pro-grammes aimed at redistributing public land are supported by tech-nical guidance, credit, marketing and infrastructure (Hayami, 1991).[15]

ii) Alternatively, if the land market does not redistribute land as desired, the government may have to intervene. One option is that it buys the land and compensates the owners at market prices with land reform bonds instead of cash. It services the interest and principal

---

[15] The "agricultural ladder" hypothesis was suggested in studies of United States agriculture in the nineteenth century (Bell, 1990a). Young, relatively poor individuals begin as labourers and acquire sufficient skills and capital through experience, work and savings to progress through the succeeding stages of share tenancy, fixed-rent tenancy and, with good fortune, outright ownership. Although it cannot be claimed that full mobility on this scale is open to all individuals in all agrarian systems, the hypothesis in question points to the opportunities created by tenancy not only for the employment of existing family members but also for the accumulation of human and physical capital by those individuals who begin with little else but labour power and some promise as farmers.

payments, which it then recovers from the beneficiaries. In this case there are three likely outcomes:

– The beneficiaries default and the programme stops.
– Bonds have built-in features that may erode their value over time so, although landowners receive their nominal value, time erodes the real market value and the government makes no compensation for this loss. Most landowners are therefore likely to oppose such thinly disguised appropriation.
– If funds cannot be raised through internal taxes or (inflationary) monetary expansion, the government may have to borrow abroad (since grants may not be forthcoming). If the debt service burden is already high, the government may fail to repay the loan.

Because the poor cannot pay for acquiring land, and credit is likely to play a supplementary but minor role, Binswanger and Elgin (1990) surmise that the "outlook for land reforms is very bleak. Landowners will oppose any form of open or disguised expropriation, foreign grants will not materialize, and governments will not allocate domestic resources for the purpose" (p. 351). Whether this surmise is plausible or excessively pessimistic can only be judged in a specific context. Nevertheless, the financing of land reforms in the context of a pervasive financial crisis is a serious concern and warrants careful analysis.

Chapter 6
Rural credit interventions

Credit helps the poor to smooth their consumption over time, thereby enabling survival in periods of adversity. In addition, access to credit enables them to make investments in physical and human assets, which improves their long-term income prospects.

Motivated by these concerns, governments have tried to expand credit for the poor. These programmes range from tightly targeted, non-subsidized credit assistance schemes with high repayment rates to highly subsidized, corrupt programmes with high default rates, which benefit mainly the non-poor.

The failure of rural credit interventions, it has been argued in some recent contributions (e.g. Hoff and Stiglitz, 1990), is largely a reflection of the failure to understand the functioning of rural credit markets.[1] An imperfect information paradigm has been proposed which yields valuable insights into the functioning of these markets and guidelines for government intervention. It emphasizes risk in rural credit transactions as a result of information deficiencies.

---

[1] Drèze, Lanjouw and Sharma (1992) caution that the failure of institutional credit reaching the poor should not be taken to imply that it has not served any useful purpose. Their assessment, based on a meticulously researched study of Palanpur (an Indian village) is that: "Institutional credit has certainly played an important role in facilitating the major transformation of agricultural practises that has taken place in the last few decades, particularly the improvement of irrigational facilities. One of the major brakes reducing the speed of this transition has been the limited investment capacity of farmers, and in the absence of institutional credit, it would have taken most of them many years to save enough, say, to instal a Persian wheel on their land or to buy a diesel engine. Credit institutions have given their clients a bumpy ride, and their functioning is open to many compelling criticisms, but it does not follow that they have been altogether useless" (p. 21).

The absence of unambiguous and legally enforceable land titles, large variations in crop yields and weak enforcement of contractual obligations render the provision of credit both costly and risky. Some of these difficulties are compounded for small farmers (and other low-income households) by a lack of collateral and the high processing costs of small loans. An altogether different role for the government emerges from this perspective. A focal point for government interventions is information deficiencies and associated risks.

The first section in this chapter delineates some important but stylized features of rural credit markets from an imperfect information perspective. The next reviews credit interventions in developing countries with a view to distilling policy guidelines and the third section, drawing on this experience, elaborates the role of the government.

MONOPOLISTIC COMPETITION

According to Hoff and Stiglitz (1990), some stylized features of rural credit markets are:

- the coexistence of the formal and informal sectors, with formal rates considerably below those charged in the informal sector;
- credit rationing at high interest rates in the informal sector;
- segmented credit markets – interest rates charged in the informal sector vary by more than can be plausibly accounted for by differences in the likelihood of default;
- the small number of lenders in the informal sector;
- interlinkages between credit and other transactions in the informal sector; and
- the specialization of formal lenders in areas where farmers have land titles.

Neither the traditional monopoly nor the perfect market view can explain these features. As argued and demonstrated by Hoff and Stiglitz (1990), and corroborated in other studies in a recent symposium published in *The World Bank Economic Review* (Vol. 4), a monopolistically competitive formulation comes closest to explaining them. Even though corroborative evidence is limited to a few developing countries, this characterization is likely to be applicable in some other cases too.[2] The focus here is on the failure of subsidized credit programmes – especially why such interventions neither weakened the position of village moneylenders nor lowered the interest rate charged by them.

Salient features of the Hoff-Stiglitz formulation, together with some empirical illustrations, are delineated below.

The first issue is the existence of high interest rates. Given the risk of default, this is not surprising. In this context, it is helpful to distinguish two costs, viz. screening and enforcement costs. The former refer to the costs of eliminating borrowers with a high likelihood of default while the latter cover the costs of compelling repayment. If these costs are high, interest rates are likely to be high. A recent survey of rural credit in Pakistan, for example, shows that the mean interest rate was about 79 percent. While, in one region of the Philippines, 15 percent of rice farmers paid interest charges of over 200 percent per annum (Basu, 1984).

Various (direct and indirect) screening and enforcement mechanisms are employed by village moneylenders.[3] The interest rate serves both as a price and an indirect screening mechanism. The probability of default on a loan depends on the probability that the gross return on the project for which the loan is being used is less than the principal and interest due on the loan. Thus, as projects become riskier, in the sense that the probability of both very high and very low gross returns increases relative to the probability of moderate gross returns, the likelihood of default increases. With changes in the rate of interest, there may be changes in the mix of projects undertaken

---

[2] For further details, see Aleem (1990), Siamwalla *et al.* (1990), Bell (1990b) and Udry (1990). For a contrary view, together with some illustrative evidence drawn from informal financial markets in Malawi, see Bolnick (1992).

[3] Hoff and Stiglitz (1990) distinguish between direct and indirect mechanisms as follows: indirect mechanisms rely on the design of contracts by lenders such that, when a borrower responds to these contracts in his own best interest, the lender obtains information about the riskiness of the borrower and induces him to take actions to reduce the likelihood of default and to repay the loan whenever he has the resources to do so. Direct mechanisms, on the other hand, rely on lenders expending resources to screen applicants and enforce loans.

by borrowers. More specifically, the higher the interest rate, the greater the share of riskier projects would be. A lender therefore keeps the interest rate low enough to obtain a favourable risk composition of projects while also rationing available funds by other means. Thus, credit is rationed with no tendency for the rate of interest to rise or, to put it differently, the rate of interest fails to clear the market. Some direct screening mechanisms are also employed by village moneylenders. It is the high cost of these as well as enforcement mechanisms that leads to high interest rates and, what is more important, to a monopolistically competitive structure with interest rate spreads between different segments of the rural credit markets.

Moneylenders typically advance loans to borrowers from the same village, primarily because the screening costs are lower (*vis-à-vis* the costs for outsiders) and monitoring is easier. These differences in the costs of screening and monitoring lead to the segmentation of credit markets.[4]

Let us now consider some enforcement mechanisms. Interlinkages with other markets can serve as indirect or direct enforcement mechanisms. Lenders who are landlords or merchants may use the contractual terms in other exchanges to reduce the probability of default. For example, a trader-lender may offer a farmer who borrows from him lower prices on fertilizers and pesticides because the probability of default is reduced when such inputs are used. Or, as a direct mechanism, the trader-lender may enforce his claim by deducting it from the value of the crops sold to, or through, him.[5]

Banks, in contrast, rely on collateral – usually land – as they find it difficult

---

[4] In a survey of northern Nigeria, Udry (1990) notes that credit markets were almost completely segmented along kinship and geographic lines, and information asymmetries between borrowers and lenders within these markets were negligible. Loans between individuals in the same village or kinship group accounted for 97 percent of the value of those transactions.

[5] In towns with well-organized commodity markets, there may sometimes be cooperation among traders in enforcement. For example, Bell (1990b) reports from his field work in India that, if a farmer attempted to sell through an agent other than the one with whom he normally dealt, the new agent would deduct principal and interest on the loan, basing his calculations on the usual rule of thumb, relating the size of the loan to the quantity to be delivered, and hand over the amount to the first agent.

to screen and monitor borrowers directly. This explains why formal lenders tend to specialize in areas where farmers have land titles. Because land wealth and household income are strongly correlated, borrowers with above average income typically have greater access to formal sources than those with lower incomes.[6]

Some other aspects of a monopolistically competitive rural credit market are captured strikingly in Aleem's (1990) survey, as summarized below. The screening process is usually long drawn out – partial screening, for example, could be spread over two seasons (approximately one year) before an applicant qualifies for a small initial loan – and, as a result, the bulk of borrowers tend to rely on one source. The total average cost of lenders, as a fraction of the amount recovered, is comparable to the rate of interest charged. Moreover, the mean marginal cost as a fraction of the amount recovered is lower than the average interest rate charged. Each lender faces a downward sloping demand curve from borrowers tied to him, so he can price at above the marginal cost but the potential entry of new moneylenders keeps profits down to zero by driving the interest to the level of average costs. Each lender operates on a small scale with fixed costs spread over a small clientele. In short, the essential features of the Chamberlinian formulation are corroborated.

Finally, to address the issues raised at the beginning of this section, i.e. why have subsidized credit interventions failed to weaken village moneylenders and/or to lower the interest rate charged by them, consider a situation in which some borrowers have direct access to cheap funds from government agencies. If there is credit rationing at a high rate of interest in the informal sector – as a mechanism for screening potential borrowers – it is unlikely that the interest rate will fall.[7] Besides, the outcome may also depend on who has access to cheap funds from government agencies. If

---

[6] The average per caput income of Thai households borrowing from the formal sector was more than 30 percent above the mean, whereas those borrowing only from the informal sector had average per caput incomes close to the mean (Siamwalla *et al.*, 1990).

[7] In contrast, in a competitive credit market, a reduction in the demand for credit from informal sources (e.g. a village moneylender) is likely to result in a reduction in the interest rate.

moneylenders have access to these funds, as is in fact corroborated by the survey in Bell (1990b), the outcome depends on how the costs of money-lenders change and how the level of competition in the informal market changes. If access to government funds increases entry, and average costs in moneylending rise because of a smaller clientele, the interest rate may in fact rise. It is thus hardly surprising that government interventions in the form of subsidized credit failed to achieve their objectives. Instead, some other interventions that seek to overcome information deficiencies and associated risks are likely to be more successful, as elaborated in the last section of this chapter.

REVIEW OF CREDIT INTERVENTIONS

One of the largest credit assistance programmes in developing countries is India's Integrated Rural Development Programme (IRDP). This pro-gramme is designed to promote self-employment through subsidized credit tied to income-generating assets (usually dairy animals). The beneficiaries totalled 15 million households during the period 1980-1985. Indonesia has had two credit schemes with a wide coverage – KUPEDES and Badan Kredit Kecamatan (BKK). The former had 1.3 million beneficiaries in 1988 and the latter had a cumulative membership of 2.7 million households in 1982, but one of the most successful credit schemes – The Grameen Bank in Bangladesh – continues on a small scale. During the period 1976-1984, its membership was limited to 84 000 households (FAO, 1990c). As elaborated below, a great deal can be learnt from the experience of these schemes.

Schemes which offer subsidized credit (e.g. the IRDP in India) have failed for a number of reasons. Given the interest subsidy, there is an excess demand for credit, which therefore has to be rationed. Rationing tends to benefit the non-poor more than the poor, as the former are better risks and more influential. Drèze (1988) draws pointed attention to the bribery and corruption rampant in the disbursal of IRDP funds. He demonstrates that the failure of the IRDP to reach the poorest was in part attributable to "their inability to pay large bribes, influence the village headman and find them-selves 'surety guarantors'" (p. 49). In a more recent evaluation, Drèze,

Lanjouw and Sharma (1992) confirm that the representation of the affluent and influential households among the beneficiaries was far from negligible.[8] Besides, subsidized credit does not necessarily imply that the total cost of borrowing is low for the poor. Often, the procedures are excessively elaborate, long distances have to be travelled and the lending officials have to be bribed.

The most successful credit programmes typically have not subsidized credit. When loans are made at below-market rates, demand exceeds the volume of funds available, so credit has to be rationed. As was just stated, in the rationing process, it is usually the non-poor rather than the poor who obtain loans, and cheap credit thus often degenerates into a transfer programme for the non-poor.

In addition, low-interest loans may entail a number of hidden transaction costs to borrowers, so they may not be as inexpensive as they appear. These costs include transportation expenses, opportunity costs of lengthy processing time and bribes to lending officials. This may explain why the poor sometimes do not avail of subsidized credit, even if they do have access to it.[9] Yet another difficulty with subsidized credit is that it attracts borrowers with a low motivation to succeed. Pulley (1989) provides some illustrative evidence. In a panel survey of IRDP beneficiaries over a period of four years, it was found that a significant number of beneficiaries failed to retain the assets after the subsidy was withdrawn.

---

[8] In a survey of IRDP beneficiaries in the Indian village of Palanpur during 1983-1984, Drèze, Lanjouw and Sharma (1992) demonstrate that the "targeting of IRDP loans to vulnerable households has been a resounding failure" (p. 19). More specifically, "... the average household income of IRDP beneficiaries is more than twice as high as the eligibility cut-off of Rs 3 500 ..." (p. 20). Further, "... none of the beneficiary households are landless, except a shopkeeper ... who happens to be one of the very few affluent households [sic] among the landless... " (p. 20). Among others, the beneficiaries included the village head and deputy head. For other corroborative evidence, see Gaiha (1991).

[9] A study of formal credit in the Indian state of Orissa estimated that borrower transaction costs as a percentage of loan amounts were 10 percent for small landholders and 0.6 percent for larger landholders. As a result, the former have credit demands which are relatively inelastic to interest rate subsidies (Sarap, 1986).

Apart from the poor targeting of subsidized credit, the repayment rates have been rather low. As a result of the latter, such schemes are in large arrears in sub-Saharan Africa, the Near East and Latin America – with the arrears ranging from 3 to 95 percent of outstanding loans (World Bank, 1990). In this context, the experience of BIMAS, a subsidized credit programme for rice farming inputs, in Indonesia is instructive. In the initial stage (1970-1985), the repayment rate was 80 percent; however, over the next five years it fell to 57 percent (Robinson and Snodgrass, 1987). Its mounting arrears forced the government to phase the programme out in 1984. BIMAS was replaced by KUPEDES, a non-subsidized credit programme which has been highly successful. By the end of 1986, the cumulative arrears were virtually negligible – a little over 2 percent of payments due since the beginning of the programme (Robinson and Snodgrass, 1987).

The poor do actually borrow at market interest rates provided the transaction costs are low. In fact, the loans offered by KUPEDES, at a flat interest rate of 1.5 percent per month for working capital and 1 percent per month for fixed investment, are found to be quite attractive by Indonesian villagers (Robinson and Snodgrass, 1987). Similar evidence exists for Bangladesh too (World Bank, 1990).

In any case, subsidized credit schemes may not be sustainable in the long term. To the extent that the poor and others benefit from such schemes, they may become permanently dependent on them. On the other hand, credit provided at market interest rates may help mobilize savings. Banks, for example, may act more effectively as intermediaries between borrowers and savers (FAO, 1990c).

Credit tied to the purchase of specific assets or working capital is often less effective than general credit. In the IRDP in India, for example, subsidized loans are tied to the purchase of an income-earning asset – usually a dairy animal – in order to ensure a stable source of income to the beneficiaries. However, such assets often introduce greater income variances – arising from irregular fodder and feed supplies, a lack of markets for milk and the uncertain life span of animals – for the rural poor, especially landless labourers without any experience of owning assets or running businesses (FAO, 1990c; Drèze, 1988). An evaluation in India of a large credit project for purchase of milch animals initially found a surprisingly high loan recovery rate (about 84 percent), only to discover later that more than 80 percent of the beneficiaries – mainly small farmers and other poor rural households – had closed their businesses by selling the animals and repaying the loans, as they did not find the investment worthwhile (Apte, 1982). An inelastic supply of such assets in the short term may have unfavourable effects on the poor. A large increase in their demand – estimated at one million additional cattle per year as a result of the IRDP (Rath, 1985) – results in a price increase. Since IRDP credits are usually fixed in a nominal value, the poor must either bear a higher financial burden or settle for lower quality animals (FAO, 1990c).

Linking borrowing terms and facilities to repayment records makes a difference. KUPEDES, for example, imposes a penalty of 0.5 percent of the amount borrowed per month for late payments, which is collected from all borrowers but subsequently reimbursed to those who repay on time (Robinson and Snodgrass, 1987). A survey of 30 credit unions in Honduras showed that repayment delinquency was closely related to borrowers' assessment of future loan opportunities (FAO, 1991a).

Group lending is often associated with improved repayment rates. A case in point is Bangladesh's Grameen Bank. Its repayment rate of close to 100 percent is impressive by any standard while the productivity of its loans has also been high. Of considerable significance is the high proportion of women among the bank's beneficiaries (about 83 percent) (World Bank, 1990). Women are typically excluded from credit programmes – especially in parts of South Asia – because of their lack of landownership rights and their consequent inability to offer collateral.

Under group lending, usually a small group of members forms the basic unit for receiving a loan and the same group is collectively responsible for loan repayment. Joint liability among the members reduces the risk of default, since one member's failure to repay jeopardizes the entire group's access to future credit. Group lending also reduces administrative costs. Although, initially, the costs may be high since new branches have to be set up, within a few years there is a significant reduction. In the case of the Grameen Bank, for example, the administrative costs were initially as much as 16 to 25 percent of the loan capital for new branches. But, after three years, these costs declined to 6 percent (World Bank, 1990).

The experience with group lending, however, has not been uniformly good. Some pointers emerge from a review of the experience. Group size is directly related to delinquency rates. The impressive loan recovery rate of the Grameen Bank, for example, is in large measure due to the small size of borrowing groups (i.e. five persons). Joint liability is more easily imposed on small groups and, with higher repayment rates, overall lending costs are significantly reduced (Huppi and Feder, 1990). Group homogeneity and cohesiveness also matter. Peer pressure is greater among members of such groups (Schaefer-Kehnert, 1983; Hossain, 1988). Self-managed groups tend to perform better than those supervised by outsiders such as extension agents or representatives of financial intermediaries. Finally, previous experience with group activities in general – particularly group borrowing – helps improve the group's performance (Bratton, 1986).

Credit cooperatives are also designed to ensure high repayment rates and to lower transaction costs among both the borrowers and lenders. However, their performance has been uneven. In particular, high delinquency rates have been a pervasive symptom of failure. Following a recent assessment (Huppi and Feder, 1990), a key factor in the performance of credit cooperatives is whether they are single-purpose or multipurpose organizations. The latter possess several advantages as they cater to diverse needs of customers at the same place: they facilitate the mobilization of savings while the granting of loans can be coordinated with the supply of inputs. A successful example is Kenya's Cooperative Savings Scheme under which receipts from the coffee crop are credited directly to the members' interest-bearing accounts. As a result, there is a greater availability of funds for rural credit. However, Huppi and Feder (1990) are wary of generalizing from this limited experience – especially because coffee is an export crop and the cooperative is virtually the farmers' only outlet. In fact, multipurpose organizations are often more prone to managerial, financial and other problems. Combining several different functions in an organization with limited managerial and financial resources is likely to impede its smooth and efficient functioning. In addition, multipurpose cooperatives are more likely to be exploited by politicians to promote numerous policies – a case in point is farmers' associations in Taiwan Province of China which were undermined because of a diversion of resources from profitable credit operations (Huppi and Feder, 1990). For the success of credit cooperatives, therefore, it is vital that they be allowed to concentrate on their main function, i.e. providing credit. Diversification may be feasible provided managerial capabilities can cope with it, as illustrated by the step-by-step development of a national cooperative system in the Republic of Korea (Huppi and Feder, 1990).

The potential of informal credit systems has not been exploited fully. Informal systems have several advantages: the administrative costs are lower, the procedures are more flexible (e.g. they accept reimbursement in kind or in labour), the disbursement of loans is quicker, etc. However, such systems cannot function as widely seperated intermediary surplus and deficit units – a function which can only be performed by a formal financial institution. Hence, a cost-effective approach to lending might be to utilize existing informal credit systems at the local level and link them to formal financial institutions at a more aggregate level.

GOVERNMENT'S ROLE

In this section, an attempt is made to define an appropriate role for the government, mainly from an imperfect information perspective. As pointed out earlier, in the light of the available empirical evidence, the emphasis has to shift from the provision of subsidized credit to overcoming information deficiencies and associated risks. Also, to the extent feasible, efforts have to be made to reduce the transaction costs for the rural poor, especially women. The guidelines presented below reflect these concerns.

i) Although the domain of government intervention is considerably restricted, it nevertheless has a potentially important role in reducing information and enforcement costs. If there are positive externalities of an efficiently functioning land market or credit market, for instance, it would be worthwhile for the government to help develop and enforce improved systems of property rights (Hoff and Stiglitz, 1990). Information costs may also be reduced through the development of infrastructure, e.g. roads and communication networks. However, a caveat is in order: as emphasized by

Besley (1992), property rights in certain contexts may not be easy to formalize and enforce, e.g. in dealing with tribal claims to certain properties.

ii) Group lending is essentially a response to information problems in rural credit markets (Hoff and Stiglitz, 1990). The person responsible for organizing a group confers a positive externality on all those members who, on their own, would not have succeeded in securing a loan. Since an externality is typically undersupplied, the government could act as a catalyst in promoting group lending. In doing so, it is crucial to ensure that group size is small, the members belong to a homogeneous group and that they have an affinity with the group leader.

iii) As regards credit cooperatives, staff training is crucial for effective management, especially at the grassroots level. In Nigeria, when training was provided only to officials of government cooperatives, conflicts among management, local staff and members undermined the cooperative's performance. This is not to underrate the importance of training and strong management at the regional or national level. Accounting systems and external supervision are essential if the local population does not have the necessary skills to check on the performance of local managers. Both the Republic of Korea's agricultural cooperatives and the Comilla Projects in Bangladesh benefited from sound planning and management at the top. In these cases, however, the umbrella organization played a vital role in training local leaders and individual members (Huppi and Feder, 1990).

iv) There is some evidence that transaction costs (as a percentage of loan amount) are higher for small landholders. As a result, their credit demands tend to be relatively inelastic to interest subsidies. The lowering of transaction costs through easier access to banks, the simplification of procedures and quicker disbursement of loans may, therefore, significantly enhance the access of smallholders to formal credit. Successful schemes to lower transaction costs of formal credit were initiated in Indonesia by the Badan Kredit Kecamatan (BKK), which established offices in 35 percent of all villages, used simple forms and made quick decisions.[10]

---

[10] For an account of other innovative attempts, see FAO (1991a).

v) Expanding the range of assets that are acceptable as collateral may be important in increasing the availability of credit, particularly for women. In many countries, the only collateral accepted by formal credit institutions is land. But land is registered only under the names of male household members and, thus, women are deprived of access to formal credit. If, instead, assets controlled by women, such as jewellery, were to be accepted as collateral, their access to formal credit would be easier (FAO, 1991a).

Chapter 7
Rural public works

Even if land reforms – especially land redistribution – are carried out successfully and the beneficiaries are provided with access to credit and modern agricultural inputs, a large fraction of the rural poor in a densely populated agrarian economy (such as those of India and Bangladesh) is likely to remain unaffected simply because there is not enough surplus land to distribute among the poor. Furthermore, the beneficiaries may find that the income from cultivation of small plots falls short of subsistence requirements. Most of those without access to land are forced to rely primarily on agricultural employment with long seasonal spells of inactivity. In such a context, rural public works (RPW) have a potentially significant role in poverty alleviation. Indeed, it is arguable that, even without participating in RPW, agricultural labourers may benefit, as their bargaining power *vis-à-vis* their employers may increase. The gain may well be substantial in oligopsonistic rural labour markets provided, of course, RPW are initiated on a large scale.[1] Also, given the difficulties of targeting anti-poverty interventions, there is a strong incentive case for RPW. Specifically, through a work requirement, RPW tend to exclude the more affluent sections. For all these reasons, RPW are now an integral part of a poverty-alleviation strategy – especially in densely populated agrarian economies.

---

[1] In a variation on this argument Drèze (1988) emphasizes the empowerment of the rural poor in the Indian state of Maharashtra. He observes, "In a country where the enfranchisement of the rural poor is a notoriously arduous task, the reliable availability of public employment seems to provide the poor with a unique opportunity to organize around common interests, besides improving their bargaining position in the rural society" (p. 75-76).

In this chapter, the rationale of RPW is spelled out with the support of incentive arguments. In order to analyse the impact of RPW on the poor, a distinction is then drawn between transfer and stabilization benefits, while the trade-offs between them are also indicated. Following this, a distillation of developing countries' experiences with RPW is given and some aspects of the cost-effectiveness of RPW are examined. Finally, simulation results based on Indian data are reviewed and choices in designing RPW with a view to enhancing their cost-effectiveness are addressed.

RATIONALE

The incentive case for RPW rests on two distinctive arguments: a screening argument and a deterrent argument. While screening is concerned with directing support towards the truly needy, the deterrent argument emphasizes that public assistance to the poor should not deter them from making poverty-alleviating investments. These arguments are considered in detail below.

In developing countries, it is usually difficult to target assistance on the poor. One reason is the lack of income distribution data. But even if the data are not a constraint and the poor can be identified accurately, funds meant for the poor seldom reach them because of weak and corrupt administrative systems. Hence self-targeting interventions have been widely used. Rural public works, with a work requirement as a screening mechanism, are one such intervention.

Work requirement is usually effective in screening the poor.[2] This is because the opportunity cost of their time is relatively low. Given the RPW wage, the net gain of the participants depends on income foregone and other costs of participation, e.g. transportation. If these costs are high, an un-

---

[2] That the screening function is in itself a decisive consideration favouring RPW is demonstrated by Besley and Coate (1990). It could be argued, for example, that work requirement may be a costly screening device if it results in individuals doing less work in agriculture. Besley and Coate (1990) show that, under certain conditions, the benefits of screening outweigh the loss of output in other activities. In general, the loss of output may not be an important consideration if RPW are concentrated in agricultural slack periods.

targeted transfer may well be more cost-effective than RPW. Even though RPW are usually well targeted on the poor, the project authorities have some discretion in selecting the participants. Given the poor structure and weak administrative machinery, it is unlikely that the discretion is exercised in favour of the poor. One way of countering this is to add to the awareness of the poor and guarantee employment for all. But, more important, RPW as a poverty-alleviation measure has one major limitation – it excludes specific subsets of the poor such as the disabled, the old and the infirm. For these subsets transfers are necessary.

The deterrent argument for work requirement focuses on the origins of poverty. Are individuals poor just because they experienced bad luck or because of choices made earlier in life? In case the latter is true, public assistance may make individuals dependent on such support and weaken their incentives to invest in poverty-reducing activities.[3] More specifically, welfare programmes could weaken incentives to acquire the human capital necessary to avoid poverty. In order to get round this difficulty, poverty relief could be made less attractive. Again, this could be accomplished through a work requirement.[4] This argument is made more precise in a model of human capital formation, formulated by Besley and Coate (1990). They show that, if a work requirement is imposed at all, it should be a large one, i.e. the poor must work longer hours than they would have done in the absence of intervention.[5] Unfortunately, the link between forms of public

---

[3] Mill's (1848) characterization of the poverty alleviation problem is particularly apt here: how to give the greatest amount of needful help, with the smallest encouragement to undue reliance on it? (Book V, p. 334).

[4] In England, this logic motivated the 1834 Poor Law Commissioners' proposal to place the poor in workhouses. The idea was that the "condition of the able-bodied pauper be 'less eligible' – desirable, agreeable, favourable – than that of the 'lowest class' of independent labourer". The Poor Law regarded this as essential: "It is only ... by making relief in all cases less agreeable than wages that anything deserving the name of improvement can be hoped for" (quoted in Himmelfarb, 1984).

[5] Besley and Coate (1990) provide a formal exposition of the screening and deterrent arguments to support the case for workfare. This exposition is based on a "non-welfarist" definition of poverty. In other words, poverty is characterized by low income and low utility. If the emphasis shifts to utility, the screening argument goes through largely unscathed. The

assistance and investment in human capital has not been empirically investigated. It is possible that this link is not particularly strong when poverty-alleviating policies lack credibility.

TRANSFER AND STABILIZATION BENEFITS

In principle, RPW confer transfer and stabilization benefits. Both benefits matter in poverty alleviation (Ravallion, 1991a; 1991b). The transfer benefits can be direct – the gross benefit to participants less any cost they incur in participating – or indirect – including the share of the poor in the extra income generated by the scheme's output, and any other second-round effects or income from other sources. The stabilization benefits arise mainly from the scheme's effect on the risk faced by the poor of a decrease in consumption. Since many of the poor only just manage to survive, a reduction in the risk of income/consumption falling below a subsistence level matters a great deal.

As regards the direct transfer benefits, an important issue is whether the creation of an extra job under RPW has a significant effect on wages and employment in other activities – especially in agriculture. If this effect is weak or negligible, the participant's income gain is roughly equivalent to the wage rate under RPW. But this may not be the case: in quite different ways, RPW may exert an upward pressure on agricultural wages. RPW may, for example, strengthen the bargaining position of agricultural labourers and, as a consequence, the higher the agricultural wage rate may be.[6] However, a higher wage rate may result in a reduction in demand for agricultural labour. Thus, the income gain to a participant in RPW may diverge from the wage rate. Indirect transfer benefits arise mainly from the

---

deterrent argument does not, however, make sense in the welfarist case. If the government cared about utility, then work requirement would be self-defeating, as it would necessitate a compensating increase in income to preserve the individual's utility level.

[6] It is widely believed that the Employment Guarantee Scheme (EGS) wage rate has influenced the agricultural wage rate in the Indian state of Maharashtra. The guarantee makes the EGS wage a credible threat in bargaining over agricultural wages. Indeed, an effective guarantee can enable enforcement of a minimum wage in agriculture (Ravallion, Datt and Chaudhuri, 1990).

assets created by RPW. One issue is whether assets created by RPW (e.g. percolation tanks, rural roads) have sizeable output effects. Another is the extent to which the poor share the project outputs. While infrastructure is known to contribute to agricultural growth, in some cases it is the location of an "asset" that determines whether the poor will benefit from it. If, for example, a percolation tank is built in a relatively poor area with small plots of land, the poor cultivators in its vicinity are likely to benefit from the rise in the water-table. Alternatively, if it is located in an affluent area with just a few large plots, the benefits are likely to accrue mainly to the more affluent cultivators.

As noted earlier, RPW are often advocated for stabilizing incomes, thus decreasing the risk of a sharp fall in consumption of low-income households, during a monsoon failure, for instance. Two issues are important: one is whether the concentration of RPW activity in lean periods or when there is a local crop failure would displace existing private and non-governmental social insurance arrangements. The other is the trade-off between transfer and stabilization benefits, since the former are likely to be more substantial in peak periods (Ravallion, 1991b).

Family or community support may decline following the introduction of RPW (provided, of course, the donors are altruistic).[7] This implies that, if existing risk-sharing arrangements work well, the benefits of RPW would be largely neutralized by the withdrawal of private support. Although the evidence is limited and inconclusive, it is safe to assert that, when there are highly correlated risks across households (as, for example, in a drought), these risk-sharing arrangements may break down and public intervention in

---

[7] As noted earlier, two principal motives for private transfers exist. One is altruism: adults, for example, might give to their parents because they care about them. Another is self-interested exchange: family members, for example, might help with home production in exchange for financial transfers. Such exchanges could be contemporaneous or part of a long-term, possibly implicit, contract. Motivation matters because it determines the outcome of public transfers. When altruism is at work, changes in public transfers are simply offset by corresponding changes in private ones. In the case of self-interested exchanges, public and private transfers may be unrelated (Cox and Jimenez, 1990).

some form would be necessary. Further, even if transfers are self-interested exchanges, high discount rates may partly offset the future gains from reciprocity, thus restricting the magnitude of self-interested exchanges. There is some evidence that discount rates tend to be high in risky environments (Ravallion, 1991a).

The trade-off between the transfer and stabilization benefits may not be negligible. If the wage rate is lower in the lean period and if the wage elasticity of demand for agricultural labour is unity in the lean period and less than unity in the peak period, the transfer benefits would be larger in the peak period (Ravallion, 1991b). Yet, provision of RPW in the peak period is often opposed on the grounds that the social value of the output foregone is higher in the peak period than at any other time.[8] Also, to the extent that there is an aversion for poverty, there is a strong case for shifting some RPW activity to lean periods.

To put it differently, the stabilization benefits are larger in lean periods. Failure to protect consumption levels during lean periods may force the poor to make costly adjustments, sometimes with serious long-term implications. Under certain conditions, an optimal seasonal allocation is thus given by a combination of RPW activity in peak and lean periods (Ravallion, 1991b). However, this result does not rule out other, more cost-effective solutions. One possibility is to maximize the transfer benefits by concentrating RPW activity in peak periods, while the assets generated could be used for mitigating stress during lean periods. Another possibility is to combine RPW and credit schemes to enable workers in lean times to borrow from their future labour incomes, paying the loan back through RPW wages (Ravallion, 1991b).

EXPERIENCE WITH RPW[9]

RPW have long been used in many developing countries in emergency situations, such as during periods of drought and famine (and, more recently,

---

[8] The EGS in Maharashtra, for example, is terminated as soon as harvesting begins.
[9] This section relies mainly on examples cited in FAO (1990c; 1991b) and Ravallion (1991a).

during periods of macroeconomic stabilization and adjustment) as well as when there is large-scale transitory unemployment and underemployment in the rural sector. However, in recent times, many developing countries have incorporated such schemes as regular elements in their anti-poverty strategies. Some major schemes are reviewed below.

Public employment schemes were used extensively in sub-Saharan Africa during the droughts and famines that occurred in the 1980s. The Labour-Based Relief Programme (LBRP) of Botswana is one of the better known drought relief programmes in this region. This programme, which offered opportunities for wage employment in village improvement schemes to the rural poor, employed 60 000 to 90 000 people each year and replaced almost one-third of lost incomes during the 1983-85 drought period (World Bank, 1990).

In South Asia, RPW form the core of government anti-poverty strategies. One of the most successful programmes is the EGS in Maharashtra. It is unique in that it guarantees work for all registered workers within 15 days of work being requested. Unlike other schemes in South Asia (and other parts of the world), which have had a large direct employment impact over limited time periods, the EGS generates a large number of rural jobs year after year. For instance, the EGS is estimated to have directly created between 100 million and 200 million person-days of work each year, thus employing between one-sixth and one-third of the unemployed and under-employed in the state (FAO, 1990c).

Many countries in Latin America, such as Bolivia, Chile and Peru, have used public employment schemes (including public works) to counter the temporary drops in labour demand that occurred during periods of structural adjustment or macroeconomic shocks. In 1983, at the peak of recession and when unemployment was running at 20 percent, Chile's public employment programme provided employment to an impressive 13 percent of the labour force. As the labour market recovered, the programme was scaled back and virtually eliminated by 1989. At its peak in 1986, Peru's Programa de Apoyo al Ingreso Temporal (PAIT) employed 3.5 percent of the labour force.

By stabilizing incomes over time or across seasons, RPW can significantly reduce the risk of *transitory* poverty. Walker, Singh and Asokan (1986), for

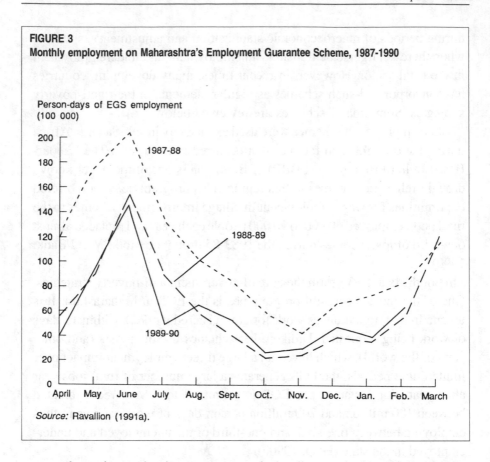

FIGURE 3
Monthly employment on Maharashtra's Employment Guarantee Scheme, 1987-1990

Person-days of EGS employment
(100 000)

Source: Ravallion (1991a).

example, estimate that income streams in landless agricultural households in two villages where the EGS operated were 50 percent less variable (as measured by the coefficient of variation) than in a third village in an agroclimatically similar region where no such scheme existed. Two pieces of evidence are self-explanatory.

i) EGS employment peaks each year in the dry summer period (March to June), when there is little other employment, and declines rapidly afterwards, as shown below in Figure 3.

ii) Further, participation also fluctuates from year to year, depending in large part on the vagaries of the preceding year's monsoon. As shown in Figure 3, the higher participation of 1987 reflects the monsoon failure: as in the earlier drought of 1972-73, the provision of public employment was crucial in the successful relief effort following the severe drought experienced in much of central and western India, including Maharashtra, in 1987 (Ravallion, 1991a).

As regards the famine in Bangladesh in 1974, it is arguable that, if an effective RPW scheme had existed, large-scale starvation and impoverishment would have been avoided (Ravallion, 1991a). In fact, the Food For Work Programme (FFWP) helped Bangladesh avoid famine in 1988, when conditions were not unlike those of 1974.

The long-term implications of income stabilization are no less important. Extra income at a crucial time may enable a household to avoid far more costly adjustment. For example, Cain and Lieberman (1983) find that, whereas the volume of land sales is highly correlated with the incidence of famine in a Bangladesh village, no such correlation exists in the Indian village they studied. Access to relief work (including the EGS) helped many of the poor in the Indian villages to avoid this very costly form of adjustment (Ravallion, 1991a).

Self-selection into and automatic targeting of RPW on the poor is corroborated in some recent studies. Dandekar and Sathe (1980) report that 90 percent of workers in their 1978-79 survey of 1 500 EGS participants spread over 56 projects were poor, as against a headcount index of 49 percent for rural Maharashtra (Kakwani and Subbarao, 1990). More revealing are the findings of Walker and Ryan (1990) and Bhende *et al.* (1990), based on household-level data, drawn from two Maharashtra villages in which the EGS operated over the period 1979-83. These studies demonstrate that the scheme is well targeted: days of participation on the EGS decrease rapidly with increases in wealth and participation is higher in the poorer of the two villages. The scheme effectively screens the poor, particularly in the richer village, where the potential losses from leakage are larger. However, female participation (taking into account both the number and duration) was significantly lower than male participation over the period in question (Deolalikar and Gaiha, 1992). This is somewhat puzzling since there is parity in wage rates for male and female participants and, in most cases, EGS projects are located within a radius of 5 km from a worker's residence.

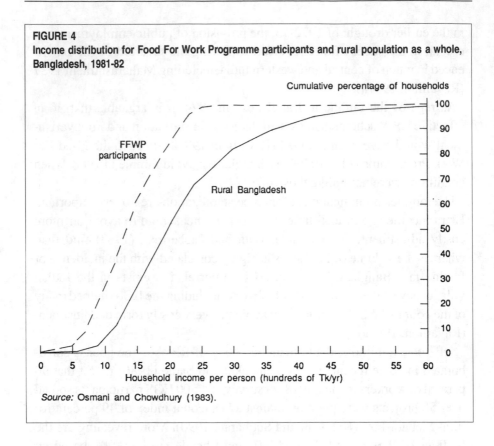

FIGURE 4
Income distribution for Food For Work Programme participants and rural population as a whole,
Bangladesh, 1981-82

Source: Osmani and Chowdhury (1983).

In case poor rural households aim for a certain minimum income, a negative covariation between male and female participation may partly explain this.

That the FFWP in Bangladesh was well targeted on the rural poor is confirmed in a recent evaluation (Ravallion, 1991a). Figure 4 combines cumulative income distributions for FFWP participants and the rural population as a whole.

For relatively low cut-off points in per caput income – 1 500 and 2 500 taka (Tk) – in 1981-82, the contrast was striking. In both cases the proportions of households with FFWP participants were markedly higher than in the aggregate sample (60 and 25 percent, respectively, for the first cut-off point and 96 and 70 percent, respectively, for the second), implying that the concentrations of poorer households among FFWP participants were higher. Also the duration of participation of acutely poor households was relatively high: 70 percent of FFWP employment accrued to 25 percent of the households with per caput incomes of less than Tk 1 500.

A characteristic of these programmes was that they paid lower than market wages. In contrast, Bolivia's Emergency Social Fund (ESF), which largely financed local infrastructure projects executed by private contractors and permitted the hiring of construction workers at market wages, was not so well targeted. Fewer than one-half of the workers employed on ESF schemes were drawn from the poorest 40 percent of Bolivian households (World Bank, 1990).

On some other criteria, RPW have not performed satisfactorily. There is some evidence to suggest that RPW have a tendency to generate inequality in access to public assets. Although the assets created under such schemes have a "public good" character and are usually sited on public land, they are generally utilized to a greater extent by the more affluent sections of the rural population. For instance, in the Maharashtra EGS, those who can make use of the groundwater generated by EGS-created percolation tanks are typically large, affluent farmers who can afford to install pumps or mechanical devices to lift water from below the ground. This inequality in utilization of public assets arises because of the absence of credit and finance organizations that could assist the small and marginal farmers participating in the EGS to purchase mechanical pumps. In addition, an institutional framework within which large farmers would pay user charges for their use of public goods, such as groundwater, would also help address the inequality problem. Unfortunately, neither type of support exists in the vast majority of rural works schemes in the developing world.

Many RPW schemes are biased in favour of creating infrastructure but not towards maintaining it adequately. As a result, facilities created by public works often fall into disrepair and, consequently, are underutilized. There is thus a need to develop postproject maintenance systems built on local capacities and technologies and on community participation, so that routine maintenance of public infrastructure is left in local hands with public intervention necessary only for essential technical tasks.

COST-EFFECTIVENESS

Few of the many empirical studies carry out a comprehensive assessment of the cost-effectiveness of RPW, taking into account the aspects discussed here. The pieces of evidence cited already are suggestive but cannot be combined for an assessment of cost-effectiveness. Not only are there gaps (no estimate is given of, for example, how large the amount of income foregone by participants in RPW is) but an appropriate benchmark is not specified. Developing a sophisticated econometric methodology consistent with the existence of involuntary unemployment, Ravallion and Datt (1992) compute a measure of the transfer efficiency of the EGS (in two villages of Maharashtra) relative to that of the uniform transfer of the same budget to all rural households.[10] The results reported are based on alternative poverty indices, including the FGT class of distributionally sensitive measures and two poverty thresholds.

Unfortunately, in the absence of a detailed discussion of the results, a critical review of this study is not feasible. However, the main findings are as follows.

The immediate net income gain from RPW employment as a proportion of total gross earnings from it is high. The income foregone is low since participation takes place largely during slack periods. However, the effect of additional income on poverty is no more than what could be achieved through a uniform allocation of the same gross budget across all rural households. This surprising result is due to losses associated with foregone income, administrative and other non-wage costs. However, if account is taken of the benefits of the output to the poor, even a modest benefit level

---

[10] A simultaneous tobit model is used to predict the amount of time devoted to a given activity (viz. wage labour, own farm work and self-employment, leisure and domestic work and unemployment) as a function of a vector of exogenous variables and the amount of time spent on the EGS. The model allows different effects across genders, and substitution effects between men and women. Such a time-allocation model can be interpreted as the solution to a household utility maximization problem in which employment on public works is rationed. This model is then used to simulate the time allocation, and hence incomes, that would be expected in the counterfactual case in which public works employment is not available. For further details, see Ravallion and Datt (1992).

(covering 40 percent of the project cost) tips the scale in favour of RPW over uniform cash transfers (Ravallion and Datt, 1992). A major limitation of this analysis however, is that it is confined to an assessment of the direct transfer benefit to RPW participants and ignores indirect transfer benefits (strengthening of the bargaining power of the participants and higher agricultural wages) and stabilization benefits. Also, as the simulations reviewed below indicate, under certain conditions RPW may confer substantial benefits on all, including the rural poor, especially in the long term.

The simulations reported in two recent complementary contributions (Narayana, Parikh and Srinivasan, 1988; Parikh and Srinivasan, 1989) supplement and extend the preceding analysis. These simulations are based on an applied general equilibrium model for India. They are designed to explore the impact that the efficiency in design, execution and targeting of RPW, as well as their financing through taxation, and the reallocation of public investment and foreign aid has on the cost-effectiveness of RPW in an economy-wide setting. Since the simulations cover the period 1980-2000, both short- and long-term effects are analysed in considerable detail. One major limitation of this analysis, however, is the failure to take into account labour market effects.[11] Nevertheless, some important policy insights emerge.

The counterfactual policy scenarios considered are: *i)* variations in public distribution system, ranging from its abolition to its extension to rural areas and making food rations free (i.e. a 100 percent subsidy); *ii)* an RPW scheme targeted on the poorest two expenditure classes with alternative assumptions regarding the efficiency of its execution as well as success in targeting; and *iii)* abolition of the fertilizer subsidy and use of part of the resources saved for augmenting aggregate investment and the remaining part spent on RPW,

---

[11] The explanation given in Parikh and Srinivasan (1989) is not particularly convincing. They explain: "The major reason for not introducing an explicit labour market is the lack of satisfactory studies of labour supply and demand. After all, even in developed countries robust estimates of labour supply elasticities are scarce" (p. 1). It is of course debatable whether this is sufficient to rule out simple but plausible formulations of the labour market in order to generate some illustrative results.

or on creating additional irrigated area. The reference scenario contains no specific redistributive policies except the continuation of public distribution of foodgrains to urban groups only. The results summarized below are relative to the reference solution.

An RPW scheme that is well designed, executed and targeted has the greatest impact on the poor. Not only do the poor improve their welfare substantially but the economy also grows faster (because of the assets created by RPW), provided the resources needed for RPW are raised through additional taxation. Specifically, the GDP in 2000 is 3.5 percent higher, amounting to an increase in the GDP growth rate of 0.22 percent per year in the period 1980-2000. The poorest rural class improves its energy intake by 70 percent, reaching a level which virtually eliminates poverty. However, in 1980, with the introduction of RPW the additional tax effort is substantial. In the reference run in 1980, taxes on non- agricultural income generate revenues of less than 2 percent of GDP and, to finance the RPW (at the level of 100 kg of wheat per person), this revenue has to be raised to around 8 percent of GDP. This is no small effort and its political feasibility, not to mention its administrative feasibility, is doubtful. But, as the economy grows over the years, by 2000 the difference in tax rates reduces to around 1 percent of GDP. This means that a serious financing problem arises only in the initial years. If foreign grants are available for a limited period, RPW could be initiated without straining the tax effort. If foreign grants are not forthcoming and tax effort is not feasible, RPW may be introduced at a modest level and gradually stepped up, thereby keeping the needed tax effort within modest limits. An important implication of these results is that RPW are not just a short-term relief measure but, given careful planning and efficient execution, can contribute substantially to both poverty alleviation and rural development in the long term as well.

However, a caveat is in order. The superiority of RPW in the counterfactual simulations should not be taken to imply that other policy interventions such as food subsidies must be abandoned.[12] As argued and elaborated in the next

---

[12] I owe this suggestion to Harold Alderman.

chapter, certain sections of the rural poor, e.g. undernourished children, pregnant and lactating women and physically handicapped people, cannot be targeted through RPW and, for them, food subsidies may be the more effective policy intervention. Also, there may be physical constraints to organizing RPW in remote and inaccessible areas. Food subsidies may well be more effective provided distribution channels exist. Thus, while RPW has decisive advantages in terms of the overall impact on the poor, specific subsets of the poor are likely to benefit more from other interventions such as food subsidies.

DESIGN

The simulation results reviewed in the previous section were based on hypothetical assumptions of efficiency in the design, execution and targeting of RPW. As there is legitimate concern about the poor design and execution of RPW in general, this particular aspect deserves careful attention. Besides, even though RPW are well targeted on the poor, an important policy question is whether, given a budget, project authorities should aim for wide or limited coverage of the poor. Finally, the trade-offs between the cost-effectiveness of RPW and their political feasibility raise some specific concerns.

Project selection, location and other considerations

Careful selection and implementation of RPW projects and access of the poor to their outputs can enhance substantially the cost-effectiveness of RPW. The returns on public investment in RPW are sensitive to the nature of the project, and the efficiency of their design and execution. Some broad guidelines distilled from the experience with RPW in South Asia are stated below.

i) If public investment substitutes for private investment, e.g. contour bunding to prevent soil erosion in a large neighbouring farm, the overall effect of this investment on that area's development would be negligible (relative to the contribution of private investment) and the bulk of the benefits would accrue to the non-poor. Public investment should therefore concentrate on public good activities, e.g. roads and flood protection structures. To the extent feasible, it should be ensured that the benefits of such activities are widely dispersed, especially among the rural poor.[13]

ii) Social returns to the assets can also be enhanced by ensuring that projects are well integrated into existing rural development plans. Projects designed largely for the immediate alleviation of poverty can often be coordinated with local and regional development plans. Besides, local village-level participation in project design and execution can help to avoid wastage and promote labour-intensive methods.[14]

iii) Since the performance of a public agency is often judged in terms of new projects undertaken and completed, the maintenance of RPW projects is seldom an important concern. RPW are sometimes associated with "roads that get washed away in the next monsoon".[15] While financial provision for regular maintenance of these assets is necessary, it is perhaps equally necessary to ensure that there is local participation in their maintenance. Greater awareness of the benefits of such assets, a deliberate community initiative in this regard and an effective enforcement mechanism would make a significant difference.[16]

Wage rates, coverage and labour intensity

i) One choice in designing RPW is to aim at a wide coverage of the rural poor or to cover a small subset. Given a fixed outlay, a wide coverage would imply low wages per participant while limited coverage would imply high enough wages to enable the participants to cross the poverty threshold. Sen (1975) drew attention to this choice and argued persuasively

---

[13] To illustrate, a road that connects a remote village to a nearby town where the unemployed may find employment during a lean period would be a better investment than a road that helps a few affluent farmers to transport their produce to the nearest wholesale market.

[14] An example is Maharashtra's new scheme, Rural Development through Labour Force (an offshoot of the EGS) which encourages village-level participation in formulating labour-intensive development plans, including specific EGS projects.

[15] This concern is raised in Basu (1981).

[16] Wade's (1987) analysis of maintenance of common property resources by villagers themselves in South India is instructive.

in favour of wide coverage of RPW. A graphic exposition (Fig. 5) may be helpful: suppose an RPW scheme is launched in a poor region and the wage offered (W_2) is high in relation to the prevailing wage. Since the wage rate that equates demand for and supply of labour (W_1) is lower, at the higher wage rate (W_2) there is an excess supply of labour (AB).[17] Quite apart from the administrative difficulty of "rationing" employment (e.g. corruption among project staff), the redistribution of the scheme's outlay is restricted to a small number of the rural poor (OM). If, as an alternative, project managers are free to hire as many workers as are needed to eliminate excess supply (for a given outlay), the demand for labour would be given by the rectangular hyperbola (AC) and ON workers would be hired at the W_3 wage rate. Thus, more work will be done and more people will be employed. It does not follow, however, that poverty will fall sharply. As pointed out earlier, the outcome depends to some extent on the poverty index – specifically, whether it is distributionally sensitive or not.

A recent analysis (Ravallion, 1989) contains some interesting results. Using Bangladesh household income distribution data, it investigates the effects of wide and low coverage of RPW on a range of poverty indices. The important results are summarized below.

When the budget is small, universal coverage of RPW with flexible benefits is less cost-effective than limited coverage with sufficiently large benefits to enable a subset of the poor to escape poverty. This result holds for both the headcount and distributionally sensitive indices (in the Foster-Grear-Thorbecke class with $\alpha > 1$). However, with a large budget and/or low administrative costs, universal coverage of RPW with flexible benefits is more cost-effective for all such indices.

The case for wide coverage assumes that the policy maker can fix the wage rate on the scheme so as to allow it to adjust to the long-term budget constraint. But, if the wage rate is (statutorily) predetermined, employment

---

[17] The vertical demand curve (MD) is implied by a fixed wage rate and a fixed component of the RPW budget earmarked for labour costs.

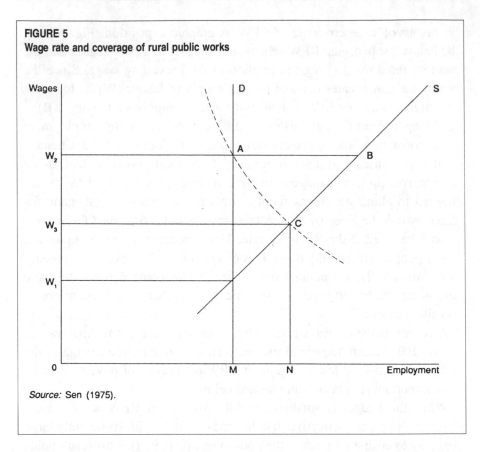

FIGURE 5
Wage rate and coverage of rural public works

Source: Sen (1975).

cannot be guaranteed without violating the budget constraint. That this may be a serious concern in some cases cannot be denied.[18]

ii) The choice between piece and time rates may also influence an RPW's performance. If piece rates are offered when time rates prevail elsewhere (which is not uncommon in lean periods), the more productive workers are likely to be attracted to the RPW, thus adding to its social opportunity cost.

---

[18] There is some evidence that substantially higher statutory minimum wages, paid under Maharashtra's EGS since 1988, have resulted in a "rationing" of employment. As a result, some of the poor have gained but others have lost (Ravallion, Datt and Chaudhuri, 1990).

A piece-rate system may thus either exclude relatively unproductive but very needy persons or result in low wages for them.[19] Hence, a combination of time and piece rates may provide a better wage schedule.

iii) The desire for promoting the employment of unskilled labour is usually reflected in a restriction on the minimum share of labour costs in total variable costs (at least 60 percent, for example, in the case of the EGS in Maharashtra). These restrictions tend to reduce the use of material inputs (tools, raw materials) to their technological minimum levels, at which substitution possibilities with labour are negligible. Such a restriction presupposes that the benefits of RPW to the poor consist of direct wage benefits only while all benefits from the output of RPW accrue to the non-poor only. To the extent that the poor share in the output benefits, optimal labour intensity may not be as high as the restrictions seem to imply (Ravallion, 1991a).

Financing

RPW can in principle be financed either through taxation or cuts in other public expenditure, borrowing or foreign aid, or a combination of some of these. New taxation may add to the existing burden and consequently weaken the incentive to work. Cuts in some items of public expenditure, e.g. health and education, may directly affect the poor. The prospects for foreign aid are not likely to improve in the foreseeable future. Thus, the financing options appear to be quite limited and the most desirable option cannot be chosen independently of the context. Whether an additional dose of taxation, for example, would be feasible can only be determined relative to the existing incidence. However, as demonstrated in the simulations by Parikh and Srinivasan (1989), there may be choices in the time-phasing of RPW and thus an unacceptably high burden of taxation in the initial stage may be avoided.

---

[19] For some recent corroborative evidence, see Deolalikar and Gaiha (1992).

Political economy considerations

Certain coalitions, as elaborated later in this report, are crucial to the political feasibility of an anti-poverty intervention. In this context, it is sometimes argued that some "leakage" of benefits to the non-poor is desirable (perhaps also unavoidable if it is a public good, e.g. a road) to ensure their support for the intervention in question. To illustrate, since the benefits of EGS projects such as percolation tanks, roads and contour bunding have accrued largely to the non-poor, this scheme has enjoyed wide support among rural landowners and others (Herring and Edwards, 1983). Also, the perception of the rural poor matters. In a semi-arid setting, characterized by a high variability of agricultural yields and incomes, the poor perceive the EGS as an insurance against crop failure. This evokes wide and spontaneous support for the scheme among them even though at any time only a subset participates in it.[20] Such a coalition of the rural poor does not guarantee political feasibility but it is undoubtedly an important contributory factor (Ravallion, 1991a).

---

[20] This is an important factor in the solidarity of the poor following the introduction of an EGS (Echeverri-Gent, 1988).

Chapter 8
Food subsidies

As argued in Chapter 7, some sections of the poor (e.g. the old, the infirm and the handicapped) are not likely to benefit from the direct anti-poverty interventions discussed so far. Neither land reforms nor RPW will help them to augment their incomes. Special interventions designed to raise their income levels are therefore necessary. Moreover, there is now sufficient empirical evidence which points to the greater vulnerability of the poor to abrupt price changes of food staples (Bliss, 1985; Gaiha, 1989c). Unanticipated fluctuations in agricultural output may, for example, cause a spurt in food prices with serious consequences for the "entitlements" of casual agricultural labourers. Typically, the effects are more severe for this group for two reasons: *i)* food accounts for a large share of their household budget and *ii)* liquidity constraints preclude the storage of food. In this context, there is a strong justification for food subsidies. However, the design and implementation of food subsidies raise many contentious issues. Such subsidies take a variety of form, e.g. general food subsidies, food rations, food stamps, and the choice of an appropriate form is often very difficult. Their effects vary, depending on whether a partial equilibrium or a multimarket analysis is carried out. If the food subsidies account for a large share of public expenditure, as is in fact the case in many developing countries (e.g. Egypt), the macro effects may well be significant. These may, for example, neutralize the favourable nutrition effects through higher inflation.

In this chapter, an analytical framework is elaborated, focusing mainly on the efficiency and welfare effects of consumer subsidies. As this is of a partial equilibrium nature, it is supplemented by an intuitive exposition of multimarket/general equilibrium considerations. Second, experiences with some major forms of food subsidy – particularly their effects on the rural poor – are reviewed. Finally, some suggestions are made to enhance their effectiveness.

FRAMEWORK

Partial equilibrium analysis

There are different ways of lowering the price of food, for example, for all consumers. One is to shift out the domestic supply curve through higher productivity. This may not be feasible in the short term. Another is to ration food demand which, in the absence of an effective enforcement mechanism, may result in the emergence of a black market. A third possibility is to augment the availability of food through imports. In what follows, the implications of food imports are analysed in a partial equilibrium framework formulated by Timmer (1986).

Suppose that the price of food imports is higher than the desired market price and that the difference is covered by a food subsidy. As shown in Figure 6, consumers respond to the lower price by increasing consumption of food; they move from d to j on the aggregate demand curve and the quantity consumed increases from Q_2 to Q_4.

Food producers move from c to g and domestic production falls from Q_1 to Q_3. Initially, the food imports were $Q_2 - Q_1$. With the introduction of a food subsidy the gap increases, resulting in larger imports, $Q_4 - Q_1$. Consequently, the foreign exchange requirements are also greater, $P_w(Q_4 - Q_3)$, as against $P_w (Q_2 - Q_1)$ without the subsidy.

Producers lose the amount a c g f, of which a b g f is transferred to consumers and b c g is deadweight efficiency loss. Consumers gain a total amount of a d j f. Total subsidy is b e j g. The sum of the subsidy and the income transfer from producers to consumers exceeds the gain in consumer surplus by the amount d e j – a deadweight efficiency loss on the consumer side.

Some additional insights into the effects of food subsidy are suggested by a disaggregation of consumers and producers by income, as shown below in Figure 7. The focus is on the impact that price changes have on the welfare of poor consumers and small farmers.

At the aggregate level, the analysis proceeds exactly as before. Hence, no

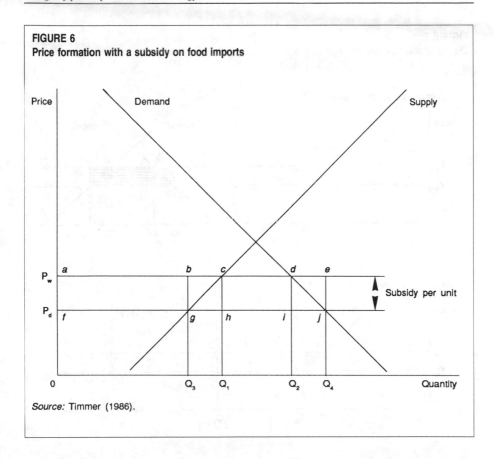

FIGURE 6
Price formation with a subsidy on food imports

Source: Timmer (1986).

comment is necessary on the top graph of Figure 7. The middle graph shows two different patterns of food consumption. Rich consumers, represented by demand curve D (rich), show no response at all to price changes. Their price elasticity of demand for food is zero. Poor consumers, however, represented by D (poor), do not enjoy such luxury. Their poverty leads them to adjust their food intake when prices change because of income and substitution effects. The quantity demanded increases from Q_{d1} to Q_{d2} and the consumer surplus is augmented by P_w m n P_d. Although the consumption of the rich does not change at all, they gain more of the total income transfer induced by the subsidy (their gain is represented by P_w u v P_d). Note that the entire efficiency loss in consumption, m l n, is borne by the poor. The

FIGURE 7
Disaggregating the impact of price policy

Aggregate supply and demand

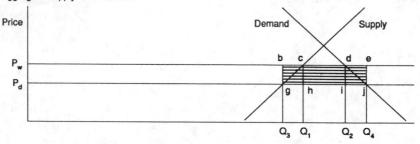

Disaggregated demand

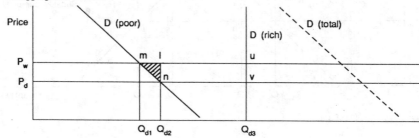

Disaggregated supply

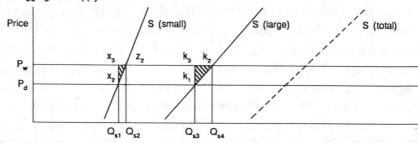

Source: Timmer (1986).

larger gain by the rich occurs for an obvious reason: they consume more of the subsidized food than do the poor. The bottom graph is constructed around a common stereotype of food producers in developing countries: small producers produce primarily for their family's subsistence needs and are not so responsive to market prices as large farmers who have more surplus production for sale. Accordingly, when the price is reduced from P_w to P_d, small producers curtail production from Q_{s2} to Q_{s1} (a small reduction) while large producers curtail from Q_{s4} to Q_{s3} (a substantial reduction). Since large producers supply a much larger quantity than small producers, the loss of producer surplus of the former is also substantially larger than that of the latter ($P_w k_2 k_1 P_d > P_w x_2 x_1 P_d$).

The framework reviewed above is useful in isolating the effects of food subsidy on different categories of consumers and producers. It also draws attention to a policy dilemma: food subsidies, for example, favour small consumers but not small producers. However, this framework cannot throw much light on the effect of food subsidies on poverty. A more specialized but somewhat limited formulation by Besley and Kanbur (1988) yields some useful insights.

The Besley-Kanbur (1988) formulation concentrates on generalized food subsidies, i.e. subsidies on food items that both rich and poor consume. This focus is justified on the grounds that means testing of a large population every year is not administratively feasible for most developing countries. The analysis is based on the Foster-Greer-Thorbecke (1984) class of additively decomposable poverty indices. Some interesting results are obtained for choosing between inframarginal and marginal subsidies and for resolving the conflict of interests between consumers and producers.

In many developing countries, food subsidies are given in the form of generalized rations through "fair price" shops. These rations are made available below the market price. If the ration can be resold at the higher free market price, the subsidy is inframarginal and equivalent to a lump sum income transfer equal to the ration quantity multiplied by the difference between the market price and the ration price. Besley and Kanbur (1988) show that the effect of an increase in the food subsidy budget on F_α is proportional to $F_{(\alpha-1)}$. Thus, for $F_{(1)} = HG$, the impact is proportional to

$F_{(o)} = H$, i.e. the headcount ratio. The intuition is simple. A small increase in the food subsidy budget increases everybody's income in the population by the same small amount. The poverty gap ($F_{(1)} = HG$) falls by the amount of increase per person multiplied by the number of poor. This result has a direct application in the location of ration shops. Suppose the population can be divided into two mutually exclusive groups by region (a generalization to many regions is straightforward). In each region, given the distribution of income, $F_{(1)}$ is computed. If the objective is to minimize $F_{(1)}$ at the national level, it follows that the region with the higher value of $F_{(0)}$ (or H) should be favoured at the margin. In other words, ration shops should be located in neighbourhoods with a high incidence of poverty as this would be most cost-effective in reducing the national poverty gap.

Alongside the subsidized ration scheme, many developing countries have food subsidy schemes which subsidize the consumption of food at the margin (Scobie, 1983). In these cases, trade in the commodity is in the hands of the government which, for example, purchases on the world market and sells to consumers at a lower price but without a ration, i.e. consumers can buy as much as they wish (similar to the general case considered at the beginning of this section). A key question is the selection of the commodity for subsidy. Besley and Kanbur (1988) show that, if the objective is to minimize the poverty gap $F_{(1)}$, the subsidy should be directed towards the commodity for which the poor's (mean) share in the mean consumption of the population as a whole is highest. The larger this share, the greater the benefit to the poor.

Some considerations in choosing between inframarginal and marginal subsidies may be noted. Inframarginal subsidies transfer purchasing power independently of current income while subsidies at the margin do so in proportion to current consumption of the commodity in question and, as a first order approximation, in proportion to income. For a given budget, therefore, inframarginal subsidies are better at alleviating poverty. However, there may be administrative difficulties in achieving full coverage of the population as well as take-up problems associated with the stigma of queuing at a ration shop. By contrast, a price subsidy made through an import subsidy, for example, is comprehensive and reaches the whole population. Besley and Kanbur (1988) show that, for $F_{(1)}$, it is better to use an inframarginal subsidy provided the mean consumption of the poor is less than the overall mean consumption. However, this conclusion rests heavily on individuals being able to benefit from ration shops and being able to turn their ration into cash.

So far, producer prices and consumer prices for food were assumed to be independent. However, often government policy operates by allowing in extra imports of food, thereby lowering prices for both consumers and producers. Clearly, depending on the fraction of the poor who are food producers and their share in the total supply of food, rural poverty may worsen. However, the government may allow in more imports and then insulate the producers from the effects of lower prices by keeping producer prices high and bearing the cost in terms of its fiscal deficit. If this is not feasible, it faces an inevitable trade-off between producer poverty and consumer poverty. Besley and Kanbur (1988) demonstrate that, for $F_{(1)}$, both the incidence of poverty among consumers and producers, taken separately, and their "exposure" to price changes (given by the mean consumption of the commodity by the poor and the mean net supply of poor producers) are crucial to the outcome.

The merit of this analysis lies mainly in providing microfoundations and precisely defining some key propositions for the designation of food subsidies in the context of poverty alleviation. Some specific indicators are identified to guide policy formulation. It may be argued, however, that its usefulness is somewhat limited. The results summarized here hold for a special case of the Foster-Greer-Thorbecke class of poverty indices, i.e. $F_{(1)} = HG$. This, as pointed out in Chapter 2, is not an appealing index. Those for the distributionally sensitive index, $F_{(\alpha > 1)}$, are rather complex and computationally demanding. A further difficulty is that transaction costs faced by the poor are given a short shrift. The case for inframarginal subsidies, for example, is weakened by the distance that the poor have to travel to get to a ration shop, the long hours of waiting and the uncertain supplies. The low take-up rates, in other words, are not so much a reflection of the stigma attached to waiting in a queue outside a ration shop as of the time lost in securing access to the rationed supplies. Finally, while a partial equilibrium focus is often useful in clarifying certain choices, in the present context, it may be limiting since a broader focus, taking into account some of the macroimplications for example, may change the results significantly.

Extension

Some of the choices considered above in a partial equilibrium framework may have a different outcome in a broader multimarket framework. In a partial equilibrium framework, for example, an import subsidy may worsen an index of aggregate poverty if the exposure of poor food producers to price changes is high. While as a general statement it has some validity, the precise effect will vary depending on whether the resources are switched to other crops. A recent analysis of agricultural pricing in Malawi (Kirchner, Singh and Squire, 1984) illustrates the sensitiveness of the results. In a partial equilibrium analysis, following a 14 percent reduction in the price of corn (the country's staple food crop), corn production declined by 6 percent and smallholder income fell by 29 million Kwacha (K). The multimarket results showed the same decline in corn production but a switch in resources, especially farm labour, led to increased tobacco and peanut production by 2 and 3 percent, respectively.[1] Because these crops are exported, foreign exchange earnings increased by K 7.5 million. The lower corn price also caused fertilizer use to drop by 15 percent. After the adjustments included in the multimarket model were accounted for, smallholders' incomes dropped by only K 18 million instead of the single market estimate of K 29 million. Thus, the effect on poor producers (as well as on the aggregate index of poverty) would be much less adverse than the partial equilibrium results suggest.

Following Timmer (1986), at a macro level, the effect of a food subsidy *may* depend on how it is financed. If there is a transfer of public expenditure from defence to food subsidies, for instance, there is no direct macro effect

---

[1] Multimarket models are applied primarily in those cases in which governments enforce fixed prices in several markets and so must plan for variable quantities if price stabilization is to be successful.

via the budget. However, if the subsidy results in a budget deficit financed through money creation, there may be a series of effects. Prices may rise with drastic income distribution changes. Wage earners may lose while owners of physical assets (e.g. land) may gain. Overvaluation of the domestic currency may result in a greater implicit subsidy on imports, including food imports. While the demand curve for food shifts out when other prices rise relative to that of food, the supply curve may shift back as other more profitable opportunities emerge, resulting in a greater depend-ence on food imports. The higher food consumption cannot be sustained for long unless foreign exchange is available to finance food imports. If there is a parallel contraction in employment (since food production is relatively labour-intensive), the short-term nutrition gain may well be wiped out.

To sum up, the linkages between food subsidy and poverty are complex. A partial equilibrium analysis can throw light on only some aspects. The illustration given above suggests that partial equilibrium results may not hold or may get modified in a broader multimarket/general equilibrium framework. From this perspective, experiences with different forms of food subsidy are reviewed below. While much of the empirical evidence is limited to the direct short-term effects of food subsidies on the poor, an attempt is made to broaden the focus by drawing on general equilibrium simulation results.

EXPERIENCE WITH FOOD SUBSIDIES

This section is in two parts: in the first, some major forms of food subsidy are reviewed, mainly taking into account the direct effects on the poor, while in the second, a general equilibrium analysis of a public distribution scheme is evaluated. The evidence reviewed yields valuable insights into how food subsidies may be targeted more towards the poor.

Direct effects

General. General food price subsidy schemes supply unlimited amounts of subsidized food to any one who wishes to buy it. The subsidy may cover a portion of the total production, storage and marketing costs. The price wedge may be administered at a point of import or at a point of

TABLE 15

Distribution of the annual income transfer from the general food subsidy, Egypt, 1981-82

Type of household and income level	Amount of transfer	Transfer as percentage of household expenditure
	(Egyptian pounds)	
Urban		
Poorest quartile	15.4	8.7
Richest quartile	18.1	3.4
Rural		
Poorest quartile	11.9	10.8
Richest quartile	15.2	2.7

Source: Alderman and von Braun, (1984) and Alderman (1991).

processing or storage. Such schemes have been extensively used in developing countries. Costs ranged from less than 1 percent of total public expenditure in Colombia in 1978-80 to 10 to 17 percent in Egypt between the mid-1970s and 1984.

The experience of Egypt is instructive. Table 15 brings out some salient features of the country's food subsidy programme.

- Although this programme is costly, it benefited the poor. The transfers to the poorest quartiles in both rural and urban areas were sizeable.
- The richest also benefited and, in fact, the absolute transfers to them in both rural and urban areas were larger.
- Both the poorest and richest quartiles in the urban areas gained more in absolute amounts than their counterparts in rural areas, suggesting an urban bias.

While general subsidies are administratively convenient – especially where private market channels exist – they tend to be costly, depending on the extent of transfers to the non-poor. All benefits going to the non-poor add to the budgetary cost of reducing poverty. In Egypt, only about 20 cents out of each dollar spent reached those in the poorest quartile (World Bank, 1990). Another difficulty is the urban bias in the distribution of the transfers. This is to some extent inevitable as market channels tend to be more extensive and efficient in urban areas.

An option, therefore, is to limit subsidies to commodities that are consumed mainly by the poor and that form a significant part of their food expenditure. Such goods are usually not available and, if they are available, are often difficult to subsidize. But there are a few examples of successful targeting: in Egypt, for example, benefits from subsidies on coarse flour accrue mainly to low-income groups.

Another option is geographic targeting. The Pilot Food Price Subsidy Scheme in the Philippines demonstrates the potential. Anthropometric investigations helped to identify poor villages with high rates of child malnutrition. Seven villages were selected to receive price discounts on rice and cooking oil – goods that accounted for a large part of food expenditures. These were sold through local retailers and were available to all villagers. The scheme improved the nutrition status of both preschoolers and adults. It was highly cost-effective; 84 cents out of each dollar spent were transferred. This, however, did not include set-up costs for extensive growth monitoring, which should be taken into account in determining overall cost-effectiveness. But few countries have an established nutrition surveillance system needed to run such schemes (World Bank, 1990).

Rationed food subsidies. An alternative to a general subsidy is to provide a quota or ration of subsidized food to households while permitting unlimited sales on the open market. Schemes of this type have been used in many developing countries. Ration schemes are designed to ensure access to a regular supply of basic staples at reasonable prices. The absolute transfer under a general ration is similar for all income groups. Thus, rations tend to be more progressive than general food subsidies.

The Sri Lankan general rice ration scheme, which operated between 1942 and 1978, had a large impact on poverty both because the benefits that accrued to the poor were large and because there was extensive coverage of different categories of the poor. To reduce costs, in 1978 the government restricted distribution to the poorest half of the population. A comparison of the targeted scheme with the general subsidy on wheat and bread during the same period shows that the benefits to the poor from the former were greater both in absolute terms and in relation to income. To illustrate, under the targeted rice ration scheme, the poorest quintile received a monthly per

TABLE 16

Urban bias in rationed food subsidies: all India, 1986/87

Commodities	Per caput monthly subsidy in Rs	
	Rural	Urban
	(Rs)	
Rice	0.625	1.352
Wheat	0.140	0.568
Pulses	0.003	0.007
Edible oils	0.315	0.711
Sugar	0.716	0.975
Total	**1.799**	**3.613**

Source: Jha (1992).

caput transfer of 11 Sri Lankan rupees (SL Rs), which worked out to be about 20 percent of per caput expenditure, while the corresponding estimates under the general wheat and bread subsidy were more than SL Rs 4 and about 8 percent, respectively. A similar pattern of transfers is seen in the distribution of food grains through fair price shops in certain states in India. In Kerala in 1977, for example, the poorest 60 percent of the population received 87 percent of the foodgrains distributed. Kerala is unique in that rations are spread fairly evenly between the rural and urban populations. In other parts of India as well as in other countries, including Bangladesh and Pakistan, the benefits of ration systems accrue disproportionately to urban consumers – although poverty is largely a rural phenomenon in South Asia (World Bank, 1990). Table 16, based on Indian data, brings out the urban bias in rationed food subsidies. Overall, the subsidy in urban areas was twice as much as in rural areas.

As is true of general subsidies, ration schemes are often limited in coverage, especially in rural areas, because the infrastructure and retail networks needed to implement them are lacking. These difficulties are compounded by a lack of political will to assist the rural poor (World Bank, 1990).

A degree of self-selection could be introduced in a different way. One possibility is to locate ration shops in slums. The transaction cost of buying a restricted quantity at a ration shop located in a slum is greater for the rich than for the poor. In northeastern Brazil, for example, small amounts of subsidized food were sold through shops in poor neighbourhoods that the well-to-do regarded as unsafe; the inconvenience of the locations and the limit on the size of purchase further discouraged them from participating. Another possibility is to restrict such schemes to commodities perceived to be inferior to the open market alternative. Self-selection was observed in Bangladesh when users of the ration shops were offered a choice of a quota of wheat flour or a larger quota of sorghum flour. Lower-income families tended to opt for the sorghum flour (Alderman, 1991).

However, while such schemes tend to be well targeted (in terms of poor beneficiaries as a fraction of total beneficiaries) their coverage of the poor beneficiaries as a fraction of the total poor is sometimes limited. This is illustrated by some recent Indian evidence. While about 60 percent of those who bought jowar – an inferior cereal – from ration shops in the rural areas were poor in 1986-87, they accounted for barely 9 percent of poor jowar consumers. By contrast, while only 40 percent of those who bought sugar were poor, they accounted for about 70 percent of the poor sugar consumers.[2] Since the differential between the ration and the open market price was also larger for sugar, it is plausible that the poor preferred sugar to jowar, as the former was associated with a larger income gain. Given the liquidity constraint, it is a fair assumption that most of the rural poor could not buy both jowar and sugar.

Food stamps. Food stamps are similar to rations except that the quota is measured in terms of a nominal currency unit rather than in commodity weights or volumes. There are, however, some important administrative differences in their functioning. Food stamps do not require the government to handle any commodities directly. They do, however, require that retailers accept a parallel currency and are able to redeem this currency conveniently. The nominal value of food stamps, of course, erodes when there is inflation.

The Sri Lankan experiment with food stamps, which began in 1979-80, was a response to a fiscal crisis which rendered it difficult to support the

---

[2] These estimates are from Jha (1992).

TABLE 17
General and targeted subsidies in Jamaica, 1988

Item	General subsidy	Targeted subsidy *(food stamps)*
Cost as share of government expenditure[1]	3.0	1.6
Proportion of transfer to:		
Poorest quintile	14.0	31.0
Richest quintile	26.0	8.0
Transfer as share of expenditure per recipient in:		
Poorest quintile	2.3	9.5
Richest quintile	0.1	1.0
Proportion of households covered in:		
Poorest quintile	100.0	51.0
Richest quintile	100.0	6.0

[1] Excluding administrative costs.
Source: World Bank (1990).

curtailed rice ration scheme and other food subsidies. The total transfer was reduced. Stamps for food and kerosene were targeted towards families with self-reported incomes of less than SL Rs 300 a month – roughly 50 percent of the population. The share of food subsidies in GNP dropped from 5 to 1.3 percent between the mid-1970s and 1984 while their share in total government expenditure fell from 15 to 3 percent over the same period. But the value of food stamps, which was fixed in nominal terms, quickly eroded in the 1980s, falling from 83 percent of the benefits of the general subsidy at the time of introduction to 43 percent in 1981-82.

Jamaica's food stamp scheme was introduced in 1984 to protect vulnerable groups from the full impact of exchange rate movements and reduced public spending. Stamps are targeted towards pregnant and lactating women and children under five through registration at primary health centres. This system encourages preventive health care and successfully screens out high-income households. Coverage is high among the intended beneficiaries and this part of the scheme is markedly progressive. Poor, aged and handicapped people who are already on welfare programmes, as well as households that report a total income of less than $J 2 600 a year, are also eligible for food stamps. This component of the scheme is less well targeted, as there is incomplete coverage of eligible households and leakage of benefits to non-target households. Nevertheless, food stamps contribute more to the incomes of the poor than the general food subsidy introduced in 1986 (see Table 17).

A much larger share of the total transfer under food stamps accrued to the poorest quintile whereas a much smaller fraction went to the richest quintile, as compared with the corresponding shares under the general food subsidy. Besides, the transfer as a proportion of the expenditure per recipient among the poorest was markedly higher under food stamps. The coverage could of course be improved. It is significant that transfers to the poorest were substantially larger at half the cost. If administrative costs are taken into account, the cost-effectiveness of food stamps would be greater. However, as in Sri Lanka, the value of food stamps eroded with inflation, thereby necessitating some adjustments.

Some general observations are in order:

- The difficulty in establishing the stamps as an alternative currency has hampered implementation of this scheme in Colombia, Egypt, Peru and Venezuela (Alderman, 1991). In the absence of a well-developed market network in rural areas, the implementation is likely to be even more difficult.
- Both the Sri Lankan and Jamaican experiments underscore the importance of sound macroeconomic management. Unless such experiments are combined with an effective anti-inflation policy, the gains to the poor may be wiped out over time.

Supplementary feeding programmes. Supplementary feeding programmes are a form of highly targeted ration or in-kind transfer scheme. Their main objective is to reduce undernutrition. Subsidized or free food is distributed through nutrition and health centres for direct or home consumption, or through schools to those deemed specifically vulnerable to nutritional and health risks.

The beneficiaries usually comprise children under five years of age, schoolchildren and pregnant and lactating women. Additional targeting on the basis of growth monitoring, location or income helps in identifying the neediest members within these groups.

The Indian experience with two supplementary feeding programmes is of particular interest, as it yields useful lessons.[3]

Initiated in 1975, the Integrated Child Development Services (ICDS) programme expanded rapidly and now covers more than 1 300 blocks of approximately 100 000 people each. It is integrated in that it aims to improve the nutrition and health of children from zero to six years of age by simultaneously providing supplementary feeding, immunization and curative medical care to children and pregnant and lactating women as well as health and nutrition education to mothers. However, the primary emphasis of the ICDS programme is on providing meals. The backbone of the ICDS is the *anganwadi*, a community centre where children and mothers gather to avail of the benefits of ICDS. Virtually all of the targeting of benefits is achieved through the location of ICDS projects in tribal and rural areas with a heavy concentration of scheduled (backward) caste households where malnutrition problems are generally most severe (Subbarao, 1989). Following are some specific comments on this programme:

- There is wide variability across ICDS projects in terms of their impact on child nutritional status. Thus, no generalization can be made from the success or failure of an individual ICDS project.
- The coverage of children under three years of age in supplementary feeding and immunization efforts is low, since such children typically need to be brought to the *anganwadi* by a parent. The coverage of pregnant and lactating women is even lower.
- Although supplementary feeding is often uneven because of erratic food supplies received by the *anganwadi*, it attracts mothers and children because of the other services included in the package.
- There is little community participation in the ICDS programme. Hence, it is viewed by potential beneficiaries as a government programme and not a community programme. As argued later, community participation is often crucial to the success of such programmes.

---

[3] For a detailed review, see Subbarao (1989).

- Although coverage of rural areas has been increasing rapidly, the ICDS has a strong urban bias.
- Finally, although it is supposed to be a *supplementary* feeding programme for undernourished preschoolers, in practice, the ICDS provides a replacement midday meal to all preschoolers who come to a centre. The lack of targeting in the programme as well as its tendency to make beneficiaries dependent on food assistance for extended periods, limits its coverage of the truly needy and also its sustainability over time.

By contrast, the Tamil Nadu Integrated Nutrition Project (TINP), initiated in 1980, has been one of the most successful nutrition intervention programmes in India. TINP is area-targeted towards the rural areas of six districts with the lowest caloric consumption in the state; age-targeted concentrating exclusively on children from six to 36 months of age; and need-targeted, depending on weight gain over a certain period. Since the children are on the supplementation programme only for the duration of time that their weight gain is below standard, it is essentially a short-term intervention that seeks to reduce long-term dependence of beneficiaries on public assistance.

Often, a problem with child supplementation programmes is that parents reduce a child's allocation at home since they view the supplementation as a substitute for home consumption. The TINP avoids this problem by serving snacks made from wheat to people who often do not consider food that does not contain rice to be a meal. Community participation is achieved by enlisting women in the project villages to assist in the preparation of the food supplement.

The TINP links the delivery of health and nutrition services. Children who do not respond to the nutrition supplementation are provided with health services, including immunization. These services are also available to pregnant and lactating women. In addition, the programme includes intensive counselling of mothers in nutrition and hygiene education.

The effects of the TINP were dramatic: "... by late 1986, preliminary findings ... pointed towards a 53 percent decline in serious and severe malnutrition, down to 8 percent of all children between seven months and five years old. Given what was happening to the economy during this period, there is fairly strong evidence that, without TINP, malnutrition rates would have been from 14 to at least 18 percent.[4] (In the untreated area studied in 1986, serious and severe malnutrition was more than 20 percent) ... children between ages four and five who had been through the program were a significant 1.75 kilograms (or 3.9 pounds) heavier than children from control villages. That the weight advantage was maintained two years after the children completed the program indicates the longer-run effects" (Berg, 1987, p. 19-25).

While a detailed comparison of the cost-effectiveness of the ICDS and the TINP is not feasible, some suggestive pieces of evidence are cited here. The annual recurrent cost of TINP in 1986-87 was SL Rs 10 per person (not per beneficiary) living in the target area, while the corresponding estimate for the ICDS was SL Rs 22 per caput. The difference in cost arises almost entirely from the fact that the ICDS is a mass feeding programme, while the TINP is a highly selective supplementary feeding programme. Also, the TINP reduced severe malnutrition among children from six to 36 months old by twice as much as the ICDS in Tamil Nadu. As the expenditure on the TINP constitutes less than 0.5 percent of Tamil Nadu's GNP, and the reduction in malnutrition was more than 50 percent, the economic justification for this programme is unquestionably strong. However, the extension of this programme to a regional or national level may be problematic for logistical reasons (Lipton and Van der Gaag, 1991).

General equilibrium analysis

As argued in the preceding section, general equilibrium results of food subsidies are likely to be different from those based on a partial equilibrium analysis, especially when food subsidies account for a large share of public expenditure. Narayana, Parikh and Srinivasan (1991) address these concerns in a recent study based on Indian data. It suffices to note here that

---

[4] Tamil Nadu had experienced a bad drought and severe economic difficulties during this period.

it is an applied general equilibrium model. The specific questions addressed in this study relate mainly to the impact of the present food procurement and distribution policies, the extension of rationing to the entire rural population and restrictions on the resale of rationed food.

Detailed simulation results are presented for the period 1980 to 2000. In addition to the level of food energy and protein intake per caput in each expenditure class, equivalent income is used as a measure of well-being. This measures the income required to obtain at the base prices a consumption basket that provides the same utility as that provided by the current basket of consumption.[5]

Although a reference scenario serves as the benchmark (it is assumed that policies regarding procurement and public distribution of foodgrains, public consumption and investment, foreign trade and aid etc., would correspond to those prevalent in the recent past), in some cases comparisons of policy scenarios are carried out for more appropriate alternatives.[6]

Impact of the present procurement and distribution policies. The comparison is between the reference scenario and another in which both procurement and urban distribution are abolished. Since public investment is unchanged, the growth rates of GDP and its components (agricultural and non-agricultural GDP) are similar in both cases. However, the distributional effects vary. The rural classes benefit from the withdrawal of the implicit procurement tax on their agricultural incomes but lose from slightly higher taxes on their non-agricultural incomes. Although there is a slight increase in the proportion of the poorest expenditure class in 2000 (compared with the reference scenario), the average energy intake and, more comprehensively, the average equivalent income of each class increase.

---

[5] For a formal definition, see Narayana, Parikh and Srinivasan (1991).

[6] The supplies for the public distribution system are obtained mainly from domestic producers at prices announced before each harvest. Since the government buys whatever is offered at these prices, regardless of the offtake from ration shops, there is often accumulation of huge stocks (23.6 million tonnes at the end of December 1986), carried at a significant cost in terms of storage and opportunity cost of resources locked up.

In contrast, the urban population loses because of the withdrawal of public distribution and the higher tax rate. Consequently, the average energy intake and equivalent income of each urban class is lower in 2000 relative to the reference solution.

Subsidized ration to both rural and urban populations. A policy scenario in which 100 kg of wheat is provided at a subsidized price (a subsidy of 20 percent) to every Indian in both rural and urban areas is compared with that in which both procurement and distribution are abolished: with an unchanged investment, the macro indicators do not change except for the average tax rate. The latter is higher in 1980, when subsidized rations are provided to both rural and urban populations, but lower in 2000. The distributional effects for the rural population in 2000 are: *i)* a reduction in the proportion of the poorest class; *ii)* a reduction in the average energy intake of all except the poorest class; and *iii)* a reduction in the average equivalent income of all classes except the poorest.

In the urban context, the corresponding distributional effects are: *i)* a reduction in the percentage of the bottom two or three classes; although *ii)* the average equivalent incomes are similar for all classes. Depending, therefore, on the feasibility of raising additional taxes, subsidized food rations to both rural and urban populations benefit the poor in the long term.

Resale restriction on rationed food. The comparison is between 100 kg of wheat sold at a subsidized price to both rural and urban populations and another scenario in which this ration cannot be resold. Since there is no change in public investment, the macro indicators are similar in both cases. Given the disincentive effect of resale restrictions, the implicit ration subsidy to be financed is lower and, consequently, the average tax rate is lower in 1980 but similar in 2000. In rural areas, both in 1980 and 2000, there is a shift of the population to lower expenditure classes. A similar shift occurs in urban areas. The welfare impacts in terms of equivalent income and food energy intake are not obvious from this analysis. However, some additional calculations, based on the assumption of identical rural and urban expenditure distributions in 1980, suggest that the poorer classes in rural and urban areas lose in terms of both equivalent income and energy intake.

To sum up, when the quantity of ration entitlement is large but the price subsidy is small, rationing with resale restrictions is regressive. The poor get less subsidy than the rich, as they are unable to buy the full ration entitlement. Further, resale restrictions do not ensure that the poor eat more. Hence, even if such restrictions could be costlessly enforced, they are not desirable.

Impact of free food distribution. A free ration entitlement of 100 kg of wheat is compared with the reference scenario (i.e. the existing policy regime and a public distribution system in urban areas). With investment being the same in both cases, the GDP figures are almost identical in 2000. There is a reduction in the proportion of the rural population in the poorest expenditure class. In urban areas, on the other hand, there is a reduction in the share of the population in the three bottom classes. As a result of higher food prices and tax rates, the equivalent incomes of all urban classes fall. In rural areas, however, the equivalent income of the poorest class rises substantially while that of the top two classes falls.

If tax rates cannot be adjusted, an alternative is to lower public investment. In that case, the GDP drops sharply in 2000. Yet, there are large reductions in the number of people in the poorest class in both rural and urban areas. This suggests that, despite the slower growth, free food rations improve the welfare of the poorest. This analysis has several merits:

- It takes into account macro implications of food subsidies – in particular, the effects on growth of GDP, financed through either higher taxes or cut-backs in public investment – in a general equilibrium framework.
- Alternative specifications of food rationing are considered: provision of subsidized food rations in urban areas and in both rural and urban areas; provision of free rations in both rural and urban areas; and restrictions on the resale of subsidized food rations.
- The impact on distribution is judged separately for rural and urban areas in terms of the share of population in different expenditure classes, average energy intake and equivalent income.

• The immediate effects of alternative specifications of food subsidies are distinguished from long-term effects.

Yet, in some respects this analysis is limited from a policy perspective. The preoccupation with untargeted food subsidies is a major limitation. As the review in the previous section emphasizes, some forms of targeted food subsidies – either in the form of food stamps or as a component of nutrition and medical care support – are more cost-effective than untargeted subsidies. Whether the case for targeted food subsidies is strengthened in a general equilibrium analysis is thus of considerable policy significance. Moreover, following on from this concern, there is a need to examine targeting mechanisms which are cost-effective without being excessively invasive (Sen, 1992a). In this context, community involvement has a potentially significant role in ensuring that those in abject poverty have access to rationed food. Following some recent contributions, notably Behrman (1991), Alderman (1991) and Narayana, Parikh and Srinivasan (1991), important issues in designing food subsidies are addressed below.

DESIGN

i) A key issue in designing food subsidies is their flexibility. Specifically, if such subsidies could be provided to the poor during a period of economic stress and phased out when conditions improve, scarce government funds would be saved for other purposes. But this is seldom feasible because of administrative and political constraints. Administratively, it is often difficult and costly to screen the beneficiaries at regular intervals. Nor is there any incentive on the part of the beneficiaries to self-report when their fortunes improve. Politically, however, the withdrawal or phasing out of subsidies may be more problematic, as there have been several instances of violent reactions in recent years. Examples of abortive attempts at reducing food subsidies include riots in Egypt in 1977, in Morocco in 1981 as well as in 1984, in Tunisia in 1984 and in Jordan in 1989. An obvious solution is to withdraw subsidies gradually but this may be ruled out when the fiscal deficit is large. Although generalizations are risky, other possibilities exist. One is that the government must publicize its rationale (Alderman, 1991). In Pakistan, for example, recent changes in food subsidies (e.g. derationing of flour) were justified on the grounds of reducing corruption and leakage. Through the extensive decontrolling of markets, it was sought to curtail the powers of a corrupt bureaucracy. If these changes are perceived to be fair as well, political support for them may be more or less spontaneous. Arguably, a prerequisite is that the subsidies must be perceived to be well-targeted. This does not of course rule out the leakage of benefits to the non-poor. Some leakage is unavoidable (as perfect screening is prohibitively costly) but perhaps also necessary to ensure political support.

ii) Since means testing at frequent intervals is unlikely to be feasible in most developing countries, more attention needs to be paid to targeting through other means. One possibility is to choose commodities or a quality of commodity consumed mainly by the poor. In this respect, as noted earlier, the Indian experience is far from encouraging. A subsidy on bajra, which is considered an inferior cereal, accrued to a small fraction of the poor. The important point is that, even if there are commodities that are only consumed by the poor, subsidized rations on their own may not necessarily raise significantly the consumption of the poor if there is a binding liquidity or income constraint.[7] Regional or area targeting is another possibility. For example, ration shops could be located in backward or poor areas. Although direct evidence on the impact of food subsidies is limited, some inferences can legitimately be drawn from the impact of regional transfers.

The evidence is, however, mixed. Some simulations reported for India in Ravallion (1992) show that, if interstate disparity in mean consumption is sought to be eliminated through transfers, the impact on poverty indices is small. Even if disparity within a state is taken into account in fixing the value of transfers, the impact is slightly greater. By contrast, similar experiments for Indonesia, where the regional disparities are acute, show substantially greater gains from regional targeting. Thus, the gains from regional targeting may vary a great deal. Besides, serious logistical problems may

---

[7] Gulati (1977) reports that, in the Indian state of Kerala, ration cards were mortgaged by the poorest to others in return for cash loans that they used for medical and other necessary expenses. Although the loans were interest-free, the implicit interest paid by the borrowers in terms of subsidy foregone exceeded 5.5 percent per month.

arise in targeting the poor in backward areas – especially in remote villages. To the extent that subsidized food distribution takes place through private trade channels, weak or non-existent trade channels in some backward areas would impede smooth distribution of food rations. Alternative distribution networks may therefore have to be utilized.[8] Using nutrition indicators for targeting, subsidized food may be distributed through rural health centres and schools. The TINP is a case in point. However, it is doubtful whether backward areas in general would be well endowed with health centres and schools. Thus, the potential for targeted food intervention in the absence of infrastructural support may be quite limited.

iii) To some extent, the transaction costs incurred by the poor would be reduced with infrastructural development. With a well-developed transport system and extensive network of ration shops, travel costs would be considerably reduced. However, the use of elaborate and complicated registration procedures tends to put the poor at a considerable disadvantage. Access to subsidized food rations in India, for example, requires a local address, which tends to exclude migrant workers. Another requirement is that at least one week's quota must be bought. This is likely to exclude daily wage workers (who are usually highly poverty prone). There is thus a strong case for simplifying procedures to enable the poor to have easier access to food rations. Allegations of corruption in the operation of the public distribution system are not uncommon. In India it is asserted that foodgrains distributed through ration shops contain a larger proportion of removable impurities (such as small stones) than the foodgrains purchased in the open market, so much so that, once the weight of the impurities and the cost (in time, if not in direct cash outlay) of removing them are taken into account, the implicit subsidy in the purchase of the ration vanishes.[9] Be that as it may, price and/or quantity controls seldom work efficiently – primarily because rent-seeking bureaucratic behaviour is pervasive. That community initiative or organizations of the poor may be successful in ensuring minimum standards of quality is plausible but has not been proved.

---

[8] For a comprehensive evaluation, see Behrman (1991).
[9] Cited in Narayana, Parikh and Srinivasan (1991).

Chapter 9
Human capital

So far the focus has been largely on direct anti-poverty interventions, essentially designed to mitigate distress and hardship among vulnerable sections of the rural population in the short term. An effective poverty alleviation strategy has to combine these measures with those that will help the poor to be more self-reliant over a period of time. The strengthening of human capital belongs to the latter category. Besides, access to some forms of human capital, e.g. primary education, is deemed to be a basic right of citizens in a democratic society. For these reasons, human capital has a key role in an anti-poverty strategy.[1]

Human capital includes education, work experience, physical fitness and stamina. As in the case of physical capital, once produced, the benefits of each of these are spread over a period of time – typically over the working life of an individual. However, there is a measurement problem. As some forms of human capital, e.g. education and physical fitness, are desirable in themselves – as is implied by the fact that access to them is a matter of right – the separation of consumption and investment aspects is problematic. While for some purposes (e.g. national income accounting) a clear separation of these components is crucial, in the present context this is not a major issue.

The relationship between human capital and poverty is a complex one in as much as each influences the other (Behrman, 1990). Lack of human

---

[1] Although this chapter is structured along the lines of Anil Deolalikar's background work for the Third Progress Report on WCARRD Programme of Action (FAO, 1991a), and along the lines of World Bank (1986; 1988) and Jimenez (1987), it extends the policy perspective in Drèze and Sen (1989).

capital among the poor takes a variety of forms – illiteracy, lack of income-augmenting skills, morbidity resulting in loss of physical stamina. This tends to perpetuate their poverty. On the other hand, given limited facilities for acquiring human capital in rural areas, acutely poor households fail to invest in human capital. Once caught in this vicious circle, poverty reinforces itself.

The production of human capital takes time. The provision of primary education in rural areas, for example, may be impeded by a lack of buildings and trained teachers. Even when the infrastructure and key inputs exist, primary education usually takes four to five years of classroom instruction. Whatever the benefits of this education (e.g. higher wages and a more efficient allocation of resources in farming), these are likely to materialize after the completion of the course. Although adult literacy and training programmes are of shorter duration, they cannot be regarded as substitutes for primary education. Given the lags in the production of human capital, there are no immediate benefits to the poor.

This chapter addresses issues in the reallocation of resources in education. In particular, a case is made for allocating a larger share of public expenditure to primary education. Attention is drawn to gender disparity in access to education and some specific proposals designed to ameliorate this disparity are reviewed. Second, the role of extension in the modernization of agriculture is critically evaluated. Some major shortcomings of extension programmes are pointed out and suggestions are made to enhance their benefits to (sections of) the rural poor. Third, the allocation of health expenditure and its cost-effectiveness are examined in detail. Specifically, given the "public good" nature of communicable disease control and other preventive programmes, and emphasizing that there is willingness to pay for curative care (provided through hospitals for example), a case is made for shifting the allocation of public expenditure in favour of preventive care. While such a shift in allocation will potentially benefit the poorer sections, utilization of public services by them cannot be taken for granted. Finally, as part of the focus on combining the market mechanism with public action, the vital role of community initiative in ensuring that the poor utilize these services is elaborated.

TABLE 18
Average social and private rates of return to education, by region

Region	Social			Private		
	Primary	Secondary	Higher	Primary	Secondary	Higher
Africa	27	19	14	45	28	33
Asia	18	14	12	34	15	18
Latin America	35	19	16	61	28	26

Source: Schultz (1988).

EDUCATION
Rationale

Education contributes to human well-being in different ways. By improving people's ability to acquire and use information, education deepens their understanding of the economic environment, broadens their perspective and improves the choices they make as consumers, producers and citizens. Education strengthens their ability to meet their wants and those of their family by increasing their productivity and their potential to achieve a higher standard of living. By improving people's confidence and their ability to create and innovate, it expands their opportunities for personal and social achievement.

An overall measure of the contribution that investment in education makes is given by its internal rate of return. Both private and social rates of return at different levels of education are given in Table 18.[2] These reveal an interesting pattern. First, the returns are highest in Africa and Latin America and lowest in Asia. Second, the returns fall with the level of education, reflecting the diminishing marginal efficiency of investment, and third,

---

[2] Private returns are typically the internal rate of return to investments made by individuals in their own education. The investments include both the explicit (tuition fee, cost of uniform and books) and implicit (opportunity cost of time) costs of education. In calculating social returns, all costs of education, including public sector subsidies, are included on the cost side of the calculation. It is important to recognize that only pecuniary benefits of education, as reflected in higher wages or salaries for more educated individuals, are included in the calculation.

social returns are lower than corresponding private returns in each region because of public subsidies.

Since these rates of return are based on statistical associations between the market earnings and schooling of individuals, they do not include the effect of education on the productivity of non-market time, such as the time spent by farmers on their own cultivation and the time spent by women in home production. Available evidence suggests that these effects are significant. A detailed study for Malaysia, Thailand and the Republic of Korea found that a year of schooling was associated with a net increase in farm product of 5.1, 2.8 and 2.3 percent, respectively (Jamison and Lau, 1982). A cross-country analysis of infant mortality and under five mortality rates suggests that they have a strong inverse association with adult female literacy (Gaiha and Spinedi, 1992). In addition, female education is the single most important variable in explaining the fertility decline in virtually all developing countries (Schultz, 1988). Since there is no consensus on how these social benefits of education should be valued, they are not typically included in the standard estimates.

There is a strong case for public provision of education, as it is a merit good. Since education is important in itself, public provision of it is motivated by the concern that every citizen must acquire a certain minimum of education. The high rates of social return (even when these do not take into account all social benefits) relative to the return on public investment elsewhere (no more than 10 percent) further strengthen the case for public provision of education. As argued below, the consistently high social rates of return on primary education suggest a reallocation of public expenditure in its favour. These rates, however, are based on national-level data; and separate estimates of social rates of return for rural areas are not available. The rural rates may not be different since the patterns of subsidies and earnings at different levels of education are not likely to differ between rural and urban areas.

Issues

Inadequate and declining public support. The fact that the social returns on investment in education exceed the returns on the same investment elsewhere in the economy (usually assumed to be around 10 percent), despite a rapid expansion during the 1960s and 1970s suggests that there is a need for a further expansion of education. However, during the 1980s, macroeconomic adjustment necessitated cut-backs in public expenditure on education in many developing countries – especially in sub-Saharan Africa – resulting in a reversal of long-term trends in expected years of schooling[3] (Schultz, 1988). Given the fiscal deficits, heavy subsidization of education – especially higher education – cannot be sustained for long. It is therefore imperative to generate more resources, mainly through user cost pricing.

Misallocation of resources. Since social returns fall with the level of education, on efficiency considerations alone a larger share of public expenditure should be devoted to primary education. Yet, in many developing countries primary education is neglected while higher education is overemphasized. The divergence between private and social returns is suggestive. In Africa, for example, the average private rate of return on primary schooling is 1.67 times the social rate, that for higher education is 2.5 times the social rate, implying greater subsidization of higher education. As shown in Table 19, the lower level of cost recovery in publicly provided higher education – particularly in East and West Africa – further corroborates this bias.

Although similar evidence for rural areas is sparse, a recent survey in West Bengal corroborates that subsidies per student are much higher in higher education than in primary education (Maitra, 1988). Table 20 contains these estimates.

The subsidies rise abruptly from primary to secondary education and somewhat moderately between secondary and college education. On average, the subsidies are about 12 times higher in secondary education and about 15 times in college (or higher) education relative to those in primary education.

---

[3] Private expenditure on education also fell (World Bank, 1986).

TABLE 19

Cost recovery in public education, by region and level of schooling in 1980

Region	Percentage of unit cost recovered		
	Primary	Secondary	Higher
East Africa	6.3	16.6	2.6
West Africa	11.4	9.8	3.1
Asia	1.7	16.0	11.5
Latin America	0.9	1.7	6.6

Note: Based on data for 27 countries.
Source: World Bank (1986).

TABLE 20

Annual subsidies per student in primary, secondary and college education in rural West Bengal, 1976

Type of subsidy	Education level		
	Primary	Secondary	College
	(Rupees)		
In cash			
Fees exempted	–	6.33	6.15
Scholarship	–	2.12	5.89
Other grants	–	0.28	–
In kind			
Books	0.66	0.09	–
Meals	0.14	0.02	–
Other subsidies	–	0.52	–
All	**0.80**	**9.36**	**12.04**

Source: Maitra (1988).

The bulk of the subsidies in secondary and higher education comprise fee exemptions and scholarships while, in primary education, books and meals account for the entire subsidy. To the extent that the social rates of return are valid, this pattern of subsidies (i.e. the relatively large amounts per student in higher education) is clearly inefficient.

TABLE 21

Share of higher education subsidies by income group in selected developing countries

Country	Income group		
	Lower	Middle	Upper
	(Percentage)		
Chile	15	24	61
Colombia	6	34	60
Indonesia	7	10	83
Malaysia	10	39	51

Note: The lower-income group corresponds to the poorest 40 percent, except in Chile where it corresponds to the poorest 30 percent.
Source: World Bank (1986).

Not only is the allocation of resources within the educational sector inefficient but it is also inequitable. The bulk of public expenditure is devoted to higher education when in fact enrolments in it account for a relatively low fraction of the school-aged population. Countries in anglophone Africa, for example, spend 50 times as much per student in higher education as in primary education, with only 1.2 percent of the school-aged population enrolled in it (World Bank, 1986).

Moreover, the relatively few who benefit from higher education are usually from affluent families. The estimates given in Table 21 are illustrative. In Indonesia, for example, the poorest 40 percent of individuals receive only 7 percent of higher education subsidies, while the richest 20 percent appropriate 83 percent of the subsidies. Although it is a small sample, it is nevertheless significant that a similar pattern is observed in other countries too.

Further corroborative evidence is provided by a sample of rural West Bengal (Maitra, 1988). Students belonging to the bottom 20 percent of the population receive 7.6 percent of the subsidies in primary education and about 8 percent of the subsidies in secondary education. In contrast, those from the top 20 percent receive about 23 percent of the subsidies in primary education and about 29 percent in secondary education. Thus, both at the primary and secondary levels, but especially at the latter, the more affluent students receive substantially higher subsidies.[4]

Cost recovery in higher education. Typically, government subsidies to higher education comprise *i)* the direct costs of education (e.g. teachers' salaries, school buildings and equipment) and *ii)* living allowances (or scholarships). Exemption from full tuition fees is common in many developing countries. In addition, generous living allowances account for nearly half of all public expenditure on higher education in a sample of eight African countries. Moreover, the allowances are so generous that they exceed actual living costs of students by anywhere from 68 percent to 400 percent (World Bank, 1986). A substantial saving may thus be feasible by simply curtailing these allowances.

That there is potential for raising resources by charging full tuition fees is confirmed by recent estimates of the income and price elasticities. Consider, first, the income elasticities in Table 22. Most of these are positive, suggesting that the higher the income the higher the enrolments (or expenditure on education). With the exception of Taiwan Province of China in all other cases the price elasticities are negative and vary a great deal. Although the price responsiveness of the demand for higher education is presumably greater, it is nevertheless significant that, in more than a few cases, the elasticities are low or negligible. This suggests that the dampening effect of higher tuition fees on enrolments is likely to be small. Of particular significance is the finding that, in rural Peru, even the poor were willing to pay more than the costs of operating a new school to reduce travel time from two hours to zero (Gertler and Glewwe, 1989).

The resources saved and/or generated through a reduction in living allowances and the charging of full tuition fees (selectively) may be used for the

---

[4] The distribution of subsidies at the secondary level is reproduced at the college level, as is evident from similar concentration coefficients for secondary education and the aggregate group of all levels of education (.294 and .296, respectively). For further details, see Maitra (1988).

TABLE 22

Price and income elasticities of demand for education in selected developing countries

Area and year of data	Dependent variable	Income	Price
		Elasticity	
Colombia (1967-68)	Total spending on education	1.045	I
	Share of household budget on education	0.334	I
	Actual expenditure and predicted expenditure	1.343	−0.67
El Salvador (1980)	Total spending on education		
	• Santa Ana	0.967	I
	• Sonsonate	0.023	I
Mali (1982)	Enrolment ratio	−	−0.98
Malawi (1983)	Household enrolment ratio		−0.03
Malaysia (1976)	Proportion of children going to school		
	• 6-11 years	0.097	−0.039
	• 12-18 years	0.318	−0.012
Pakistan (1978-79)	Proportion of children going to school	0.01-0.15	−
Philippines	Years of completed schooling		
1968	• First estimate	0.111	−0.05
1968	• Second estimate	0.111	−0.008
1975	• Enrolment rates	−	−0.625
Taiwan Province of China (1950-1969)	Number of people taking college entrance examination	0.303	1.763
Tanzania, United Rep. (1981)	Total spending on education	0.03	−

I = inelastic.
− = not available.
Source: World Bank (1986).

expansion and improvement of primary education, especially in rural areas. Both efficiency and equity considerations favour such a reallocation.

Gender disparity. Despite a rapid expansion of female enrolments at different educational levels – often at rates greater than those of male enrolments – major disparities persist in large parts of the world (notably sub-Saharan Africa and South Asia). In sub-Saharan Africa, for example, there were only 77 and 59 females per 100 males in primary and secondary schools in 1987, respectively (World Bank, 1988). The lower number of females relative to males in school reflects both fewer female entrants as

TABLE 23

Gender disparity in enrolments by expenditure fractile group in rural West Bengal, 1976

Fractile group	Age group					
	6-14 years			15-17 years		
	Male	Female	All	Male	Female	All
(percentage)						
0-5	8.5	2.7	5.8	14.2	0.0	9.1
5-10	22.7	15.9	19.4	8.4	0.0	5.1
10-20	34.5	18.9	26.6	26.4	0.0	13.3
20-30	44.2	31.5	38.6	10.5	11.9	10.6
30-40	52.4	37.1	44.6	34.3	5.7	20.5
40-50	67.1	38.4	52.0	35.4	21.8	28.3
50-60	57.8	42.2	50.7	37.4	17.1	28.8
60-70	53.4	45.3	50.0	34.4	20.6	29.1
70-80	66.7	47.5	57.5	48.3	17.6	34.5
80-90	68.7	62.8	65.9	51.3	19.5	38.5
90-95	68.8	77.2	72.8	50.7	40.8	45.3
95-100	86.0	90.5	88.5	58.9	47.8	51.6

Source: Maitra (1988).

well as a higher drop-out rate among them. Table 23 brings out sharply the gender disparity in enrolment rates in rural West Bengal.

With a few exceptions, the disparity persists among all expenditure groups. Although a clear-cut pattern is not discernible, the disparity is acute among almost all fractile groups in poverty (i.e. up to the 60th percentile) and more so among children in the age group of 15 to 17 years. There is a marked reduction in disparity in the fractile groups 90 to 95 percent and 95 to 100 percent (in fact, there is a reversal for six- to 14-year-old children, with female enrolment rates exceeding male enrolment rates).

That this is inequitable is incontestable, since both male and female children must have equal access to some basic education. Lower female enrolment rates also point to inefficiency within the education sector as the social rates of return to schooling are likely to be higher at all schooling levels for women than for men (Behrman and Deolalikar, 1990; Herz, *et al.*, 1991). Unfortunately, most of the existing estimates of rates of return are flawed for two main reasons: one is their failure to correct the returns to women's schooling for market imperfections, which limit women's options more than men's and so reduce women's earnings; another is the undervaluation of women's work done outside the labour force (e.g. household chores). Even notional corrections suggest that the social returns to female education are high and exceed those to male education (Herz *et al.*, 1991).

The reasons for the gender disparity in enrolments (and educational attainments) are both cultural and economic. Girls have special needs for physical protection and tradition often demands special concern for their privacy and social reputations. In cultures where female seclusion is practised, the impact of such traditions on girls' enrolment after puberty is substantial.

These concerns prevent parents from sending girls to school, unless schools are located close to home, equipped with facilities such as separate lavatories for girls, well supervised, and served by female teachers. When parents themselves lack education, they are more reluctant to challenge tradition by educating their daughters. Traditional constraints tend to be far more severe in rural areas.[5]

Among the economic reasons for gender disparity, the high opportunity costs of sending girls to school weigh heavily in household decisions. These costs include lost chore time, children's foregone earnings and – especially for girls – mothers' foregone earnings. Suggestive pieces of empirical evidence cited below show that opportunity costs of sending girls to school are likely to be higher for poor families in rural areas.

In general, girls do more chores than boys. Girls care for siblings, fetch food and water and ease their mother's drudgery in other ways. They also contribute to household production by caring for animals, pounding grain and so forth. Time allocation studies show that girls get involved in household production tasks at a much younger age and work longer hours than boys.[6] Many girls are classified as "non-working" (not in the labour force), but most girls from poor families spend substantial amounts of time running the household. In rural Java (Indonesia), for example, girls aged ten to 15 years worked an average of 94 hours a month in the poorest

---

[5] For an illustration based on data from rural Pakistan, see Herz *et al.* (1991).
[6] For details, see FAO (1985).

households, compared with 70 hours in middle-income households and 26 hours in the wealthiest households. The corresponding averages for boys' household labour were 38 hours, eight hours, and nine hours, respectively (FAO, 1985).

Girls' household activities, especially in Asia and Africa, have more impact than boys' activities on parents' earnings. Girls' work at home often permits parents, especially mothers, to work more on the farm or in the labour force.

By sending girls to school, the family loses the income that the mother might have earned had the daughter substituted for the mother in doing home chores. This is particularly true among poor families where girls' labour may be crucial for family survival.[7]

The promotion of female enrolments is thus largely conditional on the weakening of cultural barriers and the reduction of opportunity costs. Cultural barriers may not be overcome easily but, as pointed out earlier, a faster rate of growth in female enrolments is likely if there is a larger number of female teachers and special needs of girls are provided for. As regards the lowering of the opportunity cost, some recent proposals include the introduction of flexible school hours, the provision of child care facilities and improvement in the community's supply of water and wood (Herz *et al.*, 1991). Since no empirical estimates of their impact on female enrolments are available, no further comment can be made.

Curriculum diversification and reform. Curriculum reform may be crucial to improving the quality and efficiency of education in developing countries. A diversified curriculum combines academic with some vocational education, thereby offering students a wider choice of future career opportunities than are offered by the typical technical or purely academic curricula – especially at the secondary stage. By making the curriculum

---

[7] A study based on Indian data, for example, shows that a 10 percent increase in female wages lowers the school attendance rate of girls from poor families by about 5 percent (Rosenzweig, 1980).

more relevant to the needs of the labour market, curriculum diversification may improve the employment prospects for school-leavers and also reduce wastage and repetition within schools.

However, the experience with curriculum diversification raises some concern. Recent evaluations of curriculum diversification in Colombia and the United Republic of Tanzania – where diversification has been in place since the 1970s – indicate that, while students from diversified secondary schools performed better in both vocational and academic subjects than those from traditional secondary schools, the costs per pupil in the former were considerably higher (Psacharopoulos and Woodhall, 1985; Psacharopoulos and Loxley, 1985). Furthermore, employment prospects did not improve significantly with diversified curricula. Indeed, in Indonesia, academic tracks were a better investment than vocational courses (Clark, 1983). Since curricular diversification is often carried out in an ad hoc manner, it is not surprising that the results have been mixed. Vocational training programmes are particularly prone to this difficulty, as illustrated by recent attempts in India.

As part of the IRDP, two vocational training schemes, viz. Training of Rural Youth for Self-employment (TRYSEM) and Development of Women and Children in Rural Areas (DWCRA), were launched recently. TRYSEM was undertaken to equip rural youth (in the age group 18 to 35 years) who are below the poverty threshold with necessary skills and technical knowledge to enable them to seek self-employment. In 1983, the scope of TRYSEM was extended to include wage employment. Training is imparted through institutions such as agricultural universities as well as through master artisans. There was a stipulation that 30 percent of the trainees should be women. However, the performance in terms of both overall targets and the training of women was unsatisfactory. Also, less than 50 percent of the trained youth were able to achieve self-employment (FAO, 1991b).[8] Given

---

[8] Although 64 trades or skills were identified, the training was confined largely to traditional skills and crafts. As a result, it is not surprising that many participants in TRYSEM found themselves ill-equipped for wage self-employment (FAO, 1991b).

the negligible participation of women in TRYSEM, DWCRA was introduced. Although a detailed evaluation of DWCRA is not available, there are
reasons to doubt that it will match up to expectations.

EXTENSION
Rationale

Agricultural extension is designed primarily to ensure that farmers, in
general, and smallholders in particular are made aware of new agricultural
techniques and practices and have access to them. In recent years, considerable emphasis has been given to assistance in supply of inputs, forming
community organizations and communicating the technical problems and
needs of farmers to agricultural research organizations.

Since information is a public good – characterized by non-rivalrous
consumption and high exclusion costs – there is a case for public intervention in extension. In helping smallholders to have easier access to improved
farming practices, extension programmes may help improve income distribution. This further strengthens the case for public intervention in extension. Although extension is largely publicly provided, a review of recent
experiences suggests that a more innovative approach, drawing on community initiative in a more substantive way, may be more effective (FAO,
1990a). So, while the case for public intervention is not questioned, alternative forms of it are being debated.

There are several approaches to agricultural extension, including *i)* the
general agricultural extension approach; *ii)* the commodity-specialized
approach; *iii)* the training and visit (T and V) approach; *iv)* the agricultural
extension participatory approach; *v)* the project approach; *vi)* the farming
systems development approach; *vii)* the cost-sharing approach; and *viii)* the
education institution approach. Each differs in terms of its assumptions about farmers' problems and behaviour, and in terms of organizational
set-up, degree of centralization, extent of cost-sharing and farmer participation and focus on a particular commodity or approach (Axinn in FAO,
1988c). While a detailed discussion of the relative strength of each approach
is beyond the scope of the present report, it should be emphasized that there
is no single approach that is universally appropriate. Depending on the

nature of local problems and the capabilities of the local research establishment and the extension system, different approaches may work in different settings. Indeed, the approaches listed above are not mutually exclusive and many countries often employ combinations of the various approaches. FAO's recently introduced Strategic Extension Campaign is an example of a combination of methods that offer considerable promise (Axinn in FAO, 1988c).

Issues

Here a brief review of the impact of extension programmes is followed by a discussion of organizational and other reforms to enhance their benefits to smallholders.

The rapid spread of HYVs of wheat, corn and rice in large parts of Latin America, Asia and, to a minor extent, Africa (in what came to be known as the Green Revolution) was in a large measure the result of agricultural extension workers effectively disseminating information about improved seeds and the fertilizer and water requirements of the new technology to farmers. The Masagana 99 Programme in the Philippines, the BIMAS programme in Indonesia and the agricultural extension system of the Republic of Korea are specific examples of extension programmes that have been successful in raising farm yields and incomes.

Evenson and Kislev (1975) carried out a pioneering evaluation of agricultural extension. Using data on agricultural productivity and public expenditure on agricultural research and extension for 15 Indian states between 1953-54 and 1970-71, they estimated the marginal rate of return to investment in extension to be 17.5 percent, after controlling for investment in agricultural research. Other more recent estimates suggest a wide range – from 75 to 90 percent in Paraguay to about 15 percent in India.[9] Also, returns differ when extension investment is differentiated by crops. In Latin America, for example, returns to extension in cereals are high while they are low

---

[9] For more detailed accounts, see Feder, Lau and Slade (1985) and Birkhaueser, Evenson and Feder (1989).

for staple crops.[10] Since policy-makers are often more concerned with the downside risk to large public investments, an assessment of the likelihood of the net returns to exceed some satisfactory benchmark is of considerable value to them. There is, for example, a 90 percent probability that the return to investment in extension in India exceeds 15 percent (Feder, Lau and Slade, 1985). Since most estimates of the rate of return on investment in extension are higher than standard cut-off points for public investment, it follows that investment in extension is socially profitable.

FAO (1990a) reports benefit-cost ratios computed for selected extension programmes in developing countries. These were obtained by dividing the increase in the annual value of agricultural production by the annual cost of the extension operation. Although the range for these ratios is large, they cannot be accepted at face value, as the entire increase in the value of agricultural production is attributed to extension. Nevertheless, some useful generalizations are suggested. Briefly, approaches that embrace large numbers of farmers, such as general, participatory and T and V approaches, have lower costs per farmer and, therefore, higher benefit-cost ratios. On the other hand, approaches that maintain high agent-farmer ratios, such as project and specialized-commodity approaches, have higher per-farmer costs and therefore lower benefit-cost ratios.

The benefit-cost ratios capture the overall impact of extension. There are few studies (Feder, Lau and Slade, 1985 – for India – being one of them) which assess the impact on smallholders. Although a definitive assessment cannot be given because of the small number of studies, it is not unlikely that smallholders are generally neglected. As elaborated below, however, there is more definitive evidence that women's access to and participation in extension programmes have been limited (FAO, 1990a). Therefore, the impact on sections of the rural poor is unlikely to be significant.

Declining public expenditure on extension. Real public expenditures declined throughout much of the 1980s. This downward trend appears to

---

[10] For details, see Birkhaueser, Evenson and Feder (1989).

have been particularly serious in Africa, where public expenditure on extension relative to agricultural GDP fell by over 50 percent between 1980 and 1988. Since the number of extension workers has not fallen (in fact, it increased in many countries during the 1980s), the burden of declining expenditure presumably fell largely on recurrent non-salary expenditure – on items such as transport and fuel – which are essential for maintaining the mobility and effectiveness of extension staff.[11]

As in the case of education, a large portion of the decline in public spending on agricultural extension can be attributed to general economic decline and the consequent need for adjustment during the 1980s. This raises the question of charging farmers a fee for extension advice. Although a blanket policy of charging all farmers may not be workable, a fee or cess system will sometimes be appropriate for commercial farmers operating on a large scale. In fact, farmer financing of extension is common in developed countries such as the Netherlands and the United Kingdom. In some cases, components of the extension system, such as those dealing with high-value crops, can be made self-sustaining or else transferred over time, to the private sector. Hence, an effective cost-sharing mechanism may have to evolve through a local community initiative (Hayward in FAO, 1990a).

Limited access of women farmers to extension. The neglect of women in agricultural extension is a major concern, since in some regions – especially Africa – they play an important role in food production, processing, storage and marketing. According to a recent estimate, female labour accounts for 90 percent of the domestic food supply in some African countries (FAO, 1988a). Yet rural women felt neglected by male extension workers who see them primarily as farmers' wives and not as key participants in food production and related activities. In addition, in Islamic countries cultural barriers prevent interaction between female farmers and male extension workers (FAO, 1988a).

There is a glaring underrepresentation of women among extension wor-

---

[11] For detailed evidence, see Swanson, Farmer and Bahal in FAO (1990a).

kers. According to a recent FAO survey, women constituted only 12.3 percent of extension workers in Africa, as against 40.2 percent in North America (Swanson, Farmer and Bahal in FAO, 1990a). There is thus a strong case for recruiting and training substantially more female extension workers (FAO, 1988a).

Some organizational changes may also help. Extension workers may, for example, operate through women's groups instead of via one-to-one contact with clients. This has been attempted in some countries, notably Burkina Faso and Nigeria in Africa, and India and Indonesia in Asia, with encouraging results (United Nations, 1989).

Exclusion of broader rural development services from extension packages. Some attempts have been made in recent years to broaden the scope of extension. In particular, activities such as home management, kitchen garden production, child nutrition, household grain storage, pond agriculture and livestock health are being combined with technology diffusion. In principle, this broadening may enhance the cost-effectiveness of extension. However, its implementation has been tardy. As a recent study (Swanson, Farmer and Bahal in FAO, 1990a) points out, despite the importance of integrating nutrition and home economics services with agricultural extension, barely 2.4 percent of extension workers in Africa are female home economics extension workers. In Asia, and the Pacific, the proportion is even smaller, i.e. 0.5 percent. In contrast, 21.4 percent of all extension workers in North America are home economics extension workers.

Inadequate client participation. Active client participation in designing and implementing extension programmes can contribute greatly to their success by making them more relevant to client needs, by inducing team spirit and by facilitating the prompt supply of inputs as well as cost-sharing. Although there are a few successful cases of client participation (such as the Small Farmers' Development Projects in Nepal and Bangladesh, Sri Lanka's Sarvodya Shramada Movement and the Puebla Project in Mexico), extension programmes continue to be largely top-heavy. A recent FAO survey (Swanson, Farmer and Bahal in FAO, 1990a) found that, even at the village level, 51 percent of the extension organizations in Africa and 70 percent of those in Asia and the Pacific had no client input.

HEALTH

Rationale

Undernutrition results in lower productivity. In Sierra Leone, a 10 percent increase in per caput calorie availability increased farm output by 3.4 percent. This effect was stronger (about 5 percent) for households with an average per caput energy intake of 1 500 calories per day (Strauss, 1986). In a sample of rural households in southern India, weight-for-height – a medium-term indicator of an individual's nutrition status – significantly raised on-farm labour productivity as well as the wage rate earned in casual agricultural labouring (Deolalikar, 1988). Similar associations have been reported for other countries too, viz. Sri Lanka, the Philippines and Indonesia (Sahn and Alderman, 1988; Haddad and Bouis, 1989). Another important health indicator is morbidity. Although the association between morbidity and productivity has not been conclusively established, available evidence suggests that morbidity has an adverse effect on productivity through absenteeism and low motivation.[12]

Undernutrition among children may also have serious consequences. Studies of Nepalese and Chinese children confirm that chronic undernutrition (as reflected in a lower height-for-age) has an adverse effect on a child's probability of school enrolment and grade attainment (Jamison, 1986; Moock and Leslie, 1986). Further, chronic undernutrition may impair cognitive development (World Bank, 1990). To the extent that schooling is

---

[12] Lipton (1983) cites some suggestive evidence from a recent tabulation of the National Sample Survey on the incidence of illness and loss of employment among casual rural workers in India. Of significance is the fact that non-participation as a result of sickness among these workers was markedly higher in the July-September peak than in the April-June trough. Access to medical services – which remains limited in rural areas – could reduce the incidence and duration of morbidity. This is presumably the reason why in both the cross-sections of rural households in India, analysed in Gaiha (1985), the risk of poverty among casual labour households was inversely related to the presence of medical facilities in the sample villages.

associated with higher productivity, these effects together imply a substantial loss of productivity.

Thus, investments that improve health outcomes, among both adults and children, are likely to have high private and social rates of return.

Issues

Need for government intervention. Since health is a merit good, it calls for government intervention. Individuals left to themselves may underprovide health care. It is of course debatable whether all types of health care ought to be the exclusive concern of the government. The case for government intervention is nevertheless strengthened by some recent findings suggesting that economic growth by itself will not improve significantly the health and nutrition status of the poor. For example, among the poor and allegedly malnourished individuals in rural southern India, the responsiveness of nutrient intakes to income changes was found to be very low and almost close to zero (Behrman and Deolalikar, 1987). Results from a number of other countries, including the Philippines, Indonesia and Brazil, suggest that a low nutrition response of income is common among the poor (Behrman, 1988). There is evidence, too, of health outcomes and morbidity being not very responsive to changes in household income (Behrman and Deolalikar, 1988). A cross-country study of changes in life expectancy between 1940 and 1970 found that only less than half the increase in life expectancy during this period could be explained by changes in per caput income (Preston, 1980).

There is, however, a growing concern that the state may have overexpanded its role, since some tasks (e.g. curative care) could be more efficiently handled by the private sector (under some form of state supervision). There is thus a need for creating a judicious combination of the two. As argued below, following the important contribution of Drèze and Sen (1989), even when some forms of health or medical care are publicly provided, cost-effectiveness considerations warrant reliance on aspects of the market mechanism. In particular, the price elasticity of demand for health care by income class may be used for user cost pricing for some services.

Integration of nutrition and health interventions.[13] Child nutrition programmes tend to be more cost-effective when they are combined with existing health delivery systems, as such a combination economizes on fixed investment, personnel and management. Moreover, targeting improves. Given the frequency of illness among children, the health care system can utilize these contacts to provide nutrition supplementation. Furthermore, nutrition and hygiene education may be imparted to mothers. As discussed in Chapter 8, a case in point is the TNIP in India. Replication of such a project on a large scale is, however, doubtful (Lipton and Van der Gaag, 1991). In particular, the lack of a nutrition surveillance system may be a serious impediment.

Misallocation of resources within the health sector. In general, the distribution of health subsidies by income class, shown in Table 24, is not as regressive as that of education subsidies. Exceptions are Indonesia and the Philippines where the poorest 40 percent receive only 19 and 27 percent, respectively, of government subsidies. Also, the distribution of health subsidies between rural and urban areas, shown in Table 25, is not particularly inequitable, except in China where 71 percent of total public subsidies on health are spent in urban areas, which account for only 21 percent of the population. That the poor fail to make up for the inequity in public expenditure on health through higher private expenditure is illustrated by some recent evidence for Indonesia. Specifically, the poorest 7 percent of households accounted for barely 1 percent of the household health expenditure in the country, while the richest 9 percent accounted for 41 percent of the total expenditure in 1984 (Brotowasisto *et al.,* 1988).

Another feature of government health expenditure is the overemphasis on curative care (as opposed to preventive care) and, within the former, on hospitals (as against primary health centres). Communicable disease control and immunization programmes (as part of preventive care) typically receive

---

[13] In order to make the discussion in this chapter complete in itself, some overlap with Chapter 8 is unavoidable.

TABLE 24

Public health subsidies by income group in selected developing countries

Country	Survey year	Type of health subsidy	Percentage share by income group[1]				
			Poorest 20%	20-40%	40-60%	60-80%	80-100%
Chile	1969	Public health	31 [2]		35		35 [3]
Colombia	1974	National health service	30	23	20	18	12
		Social security system hospital	8	15	29	24	23
		Health centre	25	29	23	15	8
		Overall public	20	21	20	20	20
Indonesia	1980	Overall public	19 [4]		36 [5]		45 [3]
Iran, Islamic Rep.	1977	Overall public	30	21	19	18	13
Malaysia	1974	In-patient hospital	19	27	10	24	20
		Out-patient hospital	22	20	23	14	6
		Rural clinic	28	27	19	19	8
		Overall public	21	26	15	22	17
Philippines	1975	Overall public	14	13	15	18	40
Sri Lanka	1978	Overall public	25	21	20	19	14

[1] All rows add up to approximately 100 percent.
[2] Poorest 30 percent income group.
[3] Income group 70 to 100 percent.
[4] Poorest 40 percent income group.
[5] Income group 40 to 70 percent.
Source: Jimenez (1987).

token funding. Even worse, such programmes are often the first casualty of macroeconomic adjustment while expenditure on hospitals is relatively protected.

For example, a cut of 50 percent in real government health expenditure in Indonesia during the period 1983-1987 (which coincided with a macroeconomic adjustment) was associated with a reduction of 75 percent in the expenditure on communicable disease control programmes while that on hospitals was cut by only 23 percent (World Bank, 1988).

Within curative care, a large fraction of government expenditure is devoted to hospitals when, in fact, primary health centres serve many more individuals – mostly poor – at a much lower cost (Gish, Malik and Sudharto, 1988). In the Niger, for example, the 50 percent of the health budget devoted to

TABLE 25

Government health subsidy by type of service and location in selected developing countries

Country	Year	Type of service	Percentage share of government subsidy		Percentage share of population	
			Rural	Urban	Rural	Urban
Indonesia[1]	1983	All public (Java)[2]	50	16	55	11
		All public (Outer)[2]	27	6	28	6
		All public	77	23	83	17
Malaysia[3]	1974	All public	57	43	60	40
Senegal	1981-82	All public	57	43[4]	81	19[4]
Colombia	1974	National health service hospitals	39	61	–	–
		Social security hospitals	2	98	–	–
		Health clinics	23	77	–	–
		All public	19	81	38	62
China	1981	Hospitals[5]	25	75	–	–
		Other Ministry of Public Health activities	84	16	–	–
		Medical insurance[6]	0	100	–	–
		All public	29	71	79	21

– = not available.
[1] Services include government hospitals, public health centres and community health volunteers.
[2] Percentages of all Indonesia subsidies.
[3] Services include government, district and general hospital public health centres; community health volunteers; and rural out-patient clinics.
[4] For the Cape Verde region (Dakar).
[5] Expenditures by the Ministry of Public Health. Services include hospitals of traditional medicine, communal health centres and anti-epidemic activities.
[6] Expenditures by the Ministry of Finance to provide free health care.
Note: subsidies are government expenditures less any fees received.
Source: Jimenez (1987).

hospitals in 1984 benefited 350 000 hospital patients while the other half of the budget provided services for more than ten million clients.

As elaborated in the next section, these imbalances in the allocation of government health expenditure have serious implications for the financing of such expenditure. It is arguable that the government should subsidize activities of a public good nature, such as a communicable disease control programme, for which there is typically little private willingness to pay.

On the other hand, activities such as curative care in hospitals that generate private benefits especially for middle- and high-income patients – should not be subsidized. Furthermore, within curative care, greater emphasis ought to be given to primary health centres for reasons of both efficiency and equity.

Cost recovery in health. Financing of government health expenditure in the context of structural adjustment is a major concern. A consensus is emerging that more resources must be generated by charging user fees for designated services (e.g. curative care) in selected facilities (e.g. hospital) in certain areas (e.g. urban). Preventive care – such as maternal and child health care – dispensed in rural primary health centres could be subsidized, as could communicable disease control programmes. User fees need not be onerous, as some estimates suggest that the costs range from 1.6 to 3 percent of the average household income, depending on whether only recurrent or total costs are charged (Jimenez, 1987). That charging user fees is not likely to discourage the utilization of health services is confirmed by the generally low price elasticities in Table 26. However, more detailed investigations (e.g. Gertler, Locay and Sanderson, 1987; Gertler and Van der Gaag, 1990) indicate that the price responsiveness is greater among low-income patients. This suggests that user fees should be levied only on the more affluent households or on services typically demanded by them, since an across-the-board increase in user fees may price the poor out of the organized health care system.

Gender differences in nutrition, health care and health outcomes.[14] Some region-specific evidence – mainly South Asian – points to significant gender differences in food or nutrient intake (Sen, 1988). In Punjab, although infant boys and girls had roughly equal calorie intakes, there were significant gender differences in diet, with girls consuming more cereals and boys consuming more milk and fats (Das Gupta, 1987). In rural southern India, on the other hand, the nutrient intake of girls, although not different from that of boys on average, was more adversely affected by changing food prices (Behrman and Deolalikar, 1990). Thus, girls were

---

[14] This subsection overlaps with the material on gender disparity in Chapter 2.

TABLE 26

Income and price elasticities of demand for health care in selected developing countries

Country	Latest year of data	Dependent variable	Income		Price	
			Measure	Elasticity	Measure	Elasticity
El Salvador[1]	1980	Medical expenditure	Monthly income	0.887	Distance	− 0.054
Malaysia – *Private*	1975	Out-patient visits	Monthly income	11.32	Private fee	− 0.15
					Government fee	− 0.01
					Private waiting time	− 0.25
					Private travel time	− 0.14
					Government travel time	− 0.18
– *Government*		Out-patient visits	Monthly income	− 11.43	Private fee	0.15
					Government fee	− 0.01
					Private waiting time	− 0.07
					Government travel time	0.10
					Private travel time	0.26
					Government travel time	− 0.05
Mali	1982	Willingness to pay for a health worker	Monthly income	–	Distance to dispensary	− 0.0003
					Distance to drug outlet	− 0.0001
					Quality of dispensary	− 0.18
					Quality of output	0.04
Philippines	1980	Expenditure on drugs	Monthly income	–	Distance to dispensary	− 0.002
					Distance to drug outlet	0.0009
					Quality of dispensary	− 0.45
					Quality of outlet	0.17

– = not available.
[1] For Santa Ana only.
Source: Jimenez (1987).

more vulnerable to nutrition risks during periods of food scarcity (when food prices tend to rise). Differences in food or nutrient intake, coupled with general parental neglect of female children, result in a poorer nutrition and health status for them (Bardhan, 1982; Das Gupta, 1987; Sen, 1988).

There is also evidence of higher post-neonatal mortality rates for female relative to male children (Rosenzweig and Schultz, 1982). Parental neglect of female infants is reflected in the markedly lower expenditure on medicines for them (Das Gupta, 1987). The fact that sex differentials in mortality have persisted in many parts of India despite significant increases in income, improvements in health care delivery systems and the expansion of female literacy, calls for effective intervention (Das Gupta, 1987). A prerequisite is a clearer understanding of the factors underlying the gender bias. To the extent that this is a result of economic factors, an effective solution may well be to create more income-generating activities for women (Bardhan, 1974b; Rosenzweig and Schultz, 1982). As a matter of fact, females tend to be less disadvantaged in parts of South Asia (e.g. eastern and southern India, Bangladesh and Sri Lanka) where the predominant crop is paddy which, unlike wheat, is more intensive in the use of female labour.

MARKETS, PRICES AND PUBLIC ACTION

An attempt is made in this section to draw together the major conclusions from the overall perspective of judiciously combining the market mechanism with public action (broadly interpreted to include state action and community initiative in its collaborative and adversarial forms). As pointed out in Chapter 1 of this report, disillusionment with state action may result in a heavy reliance on the market mechanism. But, given market imperfections and the low bargaining power of the poor, it is unlikely that market-based allocations of resources would yield significant gains for them either. In each of the three aspects of human capital discussed here – education, extension and health – there is a strong justification for government intervention. Provision of public education and health care is rationalized on the grounds that these are merit goods which cannot be left to individual decision-making. Left to themselves, individuals may spend much less than what is considered socially desirable. (Note that this has nothing to do with Pareto optimality or market failure. What is presumed is that, as far as these goods are concerned, individuals are incapable of judging what a desirable level of expenditure is.) The state of course knows what is socially desirable. Since the primary function of extension is the diffusion of information – a public good – it is likely to be undersupplied in a market-based allocation. This is obviously a case of market failure as the outcome is not Pareto-optimal. Government intervention is thus necessary. What further strengthens the case for government intervention in each event is that, given the inequalities in endowments, the poor are likely to be at a considerable disadvantage in a market-based allocation.

All this is straightforward. The extent and form of government intervention are, however, often difficult to specify. A basic choice, for example, is whether governments should provide these goods and services or whether they should limit their role to a regulatory one. No general answer can be given. All that might be said is that, when markets exist and are known to operate with a certain degree of efficiency, it would be futile for the government to supplant them (Drèze and Sen, 1989). In this case, the government could play an effective regulatory role. The point is that markets as allocators of resources have certain advantages – an important one being their decentralized functioning and relative efficiency in processing information. So, while the risk of market failure remains, with government intervention, there are the risks of inefficient processing of information and bureaucratic failure. However, there are other choices on which more could be said in the light of the discussion in the earlier sections of this chapter. These choices relate mainly to allocations of budget, pricing of services and distribution mechanisms for ensuring easy access of the poor to these services. To the extent that there is a willingness to pay for some services and market responses are sensitive to price changes, it is important to take them into account in designing government programmes for human capital formation. Indeed, in this context it is suggested that equity-efficiency trade-offs, which are so often emphasized in the theoretical literature, may be much less significant. The main points are as follows:

- A case was made for integrating several services in one human resource development programme. Experience suggests that this is more cost-effective than a multiplicity of programmes. Given the difficulties of access, communication and transport, it is easier to deliver a whole package of services when the target population comes in contact with development agencies. Two illustrations suffice here: one relates to a broad-based extension programme which combines a range of services, covering home management, child nutrition, social forestry, agriculture, etc., with its traditional function; another relates to the integration of child nutrition supplementation with existing health delivery systems. However, logistical problems may arise in extending their geographical coverage. Intensive programmes concentrated on a small area may therefore be better than programmes covering vast areas (Lipton and Van der Gaag, 1991).

• Allocations of public expenditure within education and health are both inefficient and inequitable. Within education, a very large share of resources is devoted to higher education while primary education is relatively neglected. Since the social rates of return are higher for the latter, efficiency considerations suggest a reallocation of expenditure in favour of primary education. The fact that a large majority of those benefiting from higher education represent the more affluent sections further strengthens the case for reallocation. Within health, the over-emphasis on curative care needs to be corrected, as it generates private benefits. On the other hand, low private willingness to pay for forms of preventive care, such as communicable disease control programmes, that are in the nature of a public good, means such care requires greater public support. Also, within curative care, emphasis must shift from hospitals to primary health centres, as the latter are more cost-effective and cater largely to the poor.

• In the context of unsustainable fiscal deficits, it is imperative that more resources are generated through appropriate user fees. Specifically, user fees could be selectively imposed on services (e.g. those provided by a hospital) for which there is private willingness to pay and on certain groups (e.g. middle- and high-income households) with the ability to pay. Such resources could then be used for expanding primary education and primary health centres in rural areas, for instance, and for improving their quality. Moreover, subsidies to the poor ought not to be discontinued as, in some cases (e.g. health care), an across-the-board increase in user fees is likely to price them out.

- In general, women have not benefited as much as men from human resource interventions. Despite their key role in food production and processing in sub-Saharan Africa, women are usually neglected by male extension workers. Similarly, even though female enrolments expanded rapidly in the 1960s and 1970s, girls continue to lag behind boys in schooling. Further, gender differences in nutrition and health outcomes continue to be quite pronounced in parts of South Asia, with female children facing a higher mortality risk than male children. Efficiency and equity considerations favour greater priority for girls and women in human resource interventions. Women's access to extension will improve if more female extension workers are recruited; female enrolments will grow faster if more female teachers are recruited, and efforts are made to reduce the opportunity cost of girls enrolling in schools, for example, through more flexible school hours, provision of child care facilities, etc; and nutrition and health outcomes for girls will be more favourable if they are exempted from user fees for health care.

  At a more fundamental level, however, to the extent that the gender bias is associated with economic considerations, the creation of more remunerative employment opportunities for women may make a substantial difference.

- In addition, community or public action in its collaborative and adversarial roles is of vital importance (Drèze and Sen, 1989). While higher shares of public spending (an aspect of public support) devoted to basic services appear to be closely related to social progress (i.e. a reduction in infant and child mortality), it should not be taken to imply that public expenditure is generally effectively targeted. It is, for example, well documented that health services are often skewed away from the people who need them most, i.e. the poor. Extra spending on these services will not automatically help the poor. The existing pattern of provision needs to be tilted in their favour in terms of both quantity and quality. A key element in effective targeting is community action (another aspect of public support). A comparative analysis of three basic amenities – food, health care and education – in Bangladesh, India, the Indian state of Kerala and Sri Lanka is revealing.[15] Both Sri Lanka and Kerala stand out with striking distinction. In the mid-1980s, Sri Lanka had one hospital bed for every 350 people as against 1 200 people in India. More important, Sri Lanka has emphasized maternal health care, which has contributed significantly to the reduction of infant mortality. As a result, almost all Sri Lankan mothers received prenatal care as against a small fraction in India. Similarly, a comparison with India's countrywide performance shows Kerala in a distinctly impressive light. For example, in 1977 there were 1 975 hospital beds per million of population in Kerala as against 791 in India as a whole. Moreover, the health care facilities were spread widely across the state instead of being concentrated in the urban areas, as is the case in the rest of India. It may be stressed, however, that it is not merely the physical volume of facilities that has made the difference. In fact, there are states in India that outperform Kerala in respect of some of the indices noted above. What has made the difference is the efficiency with which medical facilities have been used (Osmani, 1988). In Kerala, for example, a highly health-conscious population made sure that the existing facilities were effectively utilized. The educated and politicized people did not merely add to the health consciousness of the population (a collaborative role) but also ensured that the existing rural health centres were fully geared to their service (an adversarial role). More examples could be cited but the central insight remains: both the availability and the utilization of basic services by the poor depend to a large extent on community initiatives.

---

[15] For a more detailed exposition, see Osmani (1988).

Chapter 10
Freedom, coalitions and poverty

The fact that a poverty alleviation policy is cost-effective does not guarantee that it will be chosen in a democratic regime. If the policy is redistributive, the potential losers are likely to resist it while the potential gainers may support it. Depending on which coalition is more effective, the policy in question may be chosen or rejected. If the state has any autonomy, it may moderate the influence of such coalitions in policy choice. Following the resurgence of interest in the political economy of development, these issues have attracted a great deal of attention in recent years. The political feasibility of a policy is recognizably an important consideration.

The present chapter approaches these issues from a broad perspective. At a somewhat abstract level, the first section discusses the relationship between freedom and well-being, distinguishing between positive and negative freedom. A case is made for positive freedom (reflected in, for example, the capability to live a long life) as the focal point of public policy.[1] Negative freedom matters in an assessment of well-being but only in an instrumental sense. A cross-country statistical analysis (Das Gupta, 1989), linking functionings to negative freedom and liberties, is critically evaluated. Arguing that this analysis is limited in its scope – specifically, because it does not address the issue of the relative strength of different coalitions and their role in policy choice – the next section focuses on this and related issues. While some useful insights are suggested in a recent study by de Janvry, Fargeix

---

[1] As noted in Chapter 2, positive freedom has to do with what a person is actually able to do or be while negative freedom connotes absence of interference from the government, institutions and other individuals. A more detailed exposition is given in the first section of this chapter.

and Sadoulet (1992), based on multimarket/general equilibrium formulations for India and Ecuador, the question of whether coalitions of the rural poor can be made more effective is not addressed. In the third section, among other things, the role of initial conditions in voluntary collective action is emphasized. Two case-studies from an influential study (Wade, 1987) are reviewed to demonstrate that the pessimism in theoretical literature on the possibility of voluntary collective action is unwarranted. Finally, the insights that follow from these and other case-studies are then discussed.

FREEDOM, GROWTH AND WELL-BEING

A recent study (Roubini, 1989) emphasizes two-way causal relationships between freedom and growth on the one hand, and between freedom and well-being on the other. Consider first the relationship between freedom and growth. Identifying some forms of freedom with democracy, it is often argued that democracy and growth are incompatible and that an authoritarian regime is better able to follow policies that will lead to long-term economic growth. This incompatibility hypothesis takes different forms (e.g. Kahn, 1979; Olson, 1982).

According to Roubini (1989), a stylized version is as follows: policy-makers in a democratic government are short-sighted in their policies and are subject to the pressures of interest groups, trade unions, etc.; they follow policies that try to increase their political support and their chances of re-election instead of considering policies that maximize the potential of long-term growth.

On the other hand, there is another strand of literature which emphasizes the contribution that economic growth makes to democracy. Specifically, economic growth is regarded as a prerequisite to democracy (e.g. Lipset, 1959; Olson, 1968). As in the first case, different formulations have been employed. Some (e.g. Finer, 1962) have sought to establish a causal link between economic backwardness and the probability of a military coup. In case economic backwardness "causes" military coups, a related question is whether military governments have a positive effect on economic growth (e.g. Jackman, 1976). Similarly, there has been a rich crop of formulations focusing on the two-way causal relationships between freedom and economic well-being.[2]

In a democratic setting, the existence of community pressure groups may be a decisive factor in improving the standard of living of the poor (Drèze and Sen, 1989). On the other hand, poverty and unequal income distribution are often the source of social conflicts and political instability (i.e. frequent regime changes) as well as poor macroeconomic performance, sometimes paving the way for an authoritarian government.[3] With a few exceptions (notably Drèze and Sen, 1989), most of these formulations use a macro perspective. While there is nothing wrong with this perspective – indeed, it is remarkable that some relationships can be formulated at a macro level – not enough attention is paid to the meaning and implications of some of the key concepts such as freedom.

As elaborated below, freedom can be conceptualized in different ways, with quite different policy emphases (Das Gupta, 1989; Sen, 1989). In effect, the formulations are much too coarse for unravelling the complexity of the relationship between freedom and aspects of well-being, for instance. This is particularly so in empirical verification of this and other related formulations (Roubini, 1989). None of these studies, for example, throw any light on the precise relationship between freedom and measures of

---

[2] No comment is necessary on the relationship between economic growth and well-being as Chapter 3 is devoted to specific aspects of this relationship.

[3] Dornbusch and Edwards (1989) identify four phases of a "populist policy cycle", triggered by extreme poverty and inequality. In the first phase, reactivation of the economy through expansionary fiscal and monetary policies is combined with income redistribution via large increases in real wages. In the second phase, the strong expansion in demand for goods and shortage of foreign exchange reserves lead to supply bottlenecks. Inflation accelerates and the current account worsens. Then, price adjustments, devaluations, exchange rate controls and protectionist measures are introduced to cope with the external imbalance. At the same time, the budget deficit worsens dramatically. The third phase is characterized by the government trying to stabilize by cutting subsidies and by a real depreciation. Real wages fall massively and politics becomes unstable. In the fourth phase, an authoritarian government takes over and enforces a strict stabilization programme. While this stylized description has some validity in the Latin American context, it would be naive to claim that it is equally valid in other contexts.

well-being. There are other problems too. In a democratic setting, is it important to know whether some policies designed to benefit the poor are more likely to be chosen than others? If so, are these choices associated with certain coalitions that are more effective than others? These are some of the questions addressed here.

Type and content of freedom

In a number of influential writings, Sen has clarified the relationship between freedom and well-being.[4] Of particular significance in the present context is the exposition in two recent contributions (Sen, 1989; 1992b). He first distinguishes between negative and positive freedom.[5] Negative freedom refers to the independence of the individual from interference by others, including governments, institutions and other individuals. Positive freedom, on the other hand, refers to what a person is actually able to do or be. Some examples may be helpful. If a person lacks the income to buy a nutritionally adequate diet, he lacks positive freedom. But if this income shortfall is the result of interference by someone, his negative freedom is also curtailed. A more concrete case is that of a bonded labourer in rural Bihar (an Indian state) who lacks negative freedom in so far as his income-earning options are limited by ties to his present employer.[6] Sen (1989) further distinguishes between the intrinsic and instrumental values of freedom. When freedom is important in itself, it is said to have intrinsic value. On the other hand, when it is a means to other ends, it has instrumental value. This negative-positive distinction may be combined with the intrinsic-instrumental classification of freedom. An example may be helpful. Freedom to earn profit in any occupation – filmmaking, agri-

---

[4] Note that this discussion is complementary to that in Chapter 2.

[5] This distinction was first made by Berlin (1969).

[6] This distinction may, however, be an ambiguous one in the context of segmented rural credit markets, for example, which tend to restrict credit to those normally resident in a village, not because of any interference but simply as a rational response to informational asymetry. (I am grateful to Bina Agarwal for raising this issue.)

culture, handicrafts – without any restriction by a government agency, corresponds to an instrumental negative view of freedom.[7] Borrowing another example from Sen (1989), freedom from hunger is a positive freedom in so far as the underlying concern is with what people are actually able to do or be. At the same time, this freedom could be seen as possessing intrinsic value (i.e. important in itself) or as an instrument for achieving a more basic objective such as well-being or happiness.

As most of the discussion in the present report (as well as in the literature) is confined to a characterization of poverty as deprivation resulting from low income, it is necessary to examine whether this characterization is an appropriate one in the present context.[8] Sen (1992b) argues for a different characterization. First, as a broad observation, poverty may be interpreted as a drastic curtailment of freedom. More specifically, it is viewed as a failure to achieve certain basic capabilities. In the light of the discussion in Chapter 2, it may be recalled that it is capabilities and not functionings which reflect a person's freedom to lead one type of life or another.[9] Second, since transformation of resources or income into capabilities varies among individuals, the relevant concept of poverty in the income space "has to be inadequacy (for generating minimally acceptable capabilities) rather than lowness (independently of personal characteristics)" (Sen, 1992b, p. 111). To facilitate application, individuals may be grouped by gender, occupation, employment status and so on. In each case therefore, income required to achieve minimal capabilities has to be specified.

That such a shift of emphasis merits serious consideration is not an issue. What might, however, be disputed is the empirical feasibility of this approach. Contentious issues relate to the selection and weighting of the basic capabilities as well as the specification of the precise relationship between

---

[7] This is a variant of an example in Sen (1989).

[8] I am grateful to Jean Drèze for raising this issue in a personal communication.

[9] As Sen (1992b, p. 50) clarifies: "In the space of functionings, any point represents an n-tuple of functionings. Capability is a set of such functioning n-tuples, representing the various alternative combinations of functionings from which the person can choose one combination."

the capabilities and income, taking note of personal characteristics and circumstances. Sen offers a brief response. He argues that "... in dealing with extreme poverty in developing economies, we may be able to go a fairly long distance in terms of a relatively small number of centrally important functionings (and the corresponding basic capabilities, e.g. the ability to be well-nourished and well-sheltered, the capability of escaping available morbidity and premature mortality and so forth) ..." (Sen, 1992b, p. 44-45). On the question of weighting, he elaborates, a possibility is that one social state is better than another in some cases. This is the so-called "dominance partial-ordering" which allows some useful, albeit incomplete, comparisons to be made. This ranking may then be extended through an "intersection" approach for a range of weights.[10] As long as there is some agreement on the range of weights, some further comparisons of alternative states may be feasible. In other words, for a range of weights, the ranking of social states may be invariant. Surprisingly, Sen (1992b) does not suggest how to establish a causal relationship between basic capabilities and income (for groups of individuals). Since these are essentially empirical questions, an a priori resolution can hardly be persuasive.

Outcome versus distribution of resources

In Chapter 2, following Sen (1987), a case was made for shifting the focus in the measurement of living standards from access to resources for fulfilling of basic needs to the kind of life people can and choose to live. In a recent contribution, Das Gupta (1989) argues against such a shift. As far as protection of negative freedom is concerned, there is no disagreement between Sen and Das Gupta. In other words, the state must ensure that any impediments to the exercise of this freedom are removed. If, for example, an agricultural labourer chooses not to work for a particular landlord, he should be free to do so.

There is, however, a sharp disagreement in the concern for positive

---

[10] This approach takes into account the convergence of ranking social states within a specified range, even when there is no agreement on the relative weights.

freedom. While Sen (1987) is emphatic that the concern of public policy ought to be with certain capabilities (e.g. the capability to live a long, meaningful and healthy life), Das Gupta (1989) limits this concern to access to goods which are necessary for the exercise of positive freedom. As the latter correctly points out, if the basic needs are observable and measurable, in either case the outcome will be the same. However, this is generally not true. Hence Das Gupta's reasons for a limited policy focus merit consideration. First, taking a contractual view of the state, he argues that it is legitimate for the state to ensure that the goods necessary for the exercise of positive freedom (such as income or wealth) are provided.

Given this characterization of the state, Das Gupta (1989) argues, it cannot force people to use these goods as desired if they choose not to. The following example offers an illustration: Imagine a community in which all have access to adequate medical facilities but where a large number, because of deeply held religious convictions, choose not to make use of them. It is then possible that, in terms of outcomes (e.g. life expectancy at birth and morbidity rates), the community will score badly. In terms of commodity availability, however, it would score well. Besides, as Das Gupta elaborates, the concern with the outcomes may be informationally more demanding. If resources have to be provided strictly in accordance with individual needs, in order to ensure a certain outcome, there are two difficulties. One regards the assessment of needs. There are, of course, some needs that are publicly verifiable, such as those of physically handicapped people, and average needs associated with pregnancy, illness, etc. Even here, there are always interpersonal variations. But there are many needs that are not easy to ascertain in public. In these cases, the transfer of resources in accordance with specific needs, and ultimately according to person-specific well-being, is obviously not feasible. An additional difficulty in this context is that there is an incentive to exaggerate and claim a larger share of the resources than necessary. Nutritional supplementation programmes for schoolchildren are a case in point. Since the meals served at home are not publicly observable, the provision of midday meals in schools tends to attract children from affluent families. Finally, a concern limited to outcomes may distract attention from the resource costs of these achievements. Without this information, it cannot be assessed whether greater achievements could have been realized with the same overall use of resources.

The contrast is overdrawn. Sen (1987) is clearly not unaware of the difficulties pointed out by Das Gupta (1989).[11] His advocacy of capabilities or outcomes rather than distribution of resources or access to goods reflects his concern that there has been an overemphasis on the latter. Since, ultimately, what matters is well-being (as captured in some basic capabilities), it ought to be the focal point of public policy. This of course does not mean that the distribution of resources is of no consequence. It matters but only in an instrumental sense.

Brief responses to Das Gupta's (1989) specific objections suffice here.

- It is not self-evident that a contractual state would necessarily confine itself to the provision of goods for exercising positive freedom and not worry about the outcome. That contracts typically stop short of ensuring certain outcomes – a doctor, for example, can only guarantee an appropriate treatment and not a cure (Das Gupta's analogy) – is not persuasive, since some contracts are implicitly or explicitly contingent on outcomes. Implicitly, to extend the analogy, if the patient is not cured of his ailment during a certain period, he may terminate the "contract" with his doctor and enter into a new contract with another. Explicitly, as an example, piece wage rates are based on outcomes.
- Das Gupta insists that, if some needs are not observable and verifiable, outcome-based evaluations would be problematic. But this misses the point that it is as much a problem for distribution-of-resource-based evaluation as it is for outcome-based evaluation. If, for example, an unobservable metabolic disorder makes a person unable to avoid nutritional deficiency even with an amount of food that would suffice for others, then the fact that he does possess that amount of food is misleading as a basis for assessment of his nutritional status. Indeed, if a range of commodity requirements is compatible with a specific nutritional status, the case for outcome-based evaluation is strengthened.

---

[11] See, for example, Sen's (1987) reply to Hart (1987).

Moreover, if large sections of the rural poor fail to take advantage of primary health care facilities for cultural or economic reasons – as is typically the case with women – it is not particularly appealing to claim that the state has performed its contractual function of providing some merit goods. A key issue in rural poverty alleviation is not just whether these goods are publicly provided but whether they are also utilized by the poor.

• It is elementary but necessary to state that cost-effectiveness considerations involve the analysis of both distribution of resources and outcomes. Contrary to the tendency in the basic needs literature, distribution of resources by itself is not enough for such an assessment. If Sen (1987) emphasizes outcomes, he is cautioning against the temptation to view resources as valuable in themselves.

Intercountry comparisons of well-being

Das Gupta (1989) presents an interesting analysis of the relationship between negative liberties and economic growth, on the one hand, and that between growth and functionings (which Das Gupta interprets as measures of positive freedom) on the other.[12] For a sample of 50 countries, three functionings are considered: life expectancy at birth, infant mortality and adult literacy.

Two sets of observations are considered – one for 1970 and another for 1980. Economic growth denotes increase in per caput income. Quantifiable aspects of negative freedom are summarized in indices of political and civil rights for this sample of developing countries, compiled by Taylor and Jodice (1983). Averages of these indices over the period 1973-1979 are used. Political rights allow citizens to play a part in determining who governs their country and what the laws are and will be. Countries are coded

---

[12] To the extent that achievements are measured across the sample relative to a maximum attainable level, Das Gupta's interpretation is not necessarily inappropriate. A refinement, however, would be to check whether the minimum value is attainable by each developing country in the sample.

with scores ranging from 1 (highest degree of liberty) to 7 (lowest degree of liberty). Civil rights, on the other hand, are the rights the individual has *vis-à-vis* the state. Of particular importance are freedom of the press as well as other media concerned with the dissemination of information and the independence of the judiciary. The index measures the extent to which people are openly able to express their opinions without fear of reprisals because they are protected by an independent judiciary. The countries' scores (1 to 7) reflect severe deprivation of negative liberties. Citizens of 35 of the sample countries suffer from systems that score 5 or more for political rights, and those of 26 countries from systems that score 5 or more for civil rights. When these indices are combined with those of functionings, the overall picture of the developing world is chilling (Das Gupta, 1989).

Das Gupta carries out a statistical analysis primarily to check whether, at low levels of income, there are any trade-offs between economic growth and negative liberties, on the one hand, and between functionings and economic growth, on the other. Most of this analysis is based on rank correlation coefficients. The main conclusions, as summarized by the author, are:

• Political and civil liberties are positively and significantly correlated with per caput income and its growth, with increases in infant survival rates and in life expectancy at birth.

• Per caput income and its growth are positively and significantly correlated, and they in turn are significantly correlated with improvements in life expectancy at birth and infant survival rates.

• Political and civil rights are strongly and positively correlated.

• An increase in the adult literacy rate is not related systematically to per caput income or its growth, or to improvements in life expectancy

---

[13] No attempt is made by Das Gupta (1989) to explain the inverse relationship between adult literacy and negative liberties. It is possible that this may change in a more detailed analysis if account is taken of the relative share of public expenditure devoted to literacy programmes. In other words, nothing can be inferred from the rank correlation coefficients if the effect of intervening variables (omitted from this analysis) is not isolated.

and infant survival rates. However, it is negatively and significantly correlated with political and civil liberties.

Most of the results are plausible.[13] It is somewhat perplexing though that a direct relationship is sought between functionings and negative liberties. The link between them through economic growth is intuitively more appealing. The overall conclusion that there is a strong association between economic growth and negative liberties, on the one hand, and between improvements in functionings and economic growth, on the other, is comforting but needs qualification. The fact that a few countries in the sample (e.g. the Republic of Korea and Thailand) recorded impressive economic performances and improvements in functionings, despite a dismal record of political and civil liberties, suggests possible trade-offs between economic growth and negative liberties. An authoritarian government, for example, may have a better chance of implementing drastic reforms. Also, even democratic systems embody vastly differing political regimes, leading to differences in the policies formulated "and their effective implementation, with very different outcomes" for the poor. This points to a basic inadequacy in Das Gupta's analysis. However, Kohli's (1987) analysis of the political economy of poverty alleviation in India provides some valuable pointers.

Nature of the political regime

Kohli's analysis examines the redistributive role of the state in a democratic setting. His basic premise is that, within similar socio-structural conditions, differences in regime type have an importance. The analysis is based on field work in the three Indian states of West Bengal, Uttar Pradesh and Karnataka during 1978-79 and 1981. During this period, these states were governed by three different political parties, with varying degrees of commitment to and capacity for redistributive reform. A comparative analysis of their performances in land reforms, small farmer schemes and wage- and employment-generation projects helps in identifying aspects of regime type which are significant in poverty alleviation. Kohli (1987) stresses four regime characteristics: leadership, ideology, organization and the class basis of the party in power.

Despite three decades (1950-1980) of planned development in India, the central government failed to make a dent in poverty. Kohli argues that the congress party, which ruled at the centre, lacked commitment to and capacity for redistributive reform. It had no clear-cut ideology and had a loose, amorphous organization. Its close alliance with the entrepreneurial class shaped India's development. Although some impressive achievements were recorded, such as a highly diversified industrial structure, the plight of the poor strata remained virtually unchanged.

Since state governments are vested with greater responsibility for poverty alleviation (land reform, for example, is a state subject), a comparative analysis of the state governments in West Bengal, Uttar Pradesh and Karnataka is illuminating. Of these states, the performance of West Bengal's Communist government was the most impressive. Within Kohli's framework, the success of the Communist party in poverty alleviation can be traced to *i)* a coherent and stable leadership; *ii)* a clear pro-lower-class ideology; and *iii)* strong grassroots-level organization. However, while the Communist party successfully carried out tenancy reforms, its record in redistributing surplus land was disappointing. In part, this was because of the poor quality of land records. But, more fundamentally, it reflected the limited redistributive intent of the Communist party in a democratic setting (Kohli, 1987). In sharp contrast, the Janta regime in Uttar Pradesh was characterized by a fragmented leadership, confused ideology and little or no organizational base. It was largely a coalition of moderately well off and rich peasants. Not surprisingly, therefore, the poverty alleviation record of this regime was dismal. The Karnataka case lies somewhere in between. Under the congress government there had been a modicum of redistributive success. In any case, a weak organization – dominated by propertied classes – could not support drastic redistribution.

Kohli (1987) persuasively demonstrates the importance of regime type in the noted areas of poverty alleviation. Unfortunately, he does not examine the access of the poor to health and education. If the impressive record of the Communist party in West Bengal were substantiated in these areas too, Kohli's contention would be further strengthened. In other words, the analysis is narrowly focused in terms of its coverage of poverty alleviation programmes. Furthermore, it does not probe the nature and strength of coalitions that are activated by specific anti-poverty interventions. Food subsidies based on domestic procurement, for example, may be resisted by large food producers and favoured by the poor. In such a context, it is not just regime type that matters but also the relative strength of different coalitions, as elaborated below.

COALITIONS, STATE AUTONOMY AND POVERTY ALLEVIATION

Even though there is now greater awareness of the constraining influence of various pressure groups on the design and implementation of policies (e.g. Naert, 1985), systematically specified and empirically validated formulations continue to be few and far between. While some observations on the political feasibility of specific anti-poverty interventions were made earlier in this report, these were not intended to provide a comprehensive assessment of their political feasibility. To do so, it is important to understand how coalitions are formed, why some of them are more successful than others and whether the state has any autonomy in policy formulation. Even if a comprehensive framework is specified – by no means an easy task – its empirical validation is just as difficult.

Against this background, a significant recent contribution is de Janvry, Fargeix and Sadoulet (1992). It develops a sophisticated methodology to construct a political feasibility index for a wide range of anti-poverty interventions (e.g. consumer food subsidies, fertilizer subsidies, technological change, infrastructural development), taking into account alternative financing possibilities. The specification of the political feasibility index focuses on the formation of coalitions and the mechanisms that trigger collective action. The state is assumed to possess a certain degree of autonomy relative to pressure groups. An *ex post* validation of this index is followed by a detailed analysis of the political feasibility of a wide range of anti-poverty interventions. Their effects on various groups, including the rural poor, are explored in a multimarket and/or general equilibrium model. Taking advantage of three recent studies (Binswanger and Quizon, 1984 and de Janvry and Subbarao, 1986, for India; and Kouwenaar, 1988, for Ecuador) various policies are ranked in terms of their political feasibility. Whether any particular coalition favours a policy, the contribution of this coalition to its political feasibility and the factors underlying the emergence of this coalition are some of the key issues which are specifically addressed in this analysis.

Setting

A brief reference to the salient features of India and Ecuador may be helpful. In India, rural population has a very heavy weight (about 80 percent) while it is equally split between rural and urban sectors in Ecuador. In India, the rich are the large farmers, the formal sector workers and the urban capitalists. In Ecuador, they include the large farmers and medium- and high-education urban groups. In both countries the rural poor comprise the lowest two income groups (see Table 28), composed of landless workers and small farmers.

Policy interventions

The set of policy interventions for these two economies is spelt out in Table 27. To avoid cluttering the text with specific features of each policy intervention, an intervention is traced to its source (Binswanger and Quizon, for example, are abbreviated as B and Q). These interventions comprise consumer food subsidies, subsidies to food production, land reform, irrigation subsidies, fertilizer subsidies and urban housing as well as programmes of rural development – through, for example, infrastructural support.

Financing options include taxation and foreign aid. Basically, all the policies considered reduce poverty among the rural poor except for fertilizer subsidies in B and Q6, as fertilizer is labour-saving and leads to a fall in employment of the poorest rural group, and the urban housing programme in K1 which reduces the real income of family farmers (1 to 5 ha) because of the inflationary impact it creates.

Political feasibility index

A political feasibility index is constructed, relative to an economic feasibility index, taking into account expected benefits to different groups from collective action, formation of coalitions, triggering mechanisms, and state

TABLE 27

Political feasibility of poverty alleviation policies

Coalitions Rural poor with:	Rural poverty alleviation policies	Real income effects				State GDP growth	Political feasibility ranks (in ascending order)
		Rural poor	Rural rich	Urban poor	Urban rich		
Rural rich	B and Q3. Food subsidies: domestic supply and tax	+ +	+	−	− −	+	1
	dJ and S3. Food subsidies cut and transfer to all poor	+	+	−	−	+Ω	2
	dJ and S4. Food subsidies cut and producer subsidy	+	+	−	−	+Ω	3
	dJ and S5. Food subsidies cut and irrigation	+	+	−	−	+Ω	2
	K2. Subsidy to food production and tax	+ +	+ +	− −	− −	+Ω	7
Urban poor	B and Q2. Food subsidies: foreign supply and tax	+ +	−	+ +	−	0	11
	B and Q4. Food subsidies: domestic supply and procurement	+ +	−	+	−	+Ω	4
	K1. Urban housing and aid	+	−	+	−	+	8
	K4. Land reform, productivity growth and livestock	+	−	+	−	+	5
All urban	B and Q1. Food subsidies: foreign supply and aid	+ +	−	+ +	+	+ +	13
	B and Q5. Irrigation and aid	+	−	+	+	+	10
	dJ and S1. Productivity and aid	+	−	+ +	+	+	9
Rural rich and all urban	B and Q6. Fertilizer subsidies and aid	+	+ +	+	+	+	6
	dJ and S2. Productivity, aid and price support	+ +	+	+ +	+	+ +	12
	K3. Rural development and productivity	+	+	+	+	+ +	10

Note: Ω denotes a very small effect. *Author codes:* B&Q = Binswanger and Quizon; dJ and S = de Janvry and Subbarao; K = Konwanaar.
Source: Adapted from de Janvry, Fargeix and Sadoulet (1992).

autonomy in policy formulation.[14] The poor are assumed to have an asymmetric response function, resorting to collective action only when faced with the prospects of large losses. In contrast, the non-poor respond in a symmetric and gradual way to expected gains or losses. State autonomy is reflected in the importance given to the maximization of GDP, relative to average rates of income change for groups, in policy formulation.

---

[14] If *ex post* redistribution is credible and costless, income shares of different groups reflect their influence in policy formulation. Taking, therefore, their sizes and incomes into account, the economic feasibility index is constructed. A modified version of this index, as sketched above, is the political feasibility index. For details, see de Janvry, Fargeix and Sadoulet (1992).

Coalitions and state autonomy

Policies that benefit all groups and raise GNP have high political feasibility. Examples include rural development with productivity growth (K3) and technological change with price support (dJ and S2). Although aid-funded fertilizer subsidies (B and Q6) do not benefit one segment of the rural poor (i.e. the poorest), they enjoy wide support and are thus politically feasible.

Policies that benefit all groups, except the rural rich, and that raise GNP also have high political feasibility. Examples include food subsidies based on aid-funded imports (B and Q1), and aid-funded irrigation (B and Q5) and technological change (dJ and S1). The rural rich on their own are therefore not an effective coalition.

Coalitions of the rural and urban poor in two cases – food subsidies based on domestic supply and procurement (B and Q4) and land reforms, with productivity growth in livestock (K4) – are ineffective. But when the gains are large for these groups – as in the case of food subsidies that are based on foreign supply and are tax funded (B and Q2) – or, when such coalitions enjoy state support – as in the case of aid-funded housing programmes (K1) – they are more decisive.

Finally, with or without state support, coalitions of all rural groups are ineffective against those of all urban groups. Examples include food subsidies that are based on domestic supply and are tax funded (B and Q3), and the withdrawal of urban food subsidies and their replacement by income transfers to the rural poor (dJ and S3) or by producer subsidies (dJ and S4) or by irrigation (dJ and S5). However, when the gains to the rural poor and the rich are substantial even without state support, as in the case of a tax-funded producer subsidy (K2), all rural groups constitute an effective coalition.

Some insights into the effectiveness of different coalitions are suggested. The basic issue is the distribution of costs and benefits of an anti-poverty intervention across different groups. To the extent that funding of an intervention by foreign aid does not impose a cost on any group, it is not likely to be resisted. If a foreign aid-funded intervention induces growth and results in widely-shared income gains, it is likely to enjoy wide support.

Between interventions that favour only the poor and those that benefit both the poor and the non-poor (in other words, there is "leakage" of benefits to the non-poor), the latter set of interventions is likely to carry greater support. The larger the overall income gains of groups, the more decisive is their support for the intervention. Finally, effects on growth matter, since they mobilize the support of the government.

Positive and normative aspects

The de Janvry, Fargeix and Sadoulet (1992) analysis belongs to the area of positive analysis of state action, i.e. why certain poverty alleviation policies are likely to be chosen. A positive analysis may yield clues as to how some coalitions could be strengthened to make the poverty alleviation role of the state more effective.

Following Sadoulet and de Janvry (1991), two (unrelated) formulations explain why governments do what they do, given a strategic response, and how this behaviour is influenced by their structural context. One focuses on government behaviour under lobbying by interest groups, while the other emphasizes time consistency and credibility in policy-making. Both tend to restrict state autonomy. In the former, the government favours those policies that increase its probability of staying in office. The latter, on the other hand, emphasizes that time inconsistent policies lack credibility and, hence, the government is constrained to choose time-consistent policies.[15]

The de Janvry, Fargeix and Sadoulet analysis relies on the first formulation in which the government's own objective (reflected in maximization of national income) is modified by the demands from pressure groups. This arguably is a narrow and simplistic view of state autonomy. The relative impotence of the rural poor as a pressure group is somewhat exaggerated. Under certain conditions, if the number is large, their influence in policy choice may be substantial.[16] That some coalitions – especially of the rural poor – may gain strength over time is ignored. If there is an element of

---

[15] For a more detailed exposition, see Sadoulet and de Janvry (1991).
[16] The spontaneous support of the rural poor for the EGS in Maharashtra is illustrative.

"learning", the poor may become more aware of potential gains from collective action as well as becoming better organized. In that case, the asymmetric response function (i.e. the poor respond only to large losses) loses its plausibility and, consequently, the relative impotence of the rural poor as a coalition is suspect. But this also raises a normative issue in relation to the specific mechanisms through which the government may want to strengthen this and other coalitions. The analysis in question steers clear of such normative questions. As noted, these relate to politicization of the rural poor (a direct consequence of political activism) and their empowerment (through participation in rural public works) in the course of time (Drèze, 1988). In a different context, namely that of access to common property resources, Wade (1987) demonstrates that, under certain conditions, collective action is a rational, self-interested response. Other more recent evidence points to similar responses in different settings (Chopra and Kadekodi, 1991). As some generalizations follow from recent studies, a critical evaluation is presented below.

CONDITIONS FOR VOLUNTARY COLLECTIVE ACTION

Valuable insights into the possibility of collective action come from detailed microstudies, as the context cannot be fully specified in general equilibrium/multimarket formulations of the kind employed in de Janvry, Fargeix and Sadoulet (1992). In particular, certain "initial" conditions have a crucial role in inducing and sustaining collective action. Essentially, these relate to whether corporate institutions (such as village councils) exist, whether collective action will bring about substantial gains and whether mechanisms exist for enforcing rules and regulations that have been collectively agreed on.

The case-studies in Wade (1987) illustrate their importance in equitable sharing of scarce common property resources. Contrary to assertions in the theoretical literature (Olson, 1971), these case-studies demonstrate that rational, self-interested individuals often combine, without any coercion or other form of external intervention, to achieve their common or group interests. The policy implications are significant.

Under the conditions indicated above, to the extent that the poor depend on common property resources, voluntary collective action will tend to lessen their hardship. Also, as the case-studies suggest, collective action is not simply a matter of making people aware of their real common interests or promoting values that are less individualistic. As long as gains from cooperation are substantial (farmers at the tail-end of a canal in a semi-arid region with widely scattered holdings would want equitable sharing of limited water supply) and effective enforcement mechanisms exist for collectively agreed upon rules, collective action would be a self-interested response. An appropriate role for the government, therefore, is to strengthen these mechanisms (i.e. make the application of joint rules legally enforceable) and perhaps provide technical assistance to expand and maintain some of these resources better (Wade, 1987).

Setting

Wade's (1987) analysis is based on a sample of 41 villages in southern India (Kurnool district, Andhra Pradesh), out of which 31 are irrigated from canal systems while the remaining ten are dry. Some villages have a public realm, consisting of four main institutions: a village council, a village standing fund, village guards employed by the council to protect crops, and "common irrigators", also employed by the council to distribute canal water to the rice fields. The council is accountable to an annual meeting of all village residents. As argued by Wade, these institutions play a key role in sustaining collective action.

The focus of this analysis is on access to grazing and irrigation. These are designated common property or common pool resources – a subset of public goods. They are a subset in the sense that they have finite or subtractive benefits (unlike some public goods which yield infinite benefits). Common pool resources are therefore potentially subject to depletion or degradation. Two alternative views have dominated the literature.

One view is that full private property rights over the commons are a necessary condition for avoiding overexploitation (e.g. Demsetz, 1967). Another is that it is essential to give an external agency – usually the state – full authority to regulate the commons (Hardin, 1968). Wade's analysis refutes these views.

Grazing management

Salient features of the management of grazing in a (representative) village with all four institutions are described below. The description is sufficiently focused to yield insights into the rationale and effectiveness of collective action. Intervillage variations are omitted.

The holdings are widely scattered as a risk-spreading arrangement. After the rain-fed crops are harvested in February, the landowner may either use the stubble for his own animals or sell the grazing rights. In either case, the cost of safeguarding the stubble is very high, especially because the holdings are widely scattered. A market for grazing exists. The village council negotiates grazing agreements with a small group of herders. The agreement stipulates the number of animals, the time and duration of grazing and the amount payable. The herders recover part of this amount from the sale of animal manure. Village guards ensure that grazing hours are adhered to and that no damage is done to the irrigated standing crops. Instead of charging landowners a flat rate (per cultivated acre), which may be subject to free riding (since a landowner could delay payment indefinitely in the expectation that others will pay), the guards are paid from the franchise money collected by the village council.

Irrigation management

The main crop in the first wet season is rice, irrigated from government-controlled canals. The crop is transplanted in July/August and harvested in December/January. Since the rains stop by the end of September, the crop is irrigated by canal water in subsequent months. The acreage to be irrigated is decided by individual farmers. Once this decision is taken, the allocation of canal water to individual holdings is decided by common irrigators. Each holding is entitled to be "adequately wetted", but it cannot get more water until the other holdings downstream from its outlet have also been adequately wetted. Any violation of this arrangement (e.g. somebody trying to steal water) is punishable with fines. Common irrigators are paid in kind from the harvest (on a per irrigated acre basis), thus ensuring against any delay in payment, for services rendered.

Wade's (1987) example suggests an ecological basis to collective action.

He points out that corporate institutions are mainly a feature of downstream villages. These villages also have a higher proportion of black soils, which are more water-retentive than red soils. As a result, there is a wider range of rain-fed crops, higher yields and, hence, a more abundant and varied supply of stubble. Given the scarcity of canal water in downstream villages, unrestrained access to canal water is likely to result in frequent conflicts and disruptions of the crop production cycle. Similarly, unrestrained access to stubble may result in frequent conflicts and standing crop losses. Corporate institutions with an effective enforcement machinery have evolved to regulate access to water and grazing.

A definitive assessment of how effective collective action is in these villages is not feasible, however, since it is difficult to find a pair of villages similar in all respects except that one possesses corporate institutions and the other does not. All that may be conjectured is that both production and equity are likely to be greater with than without collective action (in the same villages). How general are these results? Again, a definitive assessment cannot be given for no other reason than that there is a dearth of studies similar to that of Wade (1987). Yet the results are significant as they counter the pessimism in the theoretical literature on the possibility of voluntary collective action in ensuring equitable access to a subset of public goods.

Extensions and qualifications

Further insights into collective action follow from two case-studies in Chopra and Kadekodi (1991). One is a study of successful community participation in arresting environmental degradation in Sukhomajri, a village in the foothills of the Siwalik range of the Himalayas, in the Indian state of Haryana.

Over the years, this village had witnessed severe soil erosion, forest denudation and declining land productivity and the combined efforts of the central and state governments failed to arrest the degradation. However, a successful participatory process involving the local people was initiated in 1978 with the building of a storage tank. Access to water was conditional on the villagers' stall-feeding their animals to facilitate afforestation. The villagers responded enthusiastically, since access to irrigation water was likely to augment crop yields, although conflicts soon arose over the sharing of irrigation water. The conflicts were resolved in 1981 through the formation of a Water Users' Society which regulated water usage. Following this successful experiment, the domain of community management was extended to the cutting, distribution and sale of fodder. By 1985, the participatory process became self-sustainable. This example points to the crucial role of "learning by doing" in sustaining collective action. Also, as in the case of Wade's (1987) example, sustainability of collective action is enhanced when complementarities between common property resources are fully exploited. However, given imperfect information, the process of learning may well be slow.

Another interesting example is the creation of common property resources from private property resources and their conservation with community initiative in Bhusadia, a village in the Indian state of Bihar. Most of the inhabitants were either landless or had smallholdings (0.5 to 3 acres). Land productivity was low. Forests were over exploited. In 1987, through the initiative of a local non-government agency, private land and denuded common lands were pooled and converted into community land. An agroforestry scheme with a three-tier plantation programme was worked out in collaboration with regional research centres and local expertise.[17] Participants provided labour or land and were involved in decisions relating to village development and the conservation of soil, forests and water. They shared the benefits equitably. A contribution was made to the common village fund for further investments in the village. The results were impressive, with high financial returns on a sustainable basis. The key to the success of collective action in this venture was economies of scale. The conversion of small, uneconomic private holdings (together with denuded common land) into common property, and its use for large-scale agroforestry farms and plantations augmented the earnings of all participants.

---

[17] The three-tier plantation system resulted in different cycles of production. These could be annual, such as those of cereals and vegetables, of three to four years, as for fruit plantations, or of seven to ten years, as for fuelwood and timber (Chopra and Kadekodi, 1991).

Often, however, the situation corresponds to a zero-sum game in which a group's gain is perceived by another group as its loss (e.g. wage bargaining). There are a few success stories from the point of view of the rural poor. The empowerment of the rural poor through the EGS and its favourable effects on agricultural wages is a case in point (Drèze, 1988). But this is far from typical, as the following example illustrates

Labour militancy in certain regions in two southern Indian states (Tamil Nadu and Kerala) was instrumental in raising agricultural wage rates. But the potential income gain was offset by a reduction in number of days of employment. This was a direct consequence of landowners *i)* using labour-saving machinery (e.g. tractors) and *ii)* switching to alternative, less labour-intensive crops (such as casuarina or sugar cane in Tamil Nadu, or areca nut and coconut in Kerala). Often the landowners organized first against the government to protest against water taxes, reduce interest on agricultural loans or to secure various kinds of subsidies. All these were obvious issues in which smallholders also had a stake, although the stake of the rich was proportionately higher. However, once formed, these same organizations were then used against agricultural labourers (Mencher, 1988).

GUIDELINES

Although generalizations from a few case-studies are risky, some important factors underlying collective action can nevertheless be identified. In doing so, the focus will be largely on Wade's (1987) important contribution. To the extent that the government has a role in promoting collective action – especially among the rural poor – the observations made below may help delineate the nature and areas of government intervention.

If there are intensely felt needs that cannot be met by individual action – as among farmers in downstream villages in the Kurnool district of Andhra Pradesh or among the landless and small farmers who eke out a subsistence living in Bhusadia, in Bihar – cooperation is likely. However, whether such needs are rankable seems doubtful. Wade's ranking is as follows: the safeguarding of production, followed by the enhancement of income and then education, nutrition, health and civic consciousness. However, it is debatable whether this ranking is established conclusively by his empirical analysis. Alternative rankings may be possible, e.g. nutrition and health programmes in Kerala are given high priority in community initiatives.

Corporate institutions are likely to emerge in response to such needs. How effective these institutions are – specifically in ensuring equitable access to scarce common property resources – depends, among other things, on whether they are backed by the local elite (or large landowners). In Wade's (1987) sample, elite support was guaranteed by the fact that the plots of large landowners were widely scattered. Since any individual arrangement would not have been workable, it was in everybody's interest to cooperate. The local elite thus actively participated in the framing of the rules and their enforcement. However, a qualification is necessary: as long as the village council confined its role to allocating non-privatizable goods (e.g. irrigation water), it worked effectively. An attempt to include a privatizable good (e.g. rationed sugar) was unsuccessful (Wade, 1987). This is not to suggest that the domain of village councils must be restricted, since complementarities between common property resources need to be fully exploited. At the same time, full coverage of the local community – as opposed to specific groups – vests greater authority in a village council and enables it to play a more effective role. Further, efficiency of a village council improves when it is accountable to a larger body (i.e. the village community). Simple record-keeping and budgetary control procedures help in assessing its performance. In Wade's sample, income and expenditure accounts of the council were read out at an annual meeting of the village community. Finally, the enforcement of joint rules is often restricted by a weak legal framework. Governments can play an effective role in strengthening this framework and, more specifically, by recognizing the village council as a legal identity with a specific role.

To conclude, although there are grounds for optimism, it would be naïve to presume that collective action among the rural poor can be initiated and strengthened through just government support. As emphasized earlier, given imperfect information and village power structures, organizing the rural poor is not easy. The learning process among them may be slow and frustrating. Locally powerful groups may divide the poor. Yet, in a strategy of poverty alleviation, strengthening coalitions of the rural poor deserves high priority.

Chapter 11
Concluding observations

The main conclusions of this report, together with observations on data requirements for monitoring changes in rural poverty from a broad policy perspective are presented in this chapter.

It was argued that agricultural growth by itself may not make a dent in rural poverty. Even if the growth process is such that the poor participate in it, some segments, for instance the old and infirm, are likely to be left out. In fact, there is often a large hard core of the chronically poor who fail to benefit from agricultural growth. Hence, direct anti-poverty interventions such as food subsidies and rural public works (RPW) are necessary. The nature of these interventions, complementarities between them and their financing, timing and political feasibility are among the key issues.

Empirical evidence suggests a number of reasons for the failure of anti-poverty interventions.

i) Some interventions were based on a misunderstanding of the way rural markets function. High interest rates, for example, are not exploitative. As noted in Chapter 6, interest rates are high because of high screening and enforcement costs for local moneylenders. In a monopolistically competitive credit market with rationing at high interest rates in order to ensure a favourable risk-composition of projects, subsidized credit failed to lower the interest rate or to weaken the position of local moneylenders. On the other hand, the rural poor had limited access to subsidized credit because of the high transaction costs and lack of collateral.

ii) Isolated interventions in specific markets are often counterproductive where there are linkages between markets. For example, if higher agricultural wages are statutorily fixed, the gains to agricultural labourers may be partly or wholly offset by higher interest rates in the credit market when the employer is also a moneylender.

iii) The "costs" of targeting, including those borne by the poor, are seldom taken into account. An absence of administrative and other support systems makes it difficult to implement targeted interventions. Unless these support systems evolve, self-targeting interventions such as RPW would have a major role in poverty alleviation. However, the experience with RPW has not been altogether satisfactory, mainly because of deficiencies in their design.

iv) The role of human capital (e.g. education and health) has been neglected in poverty alleviation. However, in order to make the poor self-reliant it is necessary to include the provision of human capital. Besides the inadequacy of public expenditure in this area, the allocation has been lopsided, e.g. primary education has been relatively neglected. Moreover, in the context of structural adjustment and, more specifically, the need to curb fiscal deficit, it is imperative to raise more revenue through selective user cost pricing.

v) Certain types of anti-poverty programmes have usually been abandoned or implemented half-heartedly because of resistance from some influential sections. The redistribution of land is a case in point. Strengthening the coalitions of the rural poor is likely to be crucial for the success of such poverty alleviation measures.

Following are suggestions regarding what the government can and should do for designing appropriate anti-poverty interventions.

Given the strong complementarities between different anti-poverty interventions, there is a case for simultaneous and well-coordinated interventions in land, labour and credit markets. The concern that such a strategy may exceed the administrative capabilities of most developing countries appears to be exaggerated, since government intervention would be limited in certain markets. Admittedly, even a considerably restricted role for the government may not be feasible in all cases. But this does not weaken the general case for simultaneous and coordinated government interventions in different markets.

As noted in Chapter 5, both on efficiency and equity grounds, there is a strong case for land redistribution. However, it is necessary to eliminate certain anomalies such as fixing land ceilings for some crops but not all; avoid tenancy regulations, especially restrictions on share tenancy; encourage the use of the market mechanism through, for example, a progressive land tax; and overcome political resistance through, among other changes, a lowering of land ceilings.

As discussed in Chapter 6, the case for the provision of subsidized credit is weak. Instead, more attention needs to be given to measures designed to lower the screening and enforcement costs for lenders and the transaction costs for borrowers – especially among smallholders and agricultural labourers. Group lending is an important innovation in this context. An appropriate role for the government is to help in organizing groups and ensure the strict enforcement of joint liability rules. The groups must be small, homogeneous and self-managed.

There is growing awareness that the promotion of self- employment opportunities is likely to benefit only a limited segment of the rural poor and, therefore, RPW can play a more significant role in poverty alleviation. An important feature of RPW is that they are self-targeting: only the needy are likely to come for manual labour (at a relatively low wage). Besides, RPW may help to organize the rural poor into an effective coalition. As discussed in Chapter 7, although RPW have been well targeted, they suffer from a number of design deficiencies. For instance, a low wage could be fixed to ensure a wide coverage. In some cases this is better than limited coverage at high wages. Rigid restrictions on a minimum wage share in total outlay tend to limit project selection. Contrary to common belief and practice, there is little justification for concentrating RPW activity in agriculturally slack periods. Also, if there are budgetary constraints to financing RPW on a large scale, they may be initiated on a small scale and expanded gradually.

The scaling down or gradual withdrawal of food subsidies as a safety net (when appropriate) is feasible if it is linked to other major policy reforms such as the decontrolling of markets. If the underlying rationale of such policy reforms is well publicized, especially their fairness to all sections, political resistance is likely to weaken. However, as noted in Chapter 8, food subsidies must continue for some specific groups of the poor such as the old, infirm and pregnant and lactating women. Since means testing at frequent intervals is prohibitively expensive, it is imperative to identify other targeting indicators, namely location. Also, the use of simple registration procedures would reduce transaction costs for the poor and enhance their access to subsidized food.

Greater emphasis on the provision of human capital is necessary to enable the poor to break out of the vicious circle of poverty. However, as emphasized in Chapter 9, allocations of public expenditure within the education and health sectors have been both inefficient and inequitable. Shifts in favour of programmes for primary education as well as for primary health care and communicable disease control are necessary. Selectively imposed user fees for services for which there is private willingness to pay (e.g. hospital care), and on certain groups (e.g. middle- and upper-income urban consumers) would yield revenues both to expand primary education and primary health care facilities in rural areas and to improve their quality. At the same time, it is important to continue subsidies on health care, food and education for the poor (provided, of course, targeting indicators exist). Women's education and health are important in their own right and warrant imaginative, wide-ranging interventions. For example, the expansion of female education requires not just a lowering of the opportunity cost of attending a school but also concerted efforts to overcome parental resistance.

Agricultural extension programmes require reorientation. Specifically, there is some concern that small farmers – especially women – have been neglected. This in part reflects the diminutive presence of women among extension workers. It is therefore, necessary to recruit and train substantially more female extension workers. Another aspect that needs emphasis is client participation. This is likely to impart greater relevance to extension programmes. Besides, it may facilitate cost-sharing which is an important issue in the context of declining public expenditure on extension. Although a blanket policy of charging farmers a fee may not be workable, a fee or cess applicable to commercial farmers operating on a large scale may be easier to administer.

Finally, as emphasized in Chapter 10, strengthening the coalitions of the rural poor is of utmost importance. While some useful insights are suggested by recent studies of community participation in the management of common property resources, few generalizations can be made about the possibility of collective action by the rural poor for more equitable allocations of private goods. In wage bargaining in an oligopsonistic rural labour market, for example, workers seldom succeed in negotiating higher wages. An effective employment guarantee may, however, add to the bargaining power of agricultural labourers.

All of this of course presumes that relevant data for monitoring changes in rural poverty and for assessing the impact of policies is not a constraint. This is seldom the case. With the exception of a few countries, income distribution and other related data continue to be scarce. Although some UN organizations have been engaged in developing a set of indicators to facilitate the collection and compilation of relevant data – a notable example being FAO's Socio-Economic Indicator Programme – the results have been far from encouraging.[1] As of now, only one cross-section of headcount ratios (a measure of the incidence of poverty) on a broadly comparable basis for rural areas is available for selected developing countries for the period 1977-1980. Although the availability of data on other indicators of well-being is better (several UN and other organizations publish them regularly), these data are also limited in some ways.

- Very few of these indicators (such as the percentage of population with access to health services, safe drinking water and sanitation) are available separately for rural and urban areas. This is a serious limitation in the context of rural poverty analysis, as inferences – which are largely conjectural – have to be drawn from national indicators.
- Another difficulty stems from the method of construction of these indicators. A few of these (e.g. life expectancy at birth) are obtained

---

[1] This programme has two complementary objectives: *i)* to assist countries in monitoring their progress in implementing the World Conference on Agrarian Reform and Rural Development (WCARRD) Programme of Action and *ii)* to assemble and update regularly a WCARRD database at FAO headquarters. Efforts under the first objective concentrated on developing concepts and definitions of appropriate socio-economic indicators and methods for their application, which culminated in a set of guidelines in FAO (1988b). For a review, see FAO (1991c).

from life tables which are updated periodically but usually on the basis of limited evidence. Hence, precise comparisons of changes in these indicators over time are difficult.

- In general, these indicators (e.g. infant mortality rate) are not available for different socio-economic categories, making it difficult to correlate changes in poverty with changes in these indicators, for specific segments of the rural population (e.g. agricultural labour households). This is one reason why it is difficult to explain divergent movements in conventional income-based measures of poverty and some of these indicators of well-being.

Except for a few country-specific studies, very little is known about the relationship between rural poverty and the agricultural growth process. From a policy perspective, it is not enough to know that rural poverty and agricultural growth are inversely related since, depending on whether smallholders have access to credit and consequently to improved techniques, the strength of this relationship would vary. Additionally, as argued in Chapter 3, if there is a hard core of the poor – that subset of the poor, who even with access to land and other inputs are likely to remain poor because of certain innate disadvantages – the inverse relationship between rural poverty and agricultural growth would be further weakened. Our limited understanding of these issues is largely a direct consequence of a lack of analytical focus in sample surveys that are carried out periodically in some developing countries. An appropriate focus is suggested by Sen's (1981) entitlement framework.

This framework consists of an endowment vector/ownership bundle (e.g. arable land, agricultural implements) and an exchange entitlement mapping (i.e. command over alternative bundles of goods and services of a given ownership vector, for example over food, clothing and shelter). The command over alternative bundles of goods and services may be established through trade or production or a combination of both. Given that the poverty cut-off point represents a nutritionally adequate diet, the poor are those whose entitlements fall short of this norm. By basing sample surveys on such a framework, a detailed profile of the rural poor can be constructed and a definitive analysis of their entitlement failures (whether they are caused by a production shortfall or an adverse price movement, for example) would be feasible. It is not being suggested that this framework is easily implementable. Given the weak statistical systems, it will be some years before an appropriately designed survey may be carried out. Yet a beginning along the lines indicated is necessary to impart greater credibility to rural poverty alleviation as a major policy concern and to help design effective remedial policies. While a detailed discussion of the nature of surveys that would be useful is beyond the scope of this report, some observations are made below to put this discussion in perspective.[2]

• An important issue is the relative strengths and weaknesses of large- and small-scale surveys (including village surveys). While large-scale surveys (such as the National Sample Surveys of consumption expenditure distribution in India) have the advantage of standardized concepts and definitions and representativeness, they tend to be expensive and time-consuming. In a large country, coupled with a scarcity of trained investigators, the results of a large-scale survey are more likely to be vitiated by non-sampling errors (e.g. investigator bias). Furthermore, sometimes the gap between the collection and availability of survey results can be five years or more.[3] In the context of poverty alleviation programmes, this could be a serious constraint. This is not to suggest that small-scale surveys are necessarily better. They have their own difficulties, such as a lack of representativeness, non-uniformity of concepts and sample designs and, consequently, limited generalizability from a macro perspective. Their merits, however, are several: richness of contextual detail, participant observation and personal rapport of the researcher/investigator with the respondents, and quicker and less expensive data collection.[4] Through subtle and careful interviewing of

---

[2] For a more detailed exposition, see FAO (1991c).

[3] Large-scale surveys are usually multipurpose. This necessarily forces some trade-offs which small-scale surveys do not have to face to the same degree. However, a small-sized annual rotating panel can help mitigate the impact of these trade-offs (Srinivasan, 1989). For a further note on panel surveys, see p. 216.

[4] As long as the rules of random sample selection are observed, even a few village surveys can provide reliable estimates, since what matters is the absolute size of the sample and variation in the population of the characteristic being estimated (Srinivasan, 1989).

respondents, certain qualitative and non-observable aspects (e.g. motivation) can be captured with greater success in small-scale surveys. This arguably gives such surveys an edge over large-scale surveys in capturing certain processes of change (e.g. empowerment of the rural poor).[5] The point is that, no matter how comprehensive a set of indicators is, a great deal of improvisation around them is often unavoidable, either because the researcher fails to anticipate the complexity of a phenomenon or because some aspects of it are not amenable to straightforward measurement or analysis. This imparts a certain degree of flexibility to small-scale surveys which is typically lacking in large-scale surveys.

• Another issue is whether rural poverty analysis should rely on evidence from independent cross-sections (i.e. surveys in which households are randomly selected at different points in time) or on evidence from panel surveys (in which the same set of households is surveyed successively at different points in time) when the results of the two types of surveys are known to diverge. Some recent studies (e.g. Ashenfelter, Deaton and Solon, 1986; Srinivasan, 1989) favour the use of panel surveys provided the variable or characteristic in question is positively serially correlated – for instance, households with low incomes in one period have low incomes in the next. This is particularly important in the context of income dynamics. If low-income households in one period have low incomes in the next period, panel surveys would yield a more accurate assessment of temporal changes in income over the period in question.[6] But panel surveys present their own difficulties, one of which is that the results get distorted by life cycle effects, i.e.

---

[5] See, for example, Drèze (1988).

[6] The variance of the estimate of a difference depends negatively on the covariance between the estimated means. Hence, change is measured most precisely when the covariance is as large as possible. Independent cross-sections have a zero expected covariance while a completely overlapping panel exploits the positive correlation in the raw data to maximize the covariance between the estimated means. In consequence, the most accurate estimates of change from a given sample size are obtained from pure panel data (Ashenfelter, Deaton and Solon, 1986).

ageing of the sample households as well as the dissolution of households, especially if the sample period is long.[7] It may be worthwhile to combine a small rotating panel of households annually along with a large quinquennial survey.[8]

- Finally, one general observation is in order. There are often inordinate delays in making the results of surveys available for analysis. It is arguable that this is largely a consequence of not allocating resources judiciously between data collection and the timely coding, taping, cleaning and tabulating of data. Large-scale surveys are particularly vulnerable to long delays – delays of up to five years, for example, are not unusual. There is very little point in spending large sums of money on collecting data that will not be available in time for policy analysis. It is therefore of the utmost importance that collection and tabulation of data are synchronized with policy requirements.

---

[7] As Ashenfelter, Deaton and Solon (1986) observe: " ... the further apart are the successive waves of the panel, the lower will tend to be the correlation between successive observations and thus the smaller the net advantage of the overlapping generations" (p. 6).

[8] If the interest is not merely in the change in mean between periods but also in the means of each period, a rotating panel trades off some loss of precision in estimating the change for a gain in precision in estimating means (Ashenfelter, Deaton and Solon, 1986).

References

Ahmad, S.E. 1989. *Social security and poverty alleviation: issues for developing countries.* Washington, DC, World Bank. (mimeo)

Akerlof, G.A. 1984. *An economic theorist's book of tales.* Cambridge, UK, Cambridge University Press.

Alderman, H. 1991. Food subsidies and the poor. *In* G. Psacharopoulos, ed. *Essays on poverty, equity and growth.* Oxford, Pergamon Press.

Alderman, H. & Von Braun, J. 1984. *The effects of the Egyptian food rationing and subsidy system on income distribution and consumption.* Washington, DC, IFPRI.

Alderman, H. & Paxson, C. 1992. *Do the poor insure?* Washington, DC, World Bank. (mimeo)

Aleem, I. 1990. Imperfect information, screening, and the costs of informal lending: a study of a rural credit market in Pakistan. *World Bank Econ. Rev.,* 4.

Apte, D.P. 1982. *Evaluation of an integrated dairy development scheme (Warangar).* Poona, India, Gokhale Institute of Economics and Politics. (mimeo)

Ashenfelter, O., Deaton, A. & Solon, G. 1986. *Collecting panel data in developing countries: does it make sense?* Washington, DC, World Bank. (mimeo)

Atkinson, A.B. 1970. On the measurement of inequality. *J. Econ. Theory,* 2.

Atkinson, A.B. 1975. *The economics of inequality.* Oxford, Clarendon Press.

Atkinson, A.B. 1987. On the measurement of poverty. *Econometrica,* 55.

Bardhan, P. 1974a. The pattern of income distribution in India: a review. *Sankhya,* 36 (special issue).

Bardhan, P. 1974b. On life and death questions. *Econ. Polit. Wkly,* August (special issue).

Bardhan, P. 1982. Little girls and death in India. *Econ. Polit. Wkly,* 17.

Bardhan, P. 1985. Poverty and "trickle down" in rural India. A quantitative analysis. *In* J.W. Mellor & G.M. Desai, eds. *Agricultural change and rural poverty: variations on a theme by Dharm Narain.* Baltimore, The Johns Hopkins University Press.

Bardhan, P. 1988. Sex disparity in child survival in India. *In* T.N. Srinivasan & P. Bardhan, eds. *Rural poverty in South Asia.* New York, Columbia University Press.

Basu, K. 1981. Food for Work Programme: beyond roads that get washed away. *Econ. Polit. Wkly,* 16.

Basu, K. 1984. *The less developed economy.* New Delhi, Oxford University Press.

Basu, K. 1991. The elimination of endemic poverty in South Asia: some policy options. *In* J. Drèze & A. Sen, eds. *The political economy of hunger, Vol. III.* Oxford, Clarendon Press.

Becker, G.S. 1981. *A treatise on the family.* Cambridge, MA, Harvard University Press.

Behrman, J. 1988. *Nutrient intakes and income: tightly wedded or loosely meshed?* Ithaca, Cornell University.

Behrman, J. 1990. *The action of human resources and poverty on one another.* Washington, DC, World Bank. (mimeo)

Behrman, J.R. 1991. Nutrition, health and development. *In* G. Psacharopoulos, ed. *Essays on poverty, equity and growth.* New York, Pergamon Press.

Behrman. J. & Deolalikar, A. 1987. Will developing country nutrition improve with income? A case study for rural South India. *J. Polit. Econ.,* 95.

Behrman. J. & Deolalikar, A. 1988. *How do food prices affect individual health and nutritional status? A latent variable fixed effects analysis.* Philadelphia, University of Pennsylvania. (mimeo)

Behrman. J. & Deolalikar, A. 1990. *Do Indonesian labour markets favour women?* Seattle, University of Washington. (mimeo)

Bell, C. 1990a. Reforming property rights in land and tenancy. *World Bank Res. Obs.,* 5.

Bell, C. 1990b. Interaction between institutional and informal credit agencies in rural India. *World Bank Econ. Rev.,* 4(3).

Berg, A. 1987. *Malnutrition: what can be done? Lessons from the World Bank experience.* Baltimore, The Johns Hopkins University Press.

Berlin, I. 1969. *Four essays on liberty.* London, Oxford University Press.

Berry, R.A. & Cline, W.R. 1979. *Agrarian structure and productivity in developing countries.* Baltimore, The Johns Hopkins University Press.

Besley, T. 1990. Means testing versus universal provision in poverty alleviation programmes. *Economica,* 57.

Besley, T. 1992. *How do market failures justify interventions in rural credit markets?* New Jersey, Woodrow Wilson School, Princeton University. (mimeo)

Besley, T. & Coate, S. 1990. *Workfare versus welfare: incentive arguments for work requirements in poverty alleviation programmes.* New Jersey, Woodrow Wilson School, Princeton University. (mimeo)

Besley, T. & Kanbur, R. 1988. Food subsidies and poverty alleviation. *Econ. J.,* 98.

Besley, T. & Kanbur, R. 1991. *The principles of targeting.* Policy Research and External Affairs Working Paper. Washington, DC, World Bank. (mimeo)

Bhalla, S. & Roy, P. 1988. Misspecification in farm productivity analysis: the role of land quality. *Oxford Econ. Papers,* 40.

Bhende, M.J., Walker, T.S., Lieberman, S.S. & Venkatraman, J. 1990. *The EGS and the poor: evidence from longitudinal village studies.* Hyderabad, ICRISAT. (processed)

Binswanger, H. & Elgin, M.M. 1990. Reflections on land reform and farm size. *In* C.K. Eicher & J.M. Staatz, eds. *Agricultural development in the Third World.* Baltimore, The Johns Hopkins University Press.

Binswanger, H. & Quizon, J.B. 1984. *Distributional consequences of alternative food prices in India.* Washington, DC, World Bank. (mimeo)

Birkhaueser, D., Evenson, R. & Feder, G. 1989. *The economic impact of agricultural extension: a review.* New Haven, Yale University Press. (mimeo)

Bliss, C. 1985. A note on the price variable, *In* J.W. Mellor & G.M. Desai, eds. *Agricultural change and rural poverty: variations on a theme by Dharm Narain.* Baltimore, The Johns Hopkins University Press.

Bolnick, B.R. 1992. Moneylenders and informal financial markets in Malawi. *World Dev.,* 20.

Bourguignon, F. & Fields, G. 1990. Poverty measures and anti-poverty policy. *Recherches economiques de Louvain,* 56.

Bratton, M. 1986. Financing smallholder production: a comparison of individual and group credit schemes in Zimbabwe. *Public Adm. Dev.,* 6.

Brotowasisto, G., Gish, O., Malik, R. & Sudharto, P. 1988. Health care financing in Indonesia. *Health Policy Planning,* 3.

Bruce, J. 1988. A perspective on indigenous land tenure systems and land concentration. *In* R. Downs & S. Reyna, eds. *Land and society in contemporary Africa.* Hanover, University Press of New England.

Burgess, R. & Stern, N. 1989. *Social security in developing countries: what, why, who and how?* London, STICERD, London School of Economics and Political Science. (mimeo)

Cain, M. & Lieberman, S.S. 1983. Development policy and the prospects for fertility decline in Bangladesh. *Bangladesh Dev. Stud.,* 11.

Chen, L.C. 1982. Where have the women gone? Insights from Bangladesh on low sex ratio of India's population. *Econ. Polit. Wkly,* March 6.

Chen, L.C., Huq, E. & D'Souza, S. 1980. *A study of sex-biased beha-viour in the intrafamily allocation of food and the utilization of health care services in rural Bangladesh.* Bangladesh, ICDDR and Department of Population Sciences, Harvard School of Public Health. (mimeo)

Chopra, K. & Kadekodi, G. 1991. Participatory institutions: the context of common and private property resources. *Environ. Resour. Econ.,* 1.

Clark, D.H. 1983. *How secondary school graduates perform in the labour market: a study of Indonesia.* Washington, DC, World Bank.

Cornia, G. 1985. Farm size, land yields and the agricultural production function: an analysis for 15 developing countries. *World Dev.,* 13.

Cox, D. & Jimenez, E. 1990. Achieving social objectives through private transfers: a review. *World Bank Res. Obs.,* 5.

Cripps, F., Griffith, J., Morrell, F., Reid, J., Townsend, P. & Weir, S. 1981. *Manifesto, a radical strategy for Britain's future.* London, Pan Books.

Dandekar, K. 1975. Why has the proportion of women in India's population been declining? *Econ. Polit. Wkly,* October 18.

Dandekar, K. & Sathe, M. 1980. Employment Garantee Scheme and Food for Work Programme. *Econ. Polit. Wkly*, 15.

Das Gupta, M. 1987. Selective discrimination against female children in rural Punjab, India. *Pop. Dev. Rev.*, 13.

Das Gupta, P. 1989. *Well-being and the extent of its realisation in poor countries.* London, STICERD, London School of Economics and Political Science. (mimeo)

Datt, G. & Ravallion, M. 1990. *Growth and redistribution components of changes in poverty measures: a decomposition with applications to Brazil and India in the 1980s.* Washington, DC, World Bank. (mimeo)

Deaton, A. & Muellbauer, J. 1980. *Economics and consumer behaviour.* Cambridge, UK, Cambridge University Press.

de Ferranti, D. 1985. *Paying for health services in developing countries: an overview.* Washington, DC, World Bank. (mimeo)

de Janvry, A. & Subbarao, K. 1986. *Agricultural price policy and income distribution in India.* New Delhi, Oxford University Press.

de Janvry, A., Fargeix, A. & Sadoulet, E. 1992. The political feasibility of rural poverty reduction. *J. Dev. Econ.*, 37.

Deolalikar, A. 1988. Nutrition and labour productivity in agriculture: wage equation and farm production function estimates for rural India. *Rev. Econ. Stat.*, 70

Deolalikar, A. & Gaiha, R. 1992. *Targeting of rural public works: are women less likely to participate?* Washington, DC, IFPRI. (mimeo)

Demsetz, H. 1967. Toward a theory of property rights. *Am. Econ. Rev.*, 57.

Dornbusch, R. & Edwards, S. 1989. *Macroeconomic populism in Latin America.* Cambridge, MA, NBER. (mimeo)

Drèze, J. 1988. *Social insecurity in India.* London, STICERD, London School of Economics and Political Science. (mimeo)

Drèze, J. & Sen, A. 1989. *Hunger and public action.* Oxford, Clarendon Press.

Drèze, J., Lanjouw, P. & Sharma, N. *Credit in a north Indian village – an empirical investigation.* (in press)

Echeverri-Gent, J. 1988. Guaranteed employment in an Indian state: the Maharashtra experience. *Asian Surv.*, 28.

Evenson, R.E. & Kislev, Y. 1975. *Agricultural research and productivity.* New Haven, Yale University Press.

FAO. 1985. Different perspectives: West Java project on rural household economics and the role of women. In *Women in developing agriculture.* Rome, FAO.

FAO. 1988a. *Effectiveness of agricultural extension services in reaching rural women in Africa,* Vol. 2. Rome, FAO.

FAO. 1988b. *Guidelines on socio-economic indicators for monitoring and evaluating agrarian reform and rural development.* Rome, FAO.

FAO. 1988c. *Guide to alternative extension approaches.* Rome, FAO.

FAO. 1990a. *Global consultation on agricultural extension.* Rome, FAO.

FAO. 1990b. *Rural poverty alleviation: strategies and progress.* Rome, FAO. (typescript)

FAO. 1990c. *Rural services and public works.* Background paper for the Third Progress Report on WCARRD Programme of Action. Rome, FAO. (typescript)

FAO. 1991a. *Third Progress Report on WCARRD Programme of Action.* C91/19. Rome, FAO. (mimeo)

FAO. 1991b. *Employment, wages and the rural poor.* Rome, FAO.

FAO. 1991c. *The use of socio-economic indicators for evaluating progress in implementing the programme of action of the World Conference on Agrarian Reform and Rural Development.* Rome, FAO. (mimeo) (to be published by Transaction Books)

Feder, G., Lau, L.J. & Slade, R.H. 1985. *The impact of agricultural extension: a case study of the training and visit system in Haryana and India.* Washington, DC, World Bank. (mimeo)

Feder, G., Onchan, T., Chalamwong, Y. & Hongladarom, C. 1986. *Land ownership security, farm productivity and land policies in Thailand.* Washington, DC, World Bank. (mimeo)

Feder, G. & Noronha, R. 1987. Land rights systems and agricultural development in rural sub-Saharan Africa. *World Bank Res. Obs.,* 2.

Finer, S.E. 1962. *The man on horseback.* London, Pall Mall.

Foster, J., Greer, J. & Thorbecke, E. 1984. A class of decomposable poverty measures. *Econometrica,* 52.

Gaiha, R. 1985. Poverty, technology and infrastructure in rural India. *Cambridge J. Econ.,* 9.

Gaiha, R. 1987. Impoverishment,

technology and growth in rural India. *Cambridge J. Econ.*, 11.

Gaiha, R. 1988. On measuring the risk of poverty in rural India. *In* T.N. Srinivasan & P. Bardhan, eds. *Rural poverty in South Asia.* New York, Columbia University Press.

Gaiha, R. 1989a. Rural poverty in India: an assessment. *Asian Surv.*, 29.

Gaiha, R. 1989b. Are the chronically poor also the poorest in rural India? *Dev. Change,* 20.

Gaiha, R. 1989c. Poverty, agricultural production and prices in rural India – a reformulation. *Cambridge J. Econ.*, 13.

Gaiha, R. 1991. Poverty alleviation programmes in rural India: an assessment. *Dev. Change,* 22.

Gaiha, R. 1992. On the chronically poor in rural India. *J. Int. Dev.,* 4.

Gaiha, R. & Deolalikar, A. 1992. *Permanent, expected and innate poverty: estimates for semi-arid rural south India, 1975-84.* Seattle, University of Washington. (mimeo) (also to appear in Cambridge J. Econ.).

Gaiha, R. & Kazmi, N. 1981. Aspects of poverty in rural India. *Econ. Planning,* 17.

Gaiha, R. & Spinedi, M. 1992. *Infant mortality and public policy.*

Paper prepared for presentation at the World Congress of the International Economic Association, Moscow, August 1992. (to appear in Public Finance)

Gertler, P., Locay, L. & Sanderson, W. 1987. Are user fees regressive? The welfare implications of health care financing proposals in Peru. *J. Econometrics,* 33.

Gertler, P. & Glewwe, P. 1989. *The willingness to pay for education in developing countries: evidence from rural Peru.* Washington, DC, World Bank. (mimeo)

Gertler, P. & Van der Gaag, J. 1990. *The willingness to pay for medical care: evidence from two developing countries.* Baltimore, The Johns Hopkins University Press.

Gish, O., Malik, R. & Sudharto, P. 1988. Who gets what? Utilisation of health services in Indonesia. *Int. J. Health Planning Manage.,* 3.

Government of the Philippines. 1990. Country report submitted for the Third Progress Report on WCARRD Programme of Action (C19/91). (typescript)

Greer, J. & Thorbecke, E. 1986. A methodology for measuring food poverty applied to Kenya. *J. Dev. Econ.,* 24.

Gulati, L. 1977. Rationing in a peri-urban community: case study of a squatter habitat. *Econ. Polit. Wkly,* March 19.

Haddad, L. & Bouis, H. 1989. *The impact of nutritional status on agricultural productivity: wage evidence from the Philippines.* Washington, DC, IFPRI. (mimeo)

Haddad, L. & Kanbur, R. 1989. *How serious is the neglect of intrahousehold inequality?* Washington, DC, World Bank. (mimeo)

Hardin, G. 1968. The tragedy of the commons. *Science,* 162.

Hart, K. 1987. Commoditisation and the standard of living. *In* G. Hawthorn, ed. *The standard of living.* Cambridge, UK, Cambridge University Press.

Hayami, Y. 1991. Land reform. *In* G. Meir, ed. *Politics and policy making in developing countries.* San Francisco, International Centre for Economic Growth.

Herring, R.J. & Edwards, R.M. 1983. Guaranteeing employment to the rural poor: social functions and class interests in Employment Guarantee Scheme in western India. *World Dev.,* 11.

Herz, B., Subbarao, K., Habib, M. & Raney, L. 1991. *Letting girls learn.* Washington, DC, World Bank. (mimeo)

Himmelfarb, G. 1984. *The idea of poverty.* New York, Knopf.

Hoddinott, J. 1992. *Household economics and the economics of households.* Oxford, Trinity College. (mimeo)

Hoff, K. & Stiglitz, J. 1990. Introduction: imperfect information and rural credit markets – puzzles and policy perspectives. *World Bank Econ. Rev.,* 4.

Hossain, M. 1988. *Credit for alleviation of rural poverty: the Grameen Bank in Bangladesh.* Washington, DC, IFPRI. (mimeo)

Huppi, M. & Feder, G. 1990. The role of groups and credit cooperatives in rural lending. *World Bank Res. Obs.,* 5.

Islam, R. 1986. Non-farm employment in rural Asia: issues and evidence. *In* R.D. Shand, ed. *Off-farm employment in the development of rural Asia.* Canberra, Australian National University.

Jackman, R.W. 1976. Politicians in uniform: military governments and social change in the Third World. *Am. Polit. Sci. Rev.,* 70

Jamison, D.T. 1986. Child malnutrition and school performance in China. *J. Dev. Econ.,* 20.

Jamison, D.T. & Lau, L.J. 1982. *Farmer education and farm effi-*

ciency. Baltimore, The Johns Hopkins University Press.

Jarvis, L.S. 1989. The unravelling of Chile's agrarian reform, 1973-1986. *In* W.C. Thiesenhusen, ed. *Searching for agrarian reform in Latin America.* Boston, Unwin Hyman.

Jha, S. 1992. Consumer subsidies in India: is targeting effective? *Dev. Change,* 23(4).

Jimenez, E. 1987. *Pricing policy in the social sectors: cost recovery for education and health.* Baltimore, The Johns Hopkins University Press.

Jodha, N.S. 1986. Common property resources and the rural poor in dry regions of India. *Econ. Polit. Wkly,* July 5.

Kahn, H. 1979. *World Economic Development,* London, Croom Helm.

Kakwani, N. & Subbarao, K. 1990. Rural poverty and its alleviation in India. *Econ. Polit. Wkly,* March 31.

Kanbur, R. 1987. Targeting, transfers and poverty. *Econ. Policy,* 4.

Kirchner, J., Singh, I. & Squire, L. 1984. *Agricultural pricing and marketing policies in Malawi.* Washington, DC, World Bank. (mimeo)

Kohli, A. 1987. *The state and poverty in India.* Cambridge, UK, Cambridge University Press.

Kouwenaar, A. 1988. *A basic needs policy model: a general equilibrium analysis with special reference to Ecuador.* Amsterdam, North-Holland.

Kutcher, G.P. & Scandizzo, P.L. 1981. *The agricultural economy of northeast Brazil.* Washington, DC, World Bank. (mimeo)

Levinson, D. 1989. *Family violence in cross-cultural perspective.* Newbury Park, Sage.

Lin, J.Y. 1992. Rural reforms and agricultural growth in China. *Am. Econ. Rev.,* 82 (March).

Lipset, S. 1959. Some social requisites of democracy: economic development and political legitimacy. *Am. Polit. Sci. Rev.,* 53.

Lipton, M. 1974. Towards a theory of land reform. *In* D. Lehmann, ed. *Agrarian Reform and Reformism.* Cambridge, UK, Cambridge University Press.

Lipton, M. 1983. *Poverty, undernutrition and hunger.* Washington, DC, World Bank. (mimeo)

Lipton, M. 1988. *The poor and poorest: some interim findings.* Washington, DC, World Bank. (mimeo)

Lipton, M. 1991. *Land reform as commenced business: the evidence against stopping.* Paper presented at ILO-Cornell University Conf. on State, Market and Civil Institutions: New Theories, New Practices and their Implications for Rural Dvelopment, Ithaca. (mimeo)

Lipton, M. & Longhurst, R. 1989. *New seeds and poor people.* Baltimore, The Johns Hopkins University Press.

Lipton, M. & Van der Gaag, J. 1991. Poverty: a research and policy framework. *In* M. Lipton & J. Van der Gaag, eds. *Including the poor.*

Lucas, R. & Stark, O. 1985. Motivations to remit. *J. Polit. Econ.*, 93.

Lundberg, S. & Pollak, R. 1991. *Separate spheres: bargaining and the marriage market.* Seattle, University of Washington. (mimeo)

Maitra, T. 1988. Rural poverty in West Bengal. *In* T.N. Srinivasan & P. Bardhan, eds. *Rural poverty in South Asia.* New York, Columbia University Press.

Manser, M. & Brown, M. 1980. Marriage and household decision-making – a bargaining analysis. *Int. Econ. Rev.*, 21.

McElroy, M. 1990. The empirical content of Nash bargained household behaviour. *J. Hum. Resour.*, 25.

McElroy, M. & Horney, M. 1981. Nash bargained household decision: toward a generalization of the theory of demand. *Int. Econ. Rev.*, 22.

Mencher, J. 1988. Peasants and agricultural labourers: an analytical assessment of issues in their organising. *In* T.N. Srinivasan & P. Bardhan, eds. *Rural poverty in South Asia.* New York, Columbia University Press.

Migot-Adholla, S., Hazell, P., Blarel, B. & Place, F. 1990. Indigenous land rights system in sub-Saharan Africa: a constraint on policy. *World Bank Econ. Rev.*, 5.

Mill, J.S. 1848. *Principles of political economy,* Books IV and V. Harmondsworth, Penguin Books.

Miller, B.D. 1981. *The endangered sex: neglect of female children in rural north India.* Ithaca, Cornell University Press.

Minhas, S.B., Jain, L.R., Kansal, S.M. & Saluja, M.R. 1987. *On the choice of appropriate consumer price indices and data sets for estimating the incidence of poverty in India.* New Delhi, Indian Statistical Institute. (mimeo)

Moock, P.R. & Leslie, J. 1986. Childhood malnutrition and schooling in the Terai region of Nepal. *J. Dev. Econ.*, 20.

Muellbauer, J. 1987. Professor Sen on the standard of living. *In* G. Hawthorn, ed. *The standard of living.* Cambridge, UK, Cambridge University Press.

Naert, F. 1985. The political economy of pressure groups. *J. Public Finan. Public Choice*, 55-63.

Narayana, N.S.S., Parikh, K.S. & Srinivasan, T.N. 1988. Rural works programs in India: costs and benefits. *J. Dev. Econ.*, 29(2).

Narayana, N.S.S., Parikh, K.S. & Srinivasan, T.N. 1991. *Agriculture, growth and redistribution of income.* Amsterdam, North-Holland.

Newbery, D.M.G. 1977. Risk sharing, share cropping and uncertain labour markets. *Rev. Econ. Stud.*, 44.

Olson, M. 1968. Multivariate analysis of national political development. *Am. Sociol. Rev.*, 33.

Olson, M. 1971. *The logic of collective action.* Cambridge, MA, Harvard University Press.

Olson, M. 1982. *The rise and decline of nations: economic growth, stagflation and social rigidities.* New Haven, Yale Universtiy Press.

Osmani, S.R. 1988. *Social security in South Asia.* London, STICERD, London School of Economics and Political Science. (mimeo)

Osmani, S.R. & Chowdhury, O.H. 1983. Short run impact of Food for Work Programme in Bangladesh. *Bangladesh Dev. Stud.*, 11.

Otsuka, K. 1990. *Land tenure and rural poverty: a review of issues.* Manila, Asian Development Bank. (mimeo)

Parikh, K. & Srinivasan, T.N. 1989. *Poverty alleviation policies in India: food consumption subsidy, food production subsidy and employment generation.* New Haven, Yale University Press. (mimeo)

Pigou, A.C. 1952. *The economics of welfare.* London, Macmillan.

Pingali, P. & Vo Tong Xuan. 1992. Vietnam: decollectivization and rice productivity growth. *Econ. Dev. Cultural Change,* July.

Platteau, J.-Ph. 1990. The food crisis in Africa: a comparative structural analysis. *In* J.Drèze & A. Sen, eds. *The political economy of hunger, Vol. II.* Oxford, Clarendon Press.

Preston, S. 1980. Causes and consequences of mortality declines in less developed countries during the twentieth century. *In* R.A. Easterlin, ed. *Population and economic change in developing countries.* Chicago, University of Chicago Press.

Psacharopoulos, G. & Loxley, W.

1985. *Diversified secondary education and development: evidence from Colombia and Tanzania.* Baltimore, The Johns Hopkins Universtiy Press.

Psacharopoulos, G. & Woodhall, M. 1985. *Education for development.* New York, Oxford University Press.

Pulley, R.V. 1989. *Making the poor credit worthy.* Washington, DC, World Bank. (mimeo)

Putterman, L. 1985. Extrinsic versus intrinsic problems of agricultural cooperation: anti-incentivism in Tanzania and China. *J. Dev. Stud.,* 21.

Pyatt, F. 1984. *Measuring welfare, poverty and inequality.* Washington, DC, World Bank. (typescript)

Rath, N. 1985. Garibi Hatao. Can IRDP do it? *Econ. Polit. Wkly,* February 9.

Ravallion, M. 1989. *On the coverage of public employment schemes for poverty alleviation.* Washington, DC, World Bank. (mimeo)

Ravallion, M. 1991a. Reaching the rural poor through public employment: arguments, evidence and lessons for South Asia. *World Bank Res. Obs.,* 6.

Ravallion, M. 1991b. Market responses to anti-hunger policies: wages, prices and employment. *In* J. Drèze & A. Sen, eds. *The political economy of hunger, Vol. II.* Oxford, Clarendon Press.

Ravallion, M. 1992. *Poverty comparisons.* Washington, DC, World Bank. (mimeo)

Ravallion, M. & Datt, G. 1992. *Is targeting through a work requirement effective? Some evidence for rural India.* Washington, DC, World Bank. (mimeo)

Ravallion, M. & Dearden, L. 1988. Social security in a "moral economy": an empirical analysis for Java. *Rev. Econ. Stat.,* 70.

Ravallion, M., Datt, G. & Chaudhuri, S. 1990. *Higher wages for relief work can make many of the poor worse off – recent evidence from Maharashtra's Employment Guarantee Scheme.* (unpubl.)

Ravallion, M. & Van de Walle, D. 1991. The impact on poverty of food pricing reforms: a welfare analysis for Indonesia. *J. Policy Modelling,* 13.

Rawls, J. 1971. *A theory of justice.* Cambridge, MA, Harvard University Press.

RBI. 1984. *Implementation of Integrated Rural Development Programme – a field study.* Bombay, Reserve Bank of India.

Robinson, M. & Snodgrass, D. 1987. *The role of institutional credit in Indonesia's rice intensification program.* Cambridge, MA, Harvard Institute for International Development. (mimeo)

Rosenzweig, M. 1980. Neo-classical theory and the optimising peasant: an econometric analysis of market family labour supply in a developing country. *Q. J. Econ.,* 94.

Rosenzweig, M. 1988. Risk, implicit contracts and the family in rural areas of low-income countries. *Econ. J.,* 98.

Rosenzweig, M. & Shultz, T.P. 1982. Market opportunities, genetic endowments, and intrafamily resource distribution: child survival in rural India. *Am. Econ. Rev.,* 72.

Roubini, N. 1989. *The interactions between macroeconomic performance and political structures and institutions: the political economy of poverty, growth and development.* New Haven, Yale University Press. (mimeo)

Rowntree, B.S. 1901. *Poverty – a study of town life.* London, Macmillan.

Sadoulet, E. & de Janvry, A. 1991. *Political constraints on the developmental state: alternative theoretical explanations.* Paper presented at ILO-Cornell University Conf. on State, Masket and Civil Institutions: New Theories, New Practices and their Implications for Rural Development, Ithaca. (mimeo)

Sahn, D. & Alderman, H. 1988. The effect of human capital on wages, and the determinants of labour supply in a developing country. *J. Dev. Econ.,* 29.

Sarap, K. 1986. *Small farmers' demand for credit with special reference to Sambalpur district, Western Orissa.* Ph.D. dissertation. University of Delhi.

Schaefer-Kehnert, W. 1983. Success with group lending in Malawi. *In* J.D. Von Pischke, D.W. Adams & G. Donald, eds. *Rural financial markets in developing countries: their use and abuse.* Baltimore, The Johns Hopkins University Press.

Schultz, T.P. 1988. Education investments and returns. *In* H. Chenery & T.N. Srinivasan, eds. *Handbook of development economics.* Amsterdam, North-Holland.

Scobie, G. 1983. *Food subsidies in Egypt: their impact on foreign exchange and trade.* Washington, DC, IFPRI. (mimeo)

Seligson, M. 1982. Agrarian reform

in Costa Rica: the impact of the Title Security Program. *Inter-Am. Econ. Aff.*, 35.

Sen, A. 1973. *On economic inequality.* Oxford, Clarendon Press.

Sen, A. 1975. *Employment, technology and development.* Oxford, Clarendon Press.

Sen, A. 1976. Poverty: an ordinal approach to measurement. *Econometrica,* 44.

Sen, A. 1979. Issues in the measurement of poverty. *Scand. J. Econ.,* 81.

Sen, A. 1981. *Poverty and famines.* Oxford, Clarendon Press.

Sen, A. 1983. Economics and the family. *Asian Dev. Rev.,* 1.

Sen, A. 1987. The standard of living. *In* G. Hawthorn, ed. *The standard of living.* Cambridge, UK, Cambridge University Press.

Sen, A. 1988. Family and food: sex bias in poverty. *In* T.N. Srinivasan & P. Bardhan, eds. *Rural poverty in South Asia.* New York, Columbia University Press.

Sen, A. 1989. Food and freedom. *World Dev.,* 17.

Sen, A. 1992a. *The political economy of targeting.* Washington, DC, World Bank. (mimeo)

Sen, A. 1992b. *Inequality reexamined.* Oxford, Clarendon Press.

Shaban, R. 1987. Testing between competing models of share cropping. *J. Polit. Econ.,* 95.

Sharma, N. & Drèze, J. 1990. *Share cropping in Palanpur.* London, STICERD, London School of Economics and Political Science. (mimeo)

Siamwalla, A., Pinthong, C., Poapongsakom, N., Satsanguan, P., Nettayarak, P., Mingmaneenakin, W. & Tubpun, Y. 1990. The Thai rural credit system: public subsidies, private information and segmented markets. *World Bank Econ. Rev.,* 4(3).

Singh, J.J., Wyon, B. & Gordon, J.E. 1962. Medical care in fatal illness of rural Punjab populations. *Indian J. Med. Res.,* November.

Smith, A. 1776. *An inquiry into the nature and causes of wealth of nations.* London, Routledge.

Srinivasan, T.N. 1979. *Malnutrition, some measurement and policy issues.* Washington, DC, World Bank. (mimeo)

Srinivasan, T.N. 1985. Agricultural production, prices, entitlements and poverty. *In* J. Mellor & G. Desai, eds. *Agricultural change and rural poverty: variations on a theme by Dharm Narain.* Baltimore, The Johns Hopkins University Press.

Srinivasan, T.N. 1986. *Malnutrition in developing countries: the state of knowledge of the extent of its prevalence, its causes and its consequences.* New Haven, Yale University Press. (mimeo)

Srinivasan, T.N. 1989. On studying socio-economic change in rural India. *In* P. Bardhan, ed. *Conversations between economists and anthropologists.* New Delhi, Oxford University Press.

Srinivasan, T.N. 1990. *Rural poverty: conceptual, measurement and policy issues.* Manila, AsDB.

Strauss, J. 1986. Does better nutrition raise farm productivity? *J. Polit. Econ.*, 94.

Subbarao, K. 1989. *Improving nutrition in India – pólicies and programs and their impact.* Washington, DC, World Bank. (mimeo)

Taylor, C.L. & Jodice, D.A. 1983. *World handbook of political and social indicators, Vol. 1.* New Haven, Yale University Press.

Thiesenhusen, W.C. & Melmed-Sanjak, J. 1990. Brazil's agrarian structure: changes from 1970 through 1980. *World Dev.*, 18.

Timmer, C.P. 1986. *Getting prices right: the scope and limits of agricultural price policy.* Ithaca, Cornell University Press.

Townsend, P. 1973. *The social minority.* London, Allen Lane.

Townsend, P. 1979. *Poverty in the United Kingdom.* London, Allen Lane.

Udry, C. 1990. Credit markets in northern Nigeria: credit as insurance in a rural economy. *World Bank Econ. Rev.*, 4.

United Nations. 1989. *World survey on the role of women in development.* Vienna, UN.

Wade, R. 1987. *Village republics.* Cambridge, UK, Cambridge University Press.

Walker, T.S. & Ryan, J.G. 1990. *Village and household economies in India's semi-arid tropics.* Baltimore, The Johns Hopkins University Press.

Walker, T.S., Singh, R.P. & Asokan, M. 1986. Risk benefits, crop insurance and dryland agriculture. *Econ. Polit. Wkly.*, 21.

Watts, H.W. 1968. An economic definition of poverty. *In* D.P. Moynihan, ed. *Understanding poverty.* New York, Oxford University Press.

World Bank. 1986. *Financing education in developing countries: an exploration of policy options.* Washington, DC, World Bank.

World Bank. 1988. *Education in sub-*

Saharan Africa: policies for adjustment, revitalization and expansion. Washington, DC, World Bank.

World Bank. 1990. *World Development Report, 1990.* New York, Oxford University Press.